Elgar, Vicat Cole
and the Ghosts of Brinkwells

I Rex Vicat Cole, The Labourer's Home *(1906); inscribed 'Brinkwells' by the artist*

Elgar, Vicat Cole
and the Ghosts of Brinkwells

CAROL FITZGERALD AND BRIAN W. HARVEY

Produced with the assistance of a grant from the
Paul Mellon Centre for Studies in British Art

PHILLIMORE

2007

Published by
PHILLIMORE & CO. LTD
Shopwyke Manor Barn, Chichester, West Sussex, England
phillimore.co.uk

ISBN 978-1-86077-442-3

Printed and bound in Great Britain.

Contents

'This is what I hear all day – the trees are singing my music –
or have I sung theirs? I suppose I have?'

Elgar: letter to August Jaeger, 11 July 1900

List of Illustrations

EBM Elgar Birthplace Museum
Cole Papers, Private Archive Collection

Acknowledgements

Firstly we would like to thank the following, without whose active help, advice and willing co-operation this book could not have been written – Professor Tim Barringer, who also generously agreed to write the Foreword, Ruth and Anthony Barringer, Tessa Vicat-Cole, Patrick Vicat-Cole and members of the Vicat Cole family, the staff of the Elgar Birthplace Museum (particularly Margaret Sanders, Catherine Sloan and Chris Bennett), Christine Penny and staff at Special Collections, and the staff of the Barber Institute Music Library, both at Birmingham University, the Trustees of the Elgar Foundation and of the Elgar Will Trust, and Andrew Neill, John Norris, Wendy Hillary and Ann Vernau of the Elgar Society.

We would also like to express our gratitude to the Paul Mellon Centre for Studies in British Art for a grant to assist with the photography.

A large number of people have given us the benefit of their knowledge and time either in answering our questions, reading part of the manuscript or allowing their work to be quoted or paintings in their possession to be illustrated. Amongst these we should particularly mention the following: Professor Kerry Downes, Professor Jonathan Harvey, Dr Jerrold Northrop Moore, Professor Shannon Stimson, staff of the Worthing Museum and Art Gallery and of the National Portrait Gallery, London, Peter Smith, Peter Merry, Michael Pope, Renée and the late Dr Percy Young, Sir Colin Davis, Nigel Kennedy, Professor Ian Brockington, Pauline Collett, Rosalinda Hardiman of the Portsmouth Museum and Art Gallery, Robert Walker, Paul Yule, Dr Adrian Thomas, Professor Ian Parrott, Jim Berrow, Kevin Allen, Mike Ashley, the late Hugh Bean, Sir David Willcocks, and Tim McCann and Peter Wilkinson of the West Sussex Record Office.

We are also indebted in various ways to Ian Lake, Professor David Schoenbaum, Col. Sir Brian Barttelot Bart, Professor Brian Trowell, Margaret Elgar, Toni Arden, David Jones, Donald Fraser, Alistair Hicks (Art Advisor) and Bella Beattie at Deutsche Bank, London, the landlord of the *Swan Inn*, Fittleworth, Richard Etherington, Priscilla Hastings, Martin Williams and Gillian Darby, the Rev. Anthony Irwin Smyth, Paul Spencer-Longhurst, Shane Morton, Jan and Angie at P.S.W. Paper & Print Ltd, Alan Rankin, Bridget Monahan, Judy Sayers, Valerie Metcalf, Louise Vale, and Jonathan Gibbs.

Our thanks too for the skilful work of the professional photographers who provided many of our illustrations – Chris and Charlotte Wright at Chris Wright Photography Ltd and Mike Black Photographer in the UK, and Janet Hitchen Photography in the USA. The musical examples were set by by Alan Morrison.

Finally we are grateful for the enthusiasm and support of our publishers, Phillimore & Co. Ltd, and their Managing Director Noel Osborne. Arrangements for the launch of the book were completely dependent upon the generosity of Mr and Mrs David Bowerman of Champs Hill, West Sussex, to whom we extend our heartfelt thanks.

Foreword

The remarkable efflorescence of Elgar's musical reputation in recent times can, perhaps, be dated to August 1965. In the Abbey Road studios already made famous by the Beatles, the young Jacqueline du Pré recorded Elgar's Cello Concerto, with Elgar's own orchestra, the London Symphony, under the baton of Sir John Barbirolli, who had played at the first performance. The Elgar whom the youthful cellist and seasoned conductor revealed – the poet of private lamentation, rather than the painter of spectacular orchestral panoramas, the religious mystic or the bard of British imperialism – spoke directly and powerfully to audiences in the 1960s, and has continued to do so ever since.

The magical soundscape of the Concerto, lightly orchestrated and shifting constantly from the mercurial to the lyric – from shimmering atmospherics to heartfelt peroration – was the direct outcome of Elgar's encounter with the landscapes around Brinkwells, the cottage in West Sussex which he rented from my great-grandfather, the landscape painter Rex Vicat Cole, in 1917. Like the chamber music created by Elgar among the stacked canvases in Cole's studio at Brinkwells, the Concerto seems to enshrine both the irrepressible natural beauty of West Sussex and the inescapable tragedy of the human condition. Through the silent Sussex woodlands, Elgar could hear the murderous rumble of artillery across the Channel in the dying days of the Great War.

For Rex Vicat Cole, Brinkwells held a different and perhaps even more profound personal significance. The cottage, which he had rented in about 1905, provided him and his family – his wife Hannah, and sons George and John – with an idyllic escape from their London home; a land of milk and honey; a classical *locus amoenus*. For the artist himself, the woods around Brinkwells offered limitless subject matter, and even the view from the studio window, with dark clouds inexorably gathering, provided material for one of his most memorable images [see plate V]. From the extravagant, Romantic canvases exhibited at the Royal Academy in the years around 1910, to the sparse and elegiac landscapes of the 1920s, Cole, like Elgar, found at Brinkwells a uniquely powerful *genius loci*. The family left the cottage in 1926, and Cole destroyed many of the finest works produced there, perhaps in an uncharacteristic fit of Elgarian anguish; the slashes of his knife can still be seen on surviving fragments of canvas. Yet the magic of Brinkwells lived on in memory and anecdote. Perhaps a kind of benign haunting from those childhood days in the countryside determined that Cole's two sons would become, respectively, a farmer and a landscape painter, and that both would recall into old age the joys of Brinkwells, in those last, poignant days of innocence before the First World War.

Curiously, Elgar's legion of biographers has offered relatively little on this period in his life, and even Jerrold Northrop Moore's magisterial *Elgar: A Creative Life* – one of the finest biographies of a composer ever written – seems happier with earlier, and later, moments of the composer's career. Carol Fitzgerald and Brian Harvey have created a first full, scrupulous and vivid account of the composer's years at Brinkwells, deftly weaving it together with an affectionate and perceptive interpretation of Rex Vicat Cole's life and work. Thanks to their researches, characters like Mark the handyman, and Mr Aylwin the farmer, whose names reverberate from my childhood, take on a historical reality in the pages of this book. But I am especially grateful for their attention to the artist, whose work still awaits the recognition I have always believed it to deserve. The reproductions of paintings and drawings offered here will, I hope, suggest the profound web of connections by which Elgar's and Cole's works are linked, testifying to the power of Brinkwells to excite both the aural and the visual imagination. By juxtaposing two creative lives – linked by a profound love of the tiny cottage and its bewitching environs – the authors have thrown revealing new light on both painter and composer. Their intensive researches have revealed much that is new, but, more importantly, every page of the book is imprinted with that fugitive and poignantly Elgarian quality – the spirit of the age.

TIM BARRINGER
New Haven, Connecticut
August 2006

Dramatis Personae

Atkins, E. Wulstan (1904 -2003)
Wulstan Atkins was Sir Ivor Atkins' son and Elgar's godson. He knew Elgar well at the end of the composer's life and documented the long friendship that existed between his father and Elgar in *The Elgar-Atkins Friendship* (David & Charles, 1984).He was Chairman of the Elgar Foundation and the Elgar Birthplace Trust.

Atkins, Sir Ivor Algernon (1869-1953)
Sir Ivor Atkins was organist at Worcester Cathedral between 1897 and 1950. His friendship with Elgar began in 1890 when he attended the premiere of Froissart in Worcester. Atkins was immediately drawn to Elgar's music: 'I knew that I completely understood his [Elgar's] music, and that my heart and soul went with it', he wrote. Elgar too was struck by Atkins and acknowledged the beginning of a 'real friendship'. That bond lasted until the composer's death and is recorded in their many lively letters which often used their nicknames Reynart (Elgar) and Firapeel (Atkins). As conductor of the Worcester Three Choirs Festival, Atkins promoted and regularly performed Elgar's music.

Aylwin, Thomas (1849-1923)
Tenant of the Stopham estate whose farm, Springs Farm, was close to Brinkwells, it was Farmer Aylwin who used to collect the Elgars, their visitors and their luggage at the station and take them by pony cart up to Brinkwells. He would also collect heavier items of shopping for them at Pulborough or Petworth. He worked the farm with his wife Ellen (who died in 1918) and his sons. His youngest son, Arthur, was killed in 1916 in the Great War. Thomas Aylwin's death on 2 January 1923, aged 74, after an illness of eight days, upset Elgar greatly who saw it as yet another link with Brinkwells broken.

Binyon (Robert) Laurence (1869- 1943)
Laurence Binyon's career as an art historian began in the 1890s as assistant to Sidney Colvin in the Department of Prints and Drawings at the British Museum where he specialised in Oriental art. From 1913-32 he was in charge of the collection of Oriental Prints and Drawings and became its Keeper in 1932-3. He not only published on art history but also wrote poetry and plays and he was Norton Professor of Poetry at Harvard between 1933-4. Elgar's Spirit of England sets words from Binyon's poetry collection *The Winnowing Fan* published in 1915.

Blackwood, Algernon Henry (1869-1951)
Brought up in a committed evangelical Christian family, Blackwood escaped his background through a deep interest in Eastern philosophy and religion and a passionate association with nature. An unconventional and charismatic figure, Blackwood's varied early career took him to Canada where he worked in farming, and to New York where after a period of profound poverty he worked as a journalist. His adventures in North America – particularly in the

wilderness of Ontario – became the subject for some of his uncanny and ghostly tales. He returned to England in 1899 and his first collection of stories appeared in 1906. His interest in psychic phenomena and the limits of human consciousness resulted in the creation in 1908 of his fictional character, John Silence, the psychic detective. He operated as a spy in the First World War and later in life found a new career as a broadcaster on both radio and television. He became a particular favourite of both Elgar and Alice after the composer had created music for The Starlight Express, based on Blackwood's novel *A Prisoner in Fairyland*.

Buck, Dr Charles William (1852-1932)

Dr Buck first met Elgar in Worcester in 1882. A musician as well as a doctor, he was a firm supporter of the composer. After he had qualified he returned to his native Yorkshire where he practised for the rest of his life in Giggleswick.

Burley, Rosa Campbell (1866-1951)

Rosa Burley's memoirs of her friendship with Elgar add an acerbic and perceptive voice to the many recollections written by his friends. She had been Headmistress of The Mount School in Malvern and had engaged Elgar as a young man to teach violin to her pupils. Later, Carice attended her school and Rosa became a cycling companion and friend to Elgar and travelled with the Elgars to Germany. At times critical of both Elgar and Alice, Rosa Burley nevertheless remained in touch with them until shortly after Alice's death when there was an estrangement between her, Carice and Elgar arising, it is believed, from her apparent desire to look after Elgar and take Alice's place.

Cammaerts, Emile (1878-1953)

The Belgian poet Emile Cammaerts lived in England from 1908. During the First World War his poems expressed the suffering of his homeland after its invasion. Elgar set three of his works to music and, after the first performance of Carillon, Cammaerts wrote to Elgar, 'I cannot let this day pass without thanking you again for your glorious work. I have met a good many Belgians to-day and they all wonder how you managed to share so completely our pain and out hopes.' Cammaerts was married to Tita Brand, daughter of Marie Brema who had sung the Angel in The Dream of Gerontius.

Cobbett, Walter Willson (1847-1937)

Businessman and supporter of British composers and chamber music. He was Founder of the Scandinavia Belting Company and Director of W. F. Stanley Ltd. Cobbett instituted prizes for native composers and violin makers and was Vice-President of the British Music Society and founder of the Cobbett Free Library of Chamber Music. He was also Editor and Compiler of Cobbett's *Cyclopedic Survey of Chamber Music*.

Cohen, Harriet (1895-1967)

Harriet Cohen met Elgar in Hampstead when she was a young girl and they were neighbours. She studied piano at the Royal Academy of Music where she won numerous prizes and later played with the major London and provincial orchestras. She was particularly known for her playing of Bach and her promotion of the piano music of Arnold Bax with whom she lived. She performed Elgar's Piano Quintet and recorded the piece with the Stratton Quartet in 1934. Elgar had envisaged her as a possible soloist for his Piano Concerto and in 1956 she gave a performance of the slow movement of the unfinished concerto as reconstructed by Dr Percy Young with the Boyd Neel Orchestra.

Colvin, Lady Frances (1839-1924)

By all accounts Lady Frances Colvin was a remarkable woman. Born Frances Fetherstonhaugh, she married at 16 and travelled to India with her husband, the Rev. Albert Hurt Sitwell, who had a chaplaincy in Calcutta. An outbreak of cholera in India saw their return to the East End of London and two sons were born to them. But the marriage was an unhappy one and eventually they separated. By the time of the death of her younger son in 1873 Frances was working as Secretary of the Working Men's College in Queen's Square, London. Some years before this separation, probably in the late 1860s, she had met Sidney Colvin and a close friendship had developed. In spite of the death of the Rev. Sitwell in 1894, Frances and Sidney did not marry for a further nine years until the death of Sidney's mother whom he had been supporting financially. Blessed with extraordinary beauty and a fine singing voice, Frances was celebrated by her many friends for her human warmth, wit, and sensitivity. She had first met Elgar in 1904 and he recognised her compassionate and wise nature. It was to her that Elgar wrote on the death of Carice's pet rabbit – knowing that she was one person who he could count on for sympathy. And years later it was to her and Sidney ('my dear ones' as he called them) that Elgar dedicated his Cello Concerto. She could inspire more than friendship amongst her many literary and artistic friends, however, and the young Robert Louis Stevenson fell in love with her, voicing his strong feelings in letters to his 'Madonna'. It is to her credit that after the heat of Stevenson's passion had cooled their friendship survived. After her death in 1924, two days before her friend Joseph Conrad, Sidney Colvin lived in loneliness and increasing isolation for a further three years. The tributes written after her death bear witness to the esteem in which she was held by many people.

Colvin, Sir Sidney (1845-1927)

Whilst Colvin's distinguished career was as a museum administrator and art historian, his first love was literature and he is remembered now both as a literary and art scholar. He studied at Trinity College, Cambridge, where he became a Fellow, before making his name as an art critic in London. He was then elected Slade Professor of Fine Art at Cambridge in 1873, Director of the Fitzwilliam Museum in 1876, and Keeper of the Department of Prints and Drawings in the British Museum in 1884, a post which he held until his retirement in 1912. He was knighted in 1911. He wrote on early Italian art and enjoyed a wide circle of distinguished literary friends that included, amongst others, Browning, Matthew Arnold, Joseph Conrad, Henry James, Thomas Hardy (who he hoped would collaborate with Elgar on an opera) and, particularly, Robert Louis Stevenson. Colvin published editions of Stevenson's letters sent to him from Samoa, and edited the Edinburgh edition of his works. His interest in Keats culminated in a major biography of the poet published in 1917. Sidney Colvin first met Elgar in 1904 and thereafter Sidney and Frances became part of the Elgars' circle of friends in London. In 1915 it was Colvin who first suggested that the composer should 'do a wonderful Requiem for the slain – something in the spirit of Binyon's *For the Fallen* …'. And it was both Sidney and Frances who encouraged Elgar to carry on with his settings when he withdrew on learning that the composer Cyril Rootham had already set the poem *For the Fallen*. As President of the Literary Society he also oversaw Elgar's election to the Society in 1920. It is likely that Alice and Elgar found out about Brinkwells from the Colvins who in 1917 had taken E. V. Lucas's cottage at Tillington, only a few miles away, for the summer, and it was to them that Elgar dedicated his last great work, the Cello Concerto. After Alice's death and his loss of the cottage, Elgar looked back with great nostalgia to the time he spent at Brinkwells when the Colvins would visit or he and Alice would call on them. After Frances Colvin's death in 1924, Sidney withdrew more from society, isolated both by his grief and by increasing deafness and loss of memory.

Corbett, Sir Julian (1854-1922)
A distinguished naval historian and a near neighbour of Elgar at Brinkwells, Sir Julian Corbett
started his career by studying law and writing novels. He turned to history in 1889, initially
writing popular general histories but then concentrating on naval history – the first result of
this interest being his book *Drake and the Tudor Navy*. His grasp of the essentials of conflict
and the relationship between naval and land operations meant that he played a significant
role in deciding naval policy and he was a firm supporter of Admiral Jackie Fisher and his
naval reforms. His major work, *Some Principals of Maritime Strategy* (1911), was an important
contribution to the subject. After the Great War he published with Henry Newbolt an account
of its naval operations based on official documents. He was a founding member of the Navy
Records Society and a member of the Literary Society.

Davies, Sir Henry Walford (1869-1941)
Davies began his musical career as a chorister of St George's Chapel Windsor. He studied
music at the Royal College of Music under Parry and Stanford, where he also taught between
1895 and 1903. In 1898 he was appointed organist of the Temple Church and introduced a
new repertoire and style of singing. In 1919 he became the Director of Music at the University
of Aberystwyth and on Elgar's death in 1934 he succeeded him as Master of the King's Musick.
He was knighted in 1922. As a young composer he was supported by Elgar who arranged for
a performance of Davies's oratorio, The Temple, for the Worcester Festival of 1902. Like Elgar,
Davies recognised the potential of broadcasting and gave highly acclaimed radio talks on
music between 1924 and 1941.

Dent, Professor E.J. (1876-1957)
Professor of Music at Cambridge University and Fellow of King's College. He was one of
the founders of the International Society for Contemporary Music and its first President. A
brilliant linguist, he translated a number of opera libretti into English for the Sadler's Wells
Opera Company.

Elgar, Carice Irene (1890-1970)
Elgar's only child, Carice was brought up to be ever mindful of her father's welfare and after
Alice's death she carried on the role of looking after him that had been established by her
mother. Educated at Rosa Burley's school in Malvern, her grasp of languages enabled her to
find work in the Censorship Department during the First World War. In 1922 she married
Samuel Blake who died in 1939 and thereafter she concentrated on seeing that the musical
reputation of her father would be furthered by the establishment of the Elgar Birthplace at
Broadheath.

Elgar, Caroline Alice Roberts (1848-1920)
In marrying Elgar in 1889 Alice suffered the disapproval of her family. She was the daughter of
Major-General Sir Henry Gee Roberts and was born in India where he was serving in the army.
On his retirement and return to England she was brought up at the family home Hazeldine
House, Redmarley d'Abitot. Her social situation was therefore above that of Elgar who as a
Catholic, a younger man with a father in trade, and an unsuccessful composer when he met
her, had little to recommend him to her family. But Alice, herself a writer and poet, recognised
and believed in Elgar's ability and aspirations. In the early days of their marriage Elgar set some
of her words to music and Carice recorded how proud that had made her. The force of Alice's
belief in Elgar and how that inspired him is reflected in the pattern of his musical output which
began to flourish after their marriage and sharply declined after her death.

Elgar, Susannah Mary 'Pollie' Grafton (1854-1936)

Pollie, Elgar's sister, had married Martin William Grafton in 1879 and their home became a
place of refuge for Elgar. Initially he had lived with them in Worcester after their marriage and
later when they were established at Stoke Prior where Pollie's husband was employed at the
Stoke Works he would make frequent visits for relaxation amid their family (there were five
children). The Graftons acted as witnesses for Elgar's marriage to Alice. Their daughter May
lived with the Elgars between 1904 and 1908 and after Alice Elgar's death Pollie's daughters
acted as housekeepers for the composer.

Gaisberg, Frederick (1873-1951)

Gaisberg got to know Elgar late in his career through his work with the Phonograph Company
and as Recording Artists Manager for the Gramophone Company. They became firm friends
and Gaisberg accompanied Elgar on his trip to France in 1933 to attend the Violin Concerto
rehearsals with the young Yehudi Menuhin and to visit Delius. Gaisberg also regularly visited
Elgar at Marl Bank in Worcester in the years before his death and on one visit in August 1933
Elgar played parts of his opera and of the Third Symphony on the piano for him to hear. It was
Gaisberg who suggested that Elgar might supervise a recording session by telephone from his
bed in the last weeks of his life.

Griffith, Arthur Troyte (1864-1942)

Educated at Harrow and Oriel College, Oxford, Griffith qualified as an architect and started
his practice in Malvern as architectural assistant to Edward Nevinson. Later his own practice
was to take offices in the Priory Gateway. He and Elgar met in 1897 and quickly established a
close friendship – Griffith became known as 'the Ninepin' on account of his height and later
became the subject of one of the Enigma Variations (the seventh). Elgar and Griffith shared
an interest in antiquities – in particular the architecture and history of Worcestershire – and
a deep love of nature. Griffith was also a talented watercolourist and the Elgars had examples
of his work hanging in Severn House. From 1902-42 Griffith was Honorary Secretary of the
Malvern Concert Club. After Alice's death he designed a headstone for her grave in Little
Malvern and it was to this headstone that Elgar's own inscription was also added in 1934.

Harrison, Beatrice (1892-1965)

Beatrice Harrison studied the cello at the Royal College of Music and at the Hochschule,
Berlin, where she made her debut. She was the first cellist and the youngest student ever to
win the Felix Mendelssohn Prize. She was one of four musical daughters and with her sister
May, a violinist, became friendly with Delius who wrote his Double Concerto for them.
She recorded the Elgar Cello Concerto under the composer's baton in 1919 and 1928 and
also performed it with Elgar conducting a number of times including a performance at the
Worcester Festival of 1923.

Hockman, Vera (c.1897-1963)

Vera Hockman, a violinist in Billie Reed's Croydon orchestra, and Elgar met for the first
time on 7 November 1931 at a rehearsal for a performance of Gerontius conducted by the
composer at the Croydon Triennial Festival. Vera was playing at the second desk of the violins
in an orchestra made up of members of the LSO and experienced Croydon players, led by
Elgar's great friend Billie Reed. After the rehearsal Elgar asked for an introduction and the
couple fell in love. In spite of the difference in their ages – Vera was 40 years younger than
Elgar – they were united by their shared interest in music and literature, and Vera also became
a close friend to Carice. In December 1931Elgar presented her with the MS of the Violin

Sonata signed by him with the message 'who only now knows why this was written'. Vera was married to Joseph Hockman but the marriage was unhappy and by the time of the Croydon rehearsal Vera was leading an independent life. After Elgar's death she found a new partner in Charles Henry Cheeseman, a professional double-bass player, and they enjoyed a long happy relationship overshadowed by her increasing infirmity as a result of Parkinson's Disease.

Hull, Sir Percy Clarke (1878-1968)
Sir Percy Hull was appointed assistant organist of Hereford Cathedral in 1896 under G.R. Sinclair. After Sinclair's death in 1917 Hull took over the post of organist in 1918 after his release from internment in Germany. As a pupil at Hereford Cathedral School the whole of his life up to his retirement was spent in association with the Cathedral. A keen motorist – driving was listed as his recreation in his *Who's Who* entry – he gave Elgar some driving lessons.

Jaeger, August Johannes (1860-1909)
August Jaeger is widely known as the subject of the great ninth variation 'Nimrod' in Elgar's Enigma Variations. He was born in Dusseldorf but moved to England at the age of 18 where he joined the staff of the musical publishers Novello in 1890 and began his association with Elgar in 1896 or 1897. He had a deep appreciation of the great German composers, especially Beethoven and Wagner, and he was to bring that knowledge and inspiration to his understanding of Elgar's music which he instinctively believed to be of the highest quality. Jaeger's emotional support in the face of Elgar's turbulent moods, and his honest criticism of Elgar's scores, turned their working relationship into a creative friendship. The significance of that friendship is reflected in his variation. Jaeger suffered from tuberculosis from which he died at the age of forty-nine.

Joshua, Marie (d.1918)
Elgar dedicated his Violin Sonata to his friend Marie Joshua. Her father was German whilst her mother's family had been French and at the outbreak of the First World War she wrote to the Elgars that her sympathies were entirely on the side of England and France. She had been converted to Elgar's music by Hans Richter in 1910 and thereafter became part of the Elgars' circle of friends and a staunch supporter of his work – Alice used to call her Elgar's 'prophet'. Elgar wrote to her from Brinkwells whilst he was working on the Sonata and offered the dedication. She was ill and felt undecided as to whether she could accept the honour. Her unexpected death a few days later caused Elgar to incorporate a lament for her loss into the finale and to inscribe the title page with her initials with the permission of her daughter.

Kipling, Rudyard (1865-1936)
Elgar had first thought of setting a poem by Kipling, ' Recessional', in 1900 but the project was never carried through. Sixteen years later, at the request of Lord Charles Beresford, Elgar set verses by Kipling which celebrated the small boats patrolling the seas during the First World War. Although The Fringes of the Fleet played to audiences appreciative of its popular, jaunty music, the death of Kipling's only son on the Western Front in 1915 had turned him against the idea of his verses becoming light entertainment and in November 1917 he stopped any further performances. In spite of Alice Elgar's subsequent hostility to Kipling, Elgar did set one more poem 'Big Steamers' to music in 1918. By the outbreak of the war Kipling had completed the major part of his best-known literary output and was an established figure in English literary life. He had been awarded the Nobel Prize for Literature in 1907. After the death of his son, Kipling became consumed with hatred for the Germans and possibly with

guilt over his son's death (he had used his position to get his boy a commission although still under-age). He devoted much energy to organising memorials for the fallen and became the first War Graves Commissioner.

Lucas, Edward Verrall (1868-1938)

E.V. Lucas is known as a prolific editor and writer of travel books, novels, essays and anthologies. He was an authority on Charles Lamb and published his biography in 1905. He was Chairman of Methuen & Co. and a member of the Royal Commission on Historical Monuments. A friend of the Colvins, he lent them his house in Tillington for the summer of 1917, and himself visited Brinkwells during the Elgars' stay there.

Lytton, Edward George Lytton Bulwer, 1st Baron (1803-73)

As well as an active political life as MP and Colonial Secretary, Bulwer Lytton made a second career as a novelist, playwright and poet. His greatest success in his lifetime came from his novels, many of them now forgotten. His research into psychology and metaphysics was reflected in a number of occult novels which also demonstrated his interest in clairvoyance and spiritualism. He was created a baronet in 1838 and five years later inherited the Knebworth estate in Hertfordshire, at the same time taking the name of Lytton.

Mott, Charles James (c.1880-1918)

The baritone Charles Mott studied singing in Berlin with Paul Knupfer and worked for two years at the Dessau Hofoper as principal baritone. He returned to London in 1906 where he worked at the Royal Opera. He took part in the Royal Opera's German Opera Festival in 1914 and was heard by Elgar who was so impressed by his singing that he decided to help him in his career. Mott played the organ grinder in Elgar's Starlight Express and sang in The Fringes of the Fleet, but his wartime musical career was cut short when he enlisted in the First Battalion London Regiment (Artists' Rifles). He was killed at the Front on 22 May 1918 and is buried at the Bagneux Military Cemetery near Gezaincourt.

Murdoch, William David (1888-1942)

The pianist William Murdoch was born in Australia where he began his musical training at the University of Melbourne Conservatory. In 1906 he was awarded a scholarship to study for three years at the Royal College of Music in London. Thereafter he performed as a soloist in many countries and was particularly esteemed for his playing of Chopin and Debussy. He served with the band of the Grenadier Guards in France during the Great War and in 1917 began his long association with the violinist Albert Sammons who was also in the Guards. Murdoch and Sammons played in the private concert organised by Frank Schuster in 1919 as a trial run for the first performance of Elgar's Violin Sonata and Piano Quintet – the other members of the team being W. H. Reed, Felix Salmond and Raymond Jeremy. They then performed the Sonata for the first time in public at the Wigmore Hall, London. Murdoch also composed and wrote transcriptions of Bach's organ pieces for piano.

Newman, Ernest (1868-1959)

The music critic Ernest Newman (who was born William Roberts) met Elgar in 1901 and in an article published in The Speaker in December of that year stood out against the composer's production of more choral writing and urged Elgar to concentrate on the orchestra as his medium. In spite of their differences of opinion, Elgar valued his perceptive writing and later in life their relationship had warmed to the extent that Elgar dedicated the Piano Quintet to him. Educated at Liverpool University, Newman had originally intended to work for the

Indian Civil Service but his health precluded him from that career and he concentrated instead on his musical and literary work. He became Music Critic of the *Manchester Guardian* in 1905 and of the *Birmingham Post* in 1906. In 1919 he settled in London and became music critic of *The Sunday Times*.

Powell, Mrs Richard (Dorabella) (1874-1938)

Dora Penny (later Mrs Richard Powell) met Elgar in 1895 and quickly became a friend to both Elgar and Alice – helping her with the Elgar archive and amusing him with her youthful high spirits. Elgar called her 'Dorabella' and she became the subject of Variation 10 in the Enigma Variations. Later in life she wrote an account of their friendship in *Edward Elgar: Memories of a Variation*.

Reed, William Henry (1877-1942)

Often remembered now mainly in his role of confidant and invaluable musical helper to Elgar, and as an exceptionally kind and warm-hearted individual, Reed had a distinguished musical career as a performer and also as a composer. He studied at the Royal Academy of Music in London. He was a founder member of the London Symphony Orchestra which he subsequently led from 1912, leader of the Royal Philharmonic Orchestra and the conductor of many smaller orchestras and societies, amongst them the Croydon Philharmonic Society. His compositions included chamber music, songs, symphonic poems and a violin concerto. He played a vital role in the development of Elgar's chamber music and was a welcome visitor to Brinkwells and his close friendship with the composer continued unchanged until Elgar's death. He wrote two accounts of Elgar, the earlier and more personal being *Elgar as I Knew Him* (1936). His ashes are buried below the Elgar window in Worcester Cathedral.

Ronald, Sir Landon (1873-1938)

Landon Ronald had a distinguished conducting career which included the posts of conductor at Covent Garden and conductor of the New Symphony Orchestra (originally founded by Beecham) between 1909 and 1914. In 1910 he became Principal of the Guildhall School of Music and from 1916 to 1920 he was conductor of the Scottish Orchestra. He studied composition at the Royal College of Music under Parry, as well as violin and piano, and wrote many songs which enjoyed great popularity. He met Elgar in 1910 and became a keen advocate for his music and the composer later dedicated Falstaff to the younger man in recognition of Ronald's championship of his music. Ronald was knighted in 1922.

Salmond, Felix (1888-1952)

Felix Salmond was the son of the singer Norman Salmond and had made his name as a distinguished young cellist by the time he performed Elgar's Cello Concerto. He had worked through the Concerto with Elgar at various stages in its gestation and in late July 1919 he visited Brinkwells to go through the completed score. As a result Elgar suggested that he gave the premiere of the work in London. He was one of the four players who played the Quartet's slow movement at Alice's funeral. He had trained with the cellist William Edward Whitehouse and had a distinguished career as a performer and as a teacher, becoming Head of the Cello Department at the Curtis Institute.

Sammons, Albert Edward (1886-1957)

Albert Sammons was a self-taught violinist. He began his musical career in theatre orchestras and hotel bands and was appointed 1st violinist and then leader in Thomas Beecham's orchestra. He was founder of the London String Quartet and in the years before the Great

War made a reputation as a virtuoso soloist. In 1914 he played the Elgar Concerto to great acclaim and in 1919 played in the first public performance of the chamber works. The Delius Concerto was written for him. He served in the Guards during the War, where he met William Murdoch, and thereafter continued his career as a soloist and as a chamber player. He was admired for his faultless technique and warmth of sound and was regarded as the outstanding British violinist of his generation. He taught at the Royal College of Music until 1956 when he retired suffering from Parkinson's Disease.

Schuster, Leo Francis Howard (1852-1927)
Leo Schuster was part of a large and wealthy German-Jewish family whose background enabled him to act as a patron of the arts. He was particularly interested in Elgar and his houses in London and Bray were open to the composer as retreats for work or holidays. Schuster first met Elgar in 1899 and thereafter he was always eager to further the composer's interests.

Shaw, George Bernard (1856-1950)
Shaw had been a perceptive and energetic music critic in his earlier years and his collected essays on music were published between 1888 and 1890. Elgar appreciated his criticism and Shaw welcomed him as a new voice in English music. Initially, however, Elgar found Shaw's politics and his plays unattractive. But this changed over time and they established a firm friendship based on mutual admiration of each other's work. Elgar dedicated The Severn Suite to Shaw and was encouraged by him to start the Third Symphony and The Spanish Lady.

Speyer, Edward (1837-1924)
Speyer came from a wealthy musical background: his father being an amateur composer in Frankfurt where his son Edward met Rossini. In 1885 he married the soprano Antonia Kufferath who had been a pupil of Julius Stockhausen and who counted Clara Schumann and Brahms amongst her friends. She and Alice had met many years before when Alice had gone to her father in Brussels for piano lessons. Their acquaintance was renewed in 1901 when Edward and Antonia met the Elgars at the Leeds Festival. Thereafter their house, Ridgehurst, the scene for many musical gatherings, was always open to the Elgars.

Stuart of Wortley, Lady. Alice Stuart Wortley – 'The Windflower' (1862-1936)
Alice Stuart Wortley was the third daughter of the Pre-Raphaelite painter John Millais. She was the second wife of the Sheffield Member of Parliament Charles Stuart Wortley and it was on the Elgars' visit to Sheffield in 1902 that they first met. A talented pianist and sympathetic personality, Alice Stuart Wortley played an increasingly important role in Elgar's life as both musical muse and confidant. She was the inspiration behind Elgar's planned piano concerto and it was to her that he often sent the music he was working on, trusting her musical judgement and instincts. Alice Elgar too recognised the importance of her encouragement and the two women maintained their friendship despite Elgar's closeness to his muse. He named her the 'Windflower' – a name which reflects the delicacy and beauty which Elgar found in her character. They were regular correspondents but whereas most of Elgar's letters to her have survived, the vast majority of her letters have not.

Vandervelde, Hélène 'Lalla' (1870-1964)
Lalla Vandervelde was the daughter of Edward Speyer and the wife of the Belgian socialist minister Emile Vandervelde who played an influential role in the European labour movement. During the war Emile was responsible for the Belgian refugees in England and Lalla worked

hard on their behalf at one point joining the Elgars at Brinkwells in an exhausted state as a result of her war work. She was a part-time actress and writer. In 1915 she recited *Carillon*, dramatically appearing in black before a bright red curtain – a contrast she used for dramatic effect – and on another occasion she performed wrapped in a Belgian flag. In 1917 she acted in Shaw's home front play *Augustus does his Bit* at the Court Theatre in London and in 1925 she published *Monarchs and Millionaires*. She was a frequent visitor both to Brinkwells and to Severn House and on one occasion joined the Elgars on a trip to the Lake District. Her company was enjoyed by Elgar and it was at one of her parties that he was introduced to Bernard Shaw. She moved in artistic circles and was a friend of Roger Fry who designed the interior décor of her London flat in 1916 – the result was predictably disliked by the Elgars who found the colours 'most garish'.

CHAPTER ONE

Prologue

The Magic of Brinkwells

In May 1917 Sir Edward Elgar and his wife Alice rented a cottage near Fittleworth in West Sussex ,'Brinkwells', which was to become a haven for them in the subsequent years. It was there that Elgar wrote his surviving chamber music, namely the Violin Sonata, the String Quartet, the Piano Quintet and much of what is now one of his most popular works, the Cello Concerto. It was to be, in fact, his last creative surge. After these he completed nothing more of real substance before his death in 1934. [*]

The time spent at Brinkwells was therefore of particular importance to Elgar and marked a creative period that was distinctive in his life. Brinkwells was certainly an escape from the many irritants that made his life difficult in

1 Elgar at Severn House in 1912

---

[*] He left amongst other fragments the score of an opera and of a Third Symphony incomplete and fragmentary as well as sketches for a piano concerto.

London, but it was far more than that. It was a source of profound inspiration and spiritual freedom. He went there at a time when many factors, physical, psychological and artistic, combined to relieve him at least temporarily from the burdens that had increasingly dogged his career. The music he composed there has its own flavour which in part reflects the qualities he found in Brinkwells and the surrounding countryside.

It is, perhaps, impossible to explain 'magic' – but many people, both visitors and residents, attested to the magic of the woods and paths that surrounded Elgar's cottage – and something of its character can be recaptured. There is the evidence of the Elgars themselves, and that of their visitors and friends expressed in diaries and letters. But above all there is the evidence of the music – the 'wood magic' that Lady Elgar so aptly names in her diary, recognising as she did that this was something new in her husband's oeuvre. And it is because of this particularity of the Brinkwells music that it is important to build as comprehensive a picture as possible of life at the cottage rather than regarding the music in isolation from its physical context.

Fittleworth also had a history which connected it to the arts well before the Elgars' arrival, in particular the art of landscape painting, and it was from the landscape painter Rex Vicat Cole that Elgar rented Brinkwells. Vicat Cole, a member of a family of artists, was the head-tenant of Brinkwells and it was his studio that Elgar used as his music room. This large wooden building constructed by Vicat Cole in the cottage's garden became the cradle both for Elgar's music and the many drawings, sketches and paintings, some exhibited at the Royal Academy, made by the artist in the years after 1905. Therefore Vicat Cole's work, in the context of the rural beauties of West Sussex and the trees that so influenced Elgar, constitutes a fascinating source of information, both written and visual. But his importance as an artist is clearly far greater than this. Rex Vicat Cole's individualistic and often powerful paintings represent an aspect of English art that has hitherto been unjustly neglected. The development of his style, moreover, graphically illustrates how one talented landscape artist reacted to the immense changes that took place during and after the Great War. For Vicat Cole as well as Elgar Brinkwells was a magic place in which the creative process could continue relatively undisturbed by outside pressures. His work in its Brinkwells context is analysed in more detail in chapters 6 and 11 in particular.

How far was Elgar influenced by Cole's vision, for he clearly respected the artist's work? It is tempting, perhaps, to play up the consequences of this fortuitous synchronicity, but that would be unjustified. Elgar's compositional style and conservative disposition were too well established to be susceptible to such domination by anyone else's work, musical, literary or artistic, except in the most subtle manner. When a new inspirational spark did occur it was immediately picked up by the discerning Alice. She wrote in her diary for 24 August 1918 – 'Lovely day – sunny and hot … E. writing wonderful new music, different from anything else of his. A. calls it wood magic. So elusive

2 *Rex Vicat*
Cole in his
London studio in
1899/1900

and delicate.' Although the interrelation between the composer and the artist at Brinkwells was indirect, it was nevertheless real. Not only were both men profoundly influenced by the atmosphere of the cottage and the woods, but Rex Vicat Cole had been instrumental in creating part of that atmosphere, particularly in building his studio. This was to become the creative heart at the centre of the Brinkwells experience for both men.

The truth is that the Elgars welcomed the Brinkwells interludes as an escape from the sheer dreariness of the War and the unwelcome pressures of London. Elgar, too old to take on a combative role, had responded in the early years of the War by doing his patriotic duty mainly in writing music to support the cause. The younger Rex Vicat Cole, on the other hand, was involved more directly as a member of the 1st Battalion of the United Arts Rifles. He must have been only too aware of the famous Poussin painting illustrating the adage 'Et in Arcadia ego' – the omnipresence of death even in Arcadia – and reminded of the sharp contrast between his Brinkwells life and the darkness of the War on his periods of leave in Sussex. His destruction of much of his available artistic output at the end of the War can only be explained by the strong feeling that reality lay elsewhere and he had a duty to portray it thus in the future. However, before this destruction took place Elgar lived in the cottage and worked in the artist's garden studio surrounded by examples of Vicat Cole's earlier work – 'many sketches and pictures' as Elgar enthusiastically wrote to his friend Troyte Griffith, 'which wd. [have] formed a text for much expounding of miracles on your part I know …' Their indirect influence on the composer cannot reasonably be doubted.

Alice evolved a lifestyle in Brinkwells which was centred around Elgar's needs as a composer – but which was also very different from their socially driven existence in London. Their reaction to life at Fittleworth was not identical. Alice certainly found more to contend with than Elgar did but then the weight of domestic detail fell on her at a time during the First World War when food, heating and servant problems were at their height. Nevertheless, it would be wrong to assume that she did not like being there as her diary reveals moments of near poetic rapture at the sky or the colours of the trees which remind us that she had literary and poetic aspirations of her own. At times she wished it less rural, perhaps, but she managed to maintain a social round which although not as relentless as her London activities was nevertheless satisfying. However, when she did spend a short period there on her own she found the time passing very slowly.

Elgar's reaction was more pronounced. It is clear that Brinkwells represented a type of existence which reconnected him with the happy times that he had spent at Birchwood, his cottage in deep countryside at the northern end of the Malvern Hills, and even with his birthplace at Broadheath, Worcestershire. Although the couple were to spend extended periods at Brinkwells in 1918 and 1919, it was never their primary home. And this too must have added to the poignancy of being there. To Elgar, for whom a sense of loss played a key role in his outlook on life and who was constitutionally restless, the temporary nature of their stay in Sussex must have added to the intensity of the experience. When, in 1920, they tried to buy the residue of the lease of the cottage from Rex Vicat Cole in order to live there they were unsuccessful, but one has to ask whether, after Alice's death in April of that year, Elgar would have been able to resurrect the Brinkwells experience in such altered circumstances anyway. The short visits he paid there without her suggest not.

Given the nature of Elgar's personality, his extraordinary sensitivity and changeability combined with his artistic and social aspirations, his life was never going to be easy. Extreme sensitivity sat ill with the social mores of the English upper class to which he aspired. And here too Brinkwells acted as an escape. Fittleworth residents seemed not to be unduly impressed with visiting celebrities (which Elgar often found amusing). Those who did visit were usually close friends or supporters and the limitations of the cottage itself imposed a way of life that was outside the usual manners of London society.

Everyone who visited the Elgars at Brinkwells seemed to have been enchanted with this taste of Arcadia and so echoed the feelings that the Vicat Coles had for the retreat in the woods. It is interesting that one visitor in particular was described by Alice in her diary as exactly the Brinkwells guest – a description that Elgar also agreed with – and that was Algernon Blackwood. For this designation tells us not only about Blackwood himself but about how the Elgars perceived their life in the country. The friendship between Elgar and Blackwood, moreover, was based on common, almost pantheistic, beliefs that were echoed by the immediate surroundings of the cottage.

The Brinkwells interlude was, then, up to Alice's death, a particularly successful and happy one for Elgar and part of our investigation is to try to analyse why this should have been. His 'tormented personality', so described by the perceptive Arnold Bax, [*] is particularly fascinating because of the waxing and waning of his strong creative instinct. This almost literally erupts when he encounters the Arcadian influences of Brinkwells.

Whilst the aim of this book is to concentrate on one particular period in Elgar's creative life, it would of course be impossible to regard the years between 1917 and 1921 in isolation. The recurrent problems and demands of Elgar's life and the continuity of his work override any such division. However in looking at his time at Brinkwells it is possible to see how these aspects of his creative life were modified by his time there.

This book, therefore, begins by putting Elgar's career, its problems and the reception of his work into context. Moreover, where we discuss earlier or later periods this is on most occasions purely to elucidate the context of ideas under discussion (or their resolution in old age) in the same way as a physician will dig into the past to clarify the likely cause of the patient's present pathology. Identifying the grit in Elgar's oyster is always a complex exercise but it is clear that the seemingly threadbare days during the termination of the Great War witnessed some of Elgar's finest music, subtly different from what had gone before.

---

[*] Bax, *Farewell my Youth* (1943).

CHAPTER TWO

Elgar in Context

Renaissance and Reformation in English Music

The span of Elgar's life encompassed a period of particular interest in the development of English music. For if the musical renaissance in England started in the main with the work of Sir Hubert Parry (1848-1918) and the less universally loved Sir Charles Villiers Stanford (1852-1924), the year 1934 marked the end of an important era too. This *annus horribilis* witnessed the deaths of Elgar, Holst and Delius. Holst died prematurely at only 59 but both Elgar (aged 76) and Delius (aged 72) had by then enjoyed a long creative life. Admittedly their styles were so different that an innocent ear might have difficulty in discerning any common musical factors, but each had achieved an international reputation despite being British. In fact, in contradiction to the German view that at least for a century after the death of Handel England was 'the land without music', this was never true as regards performance. In, say, 1850, choral societies, glee clubs, amateur or mixed amateur/professional orchestras, brass bands and other communal activities thrived in London (along with professional opera) and had also done so in many of the cathedral cities and provincial conurbations for much of the preceding century. These communal activities were, moreover, the background to Elgar's own development as a composer. London was also sufficiently attractive to encourage foreign musicians as residents and historically had welcomed figures such as J.C. Bach, Haydn and Clementi, as well as performers such as the great Italian cellist Cervetto, and the violinist Viotti who died in London in 1824. *

What was lacking was a truly professional orchestral/chamber music tradition fuelled by native composers of real talent, together with a moneyed upper class which valued music and the arts higher than fox hunting. The encouragement of professional orchestras and competent conductors were subjects close to Elgar's heart, having suffered on occasion from hearing his own music played badly. In the course of lectures delivered at Birmingham University as Professor of Music in 1905-6 he advocated the case for the professional training of conductors and the incorporation of the art of conducting into the Birmingham degree course.

---

* Members of the Hanoverian dynasty, for all its faults, were often keen performers and sponsors of music. See generally Brian W. Harvey, *The Violin Family and its Makers in the British Isles* (OUP 1995) chs. 5 and 7.

In making this suggestion Elgar was speaking from a perspective different from a contemporary one. As recently as 1828 Clementi had conducted from a keyboard in London, pursuing a long tradition of direction of the orchestra by the continuo player (who might be the composer – e.g. Haydn) or by the first violinist as 'Concert Master'. By the middle of the 19th century composers such as Mendelssohn, Weber, Berlioz and Wagner (who wrote a treatise on conducting in 1869) had begun the tradition of the true maestro whose interpretation of the work to be performed was paramount. They were followed by professionals in England such as Jullien, Costa and Richter. But Elgar was correct in his judgement that there were remarkably few home-grown conductors in this tradition until the Henry Wood, Beecham, Boult and Barbirolli generations became established. (Conducting of opera and oratorio, the latter in the context of the importance of the choral society in Great Britain and Ireland, has a distinct history of its own.)

Things were different in Germany, the country to which Elgar had turned for inspiration as a young man and where his music was first fully appreciated. Germany had continued to benefit throughout the 19th century from the court music tradition established in the numerous princedoms into which the country had been divided before 1866. Hitherto trained predominately in Italy, particularly Venice, German musicians also benefited by the foundation of conservatories. Mendelssohn founded the Leipzig one in 1843 and this became the conservatory most patronised by foreign students. Edvard Grieg studied there, as did his friend Delius, and it was the one to which young Elgar would have gone had his father been able to afford it. There were also important music schools in Cologne (1845), Munich (1846), Dresden (1856), Stuttgart (1857) and Berlin (1869). So powerful was the assumption that professionalism in conducting could only be attained by German-trained musicians that as late as 1912 the home-grown conductor Basil Cameron (1884-1975) felt it desirable to change his name to Hindenburg, ironically only to change it back again in 1914 when the start of the Great War brought much anti-German feeling to Britain. But by then Hans Richter (1843-1916) and August Manns (1825-1907) had shown that England was not after all *das Land ohne Musik* and had in fact produced, almost in a fit of absent-mindedness, a composer of the first international rank.

Historicity

Elgar's creative life has, along with his music, been subjected to minute scholarly analysis by such distinguished writers and musicologists as (to confine the list to more recent writers) Robert Anderson, Michael Kennedy, Diana McVeagh, Jerrold Northrop Moore, Ian Parrott, Brian Trowell and Percy Young. These and other studies reveal how Elgar's 'attitude to life' (to use his own expression) was often dominated by his black depressions.[*] He despaired at the remote

---

[*] McVeagh, in *Edward Elgar: Music and Literature*, pp. 1-9.

prospect, as he saw it, of his ever doing any good. Yet at other times when he was composing he had the true artist's firm belief in his own powers – a confidence that is unshakeably present in his music. Moreover many of his friends experienced his teasing good humour and sense of fun. His numerous letters to friends reveal both the depressed and the confident, high-spirited Elgar. Some saw one side of his character only – in other cases he only revealed the image that he wished to.

A conscious leap of the imagination is needed when trying to reconstruct events which, though 'modern' by normal historical standards, are nevertheless pre-television/electronic communications and depend very much on the testimony of those there at the time. Compare, for example the accounts by Alice Elgar and Rosa Burley of Elgar's triumphant/disastrous inaugural lecture at Birmingham University in 1905 – one would not believe that the two women were talking about the same occasion at which both were certainly present. For Alice, Elgar carried off the lecture splendidly and impressed his audience, holding them breathless with attention, whilst for Rosa the occasion represented 'one of the most embarrassing failures to which it has ever been my misfortune to listen'.[*] Alice was, of course, Elgar's staunchest supporter and constitutionally ill-equipped to deal with any criticism about him, let alone make any publicly herself, whereas Rosa Burley, to

3 Alice in 1916

whom Elgar's daughter's education had been largely entrusted, brought a much colder eye to the events she describes. (Some would discount her testimony almost entirely on the ground that after Alice's death she may have had designs on Elgar, but this view too readily dismisses the inherent verisimilitude of her earlier memories.)

Similarly, it is only comparatively recently that Elgarians have been fully let into the secrets of Elgar's late-blossoming but apparently intense love affair

---

[*] Burley, *The Record of a Friendship*, p. 183.

from 1931 with the young violinist Vera Hockman. This in turn has raised the question as to precisely how important she was to him in the composition of the Third Symphony, as now 'reconstructed' by Anthony Payne. [*] But having said that, and taken in a warning about the many contradictory impressions Elgar himself knowingly gave to his contemporaries, there are other features which make our task a little easier than it might otherwise have been.

Records and Archives

In particular, by now the great majority of relevant letters and diary entries of the composer, his wife and friends have been conveniently reproduced in books or are at the Elgar Birthplace Museum in Broadheath or the University of Birmingham Library Special Collections. (The Elgar diaries, the originals of which are at Birmingham, came by descent from Carice, her companion Sybil and the beneficiary under Sybil's will – much having previously been deposited in the Record Office of Worcestershire County Council.) Also the well-established Elgar Society, founded 1956, and now with over 1,600 members internationally, produces learned articles, books, records and definitive editions of his work.

Contrary to the impression that Elgar often gave ('nobody wants my music nowadays') in fact his music has at no time been seriously neglected in Britain. [†] Most composers' popularity dips for a time in their old age or shortly after their death. If their output is of fine quality this is invariably a temporary phenomenon. [‡] Elgar also was probably the first composer to record many of his major works for the gramophone – an invaluable legacy. [§]

Thanks in large part to the efforts of Elgar's daughter Carice (1890-1970), the public has for many years been able to picture his composing life in the greatly expanded 'Birthplace' Museum.

4 Elgar's Birthplace at Broadheath

---

[*] Allen, *Elgar in Love – Vera Hockman and the Third Symphony* (2000).

[†] See e.g. Ronald Taylor, 'Music in the Air – Elgar and the BBC' in *Edward Elgar, Music and Literature*, ed. Monk, showing that the BBC far from neglected him even in his almost entirely unproductive latter years.

[‡] See the discussion in Maine, *Works*, p.276 – 'The conflict of generations is one of the commonest features in mankind's history ...'.

[§] Sergei Rachmaninov made important recordings in the 1930s, although his recording career was not as systematic as Elgar's.

In terms of learned publications the Elgar bandwagon is running along more speedily than ever. But the conjunction of the environment at Brinkwells with Elgar's physical health, and his dependence on certain friends to light the creative spark, all at a critical juncture in his life, have been comparatively little explored. This is partly, we suspect, because Worcestershire Elgarians always regard Elgar as a Worcestershire composer, whereas Sussex Elgarians regard his Brinkwells work, and particularly the Cello Concerto, as giving them too a proprietary interest. These parochial assumptions must seem strange indeed to those looking in from abroad!

Variability in Quality

Certain aspects of Elgar's life and work have almost from the start been seen as inherent problems. One of these is the variability of his output. For example, Sir David Willcocks, one of Britain's leading choral conductors, writing a centenary tribute to Elgar in 1957, makes the fundamental point that there are really two Elgars. 'Elgar No. 1' is the genius who composed Gerontius, the two oratorios (The Apostles and The Kingdom), the Enigma Variations, the two symphonies and the concertos, the string pieces, Falstaff, and some shorter works of genius too. 'Elgar No. 2', though, is the composer who could:

> plumb the depths of banality … with wearisome melodic sequences, harmonies of mawkish sentimentality, and at times blatant vulgarity. It seems incredible … that the man who could express in Gerontius such nobility and rare poetic feeling, could in the same breath utter the trite language of the drawing room ballads. To make the problem more complex, we are told that he sincerely believed in the value of his 'popular' music and that he treated it almost as seriously as the work which we recognise as great. [*]

We had the opportunity in 2004 of checking with Sir David whether his essay still represented his views and, having re-read it, he confirmed that it did.

Today there may be disagreements on how we should categorise some of Elgar's miniatures, previously condemned almost wholesale as vulgar trifles. (It is interesting in this respect to see how Elgar regarded vulgarity as less of a sin for the composer than the common-place. Vulgarity, he believed, could be evidence of creativity.) The correct category in which to put even large-scale choral pieces such as The Apostles, The Kingdom and The Music Makers continues to be debated. Many regard them as masterpieces each in their own way – others find the two biblical oratorios uneven in inspiration, cloyingly over-chromatic in parts and unacceptably religiose for today's taste, and The Music Makers embarrassing in its verse and far too retrospectively sentimental. They feel that Richard Strauss could get away with this (e.g. in Ein Heldenleben) but it does not befit an Englishman.

[*] Willcocks in *Edward Elgar, Centenary Sketches*, p. 52.

It may be, in any case, that the categories of 'good' and 'bad' Elgar are constantly changing at the margins, particularly as the standards of performance have improved so rapidly over the last few decades. Certain pieces which would have been dismissed from serious consideration some years ago are now perceived in a different light. And as Willcocks points out, 'The music of Elgar, which demands flexibility of rhythm, subtlety of phrasing, and unusual attention to problems of balance, owing to the complexity of the texture, can suffer perhaps more than that of any other composer through a lack of sympathy and sensitivity on the parts of the executants.'[*] This also raises the problem of the 'Englishness' of much of Elgar's output and how it is received abroad. An English professional String Quartet was recently engaged as the solo quartet in a continental European orchestra's performance of the Introduction and Allegro. They reported that the European orchestra, though entirely professional, completely missed the spirit of the piece which became barely recognisable as a result. But, as we shall see, the answer to the question why this should be so remains elusive.

Personality Disorders

In a recent book the name of Elgar joins those of Schumann, Berlioz, Tchaikovsky and others as a composer thought by a respected American Professor of Psychiatry to be suffering from cyclothymia, major depression or even manic-depression, now usually termed 'bi-polar disorder'.[†] This feature of Elgar's life is not well known to the general music public and indeed some of his better informed aficionados affect to be uninterested in the phenomenon, since in their eyes it detracts from his greatness. In particular his wife Alice and his daughter Carice were clearly anxious to preserve Elgar's reputation without hint of any irregularity, or, almost, idiosyncrasy. But anyone assessing the evidence impartially in the 21st century will be compelled to conclude that Elgar could be difficult and extremely egocentric.

It may be that some pattern of depression and elation can be discerned to explain at least part of Elgar's enigma and this would accord with the experience of many creative artists. In her account of their friendship Rosa Burley describes his recurrent depression which, she believed, became a problem from his time at Plas Gwyn (the house in Hereford to which Alice and Elgar moved in 1904) until the end of his life.[‡] But there is in fact evidence of Elgar's melancholy and depression from much earlier times – e.g. his statement in a letter to his friend Dr Buck on 20 July 1884, sending him 'good wishes for your happiness, these I can give you the more sincerely since I know what it is to have lost mine forever'.

Other friends were only too aware of the cycle that was played out around his creative activity when often the 'high' of composition was followed by the

---

[*] *Ibid*, pp. 52-3.
[†] Jamison, *Touched with Fire* (1993).
[‡] Burley, *The Record of a Friendship*, p. 176.

'low' of completing a work. A clear illustration of this is his letter of 19 July 1912 to his 'muse' Alice Stuart Wortley ('the Windflower').

5 *Portrait of Alice Stuart Wortley (1887), 'The Windflower', by her father Sir John Millais*

Yesterday was the usual awful day which inevitably occurs when I have completed a work: it has always been so: but this time I promised myself 'a day!' I should be crowned, – it wd. be lovely weather, – I should have open air & sympathy & everything to mark the end of the work – to get away from the labour part & dream over it happily … Alice & Carice were away for the day & I wandered alone to the heath – it was bitterly cold – I wrapped myself in a thick overcoat & sat for two minutes, tears streaming out of my cold eyes and loathed the world, – came back to the house – empty & cold – how I hated having written anything: so I wandered out again & shivered & longed to destroy the work of my hands – all wasted. – & this was to have been the one real day in my artistic life – sympathy at the end of work. [*]

This depression continued in the days following and then manifested itself in physical illness with Elgar writing to the Windflower again on 22 July that he was not well enough to leave home.

The revealing letters to Alice Stuart Wortley also remind us how dependent Elgar was on a series of female 'muses' almost throughout his life and the Windflower was amongst the most steadfast and dependable of them. His wife Alice seemed to go along with these arrangements which, with perhaps one exception during Elgar's widowerhood, were almost certainly platonic, if fervent. He clearly had a very soft spot for handsome, intelligent women whom he thought understood him and his music. Without them he might well have found his compositional processes more erratic still and his depressions less susceptible to alleviation.

There are other examples of depression in those of Elgar's extraordinarily frank letters which contain references to his desire to 'make away with himself' – and these sentiments greatly alarmed Alice who clearly took them seriously. Thus he writes to his staunch friend Jaeger at Novello's in 1900, shortly after the first, disastrous, performance of Gerontius:

I … am at the end of my financial tether. Don't go and tell anyone but I must earn money somehow – I will not go back to teaching and I think I must try some

---

[*] Moore, *The Windflower Letters*, p. 103.

trade – coal agency or horses – I wish I were dead over and over again but I dare
not for the sake of my relatives, do the job myself. Well we shall see – I've not read
the papers yet re Gerontius & never shall now. I'm sorry you've been bothered
over it – just like my influence on everything and everybody – always evil!

As we have seen, the melancholia was often at its worst when Elgar had just
finished a major composition. There was an initial period of euphoria in which
he tended to describe those works as his best – e.g. his description of Gerontius
– 'this is the best of me … .' (quoting Ruskin) or many years later his Violin
Sonata written at Brinkwells: 'They say it is as good as or better than anything
I have done in the expressive way'.* This burst of confidence and euphoria was
then often followed by a feeling of despair during which he would announce
that he had finished with music altogether. What is of interest in this is his total
identification with his music and the sense that his inner 'self' was revealed
through his work in a way that it was not revealed in his life. This, as we shall
see later, affected his friendships and his reaction to criticism.

Modern psychiatry may be able to say in retrospect how Elgar would have
been treated today in contrast to how his hypochondria (as it was seen) and
melancholia were treated then. It may be, of course, that such treatment would
have made matters worse in creative terms, even if Elgar the man felt more at
ease with himself and the world – a very tricky problem for the enlightened
psychiatrist. Put another way, is Elgar's achievement as a composer <u>because of</u>
or <u>in spite of</u> his psychological problems?

He was certainly not alone in suffering the way that he did – many creative
artists show the same traits and indeed the flux of creativity, the characteristics
of inspiration and the contrasts between these states and 'normal' activity do
in themselves mirror some of the symptoms of bi-polar illness. The difference
is that the artistically gifted can use these states creatively. Depression and
melancholia do not in themselves guarantee creativity – but creativity, if it is
strong enough, can use them – as it did in Elgar's case. Moreover in Elgar's
example depression seemed to be inextricably linked with the ebb and flow of
his works. In some instances, when he was truly 'lit up' his rapidity of thought
and power of concentrated creative effort were exceptional. Billy Reed noted
'… the singularity of his mental processes, the originality of his methods, and
the surprising speed at which he worked' when he saw Elgar working on the
Violin Concerto by assembling and re-assembling his ideas to make a coherent
whole.† Elgar himself was aware of this state when he wrote to Rosa Burley that
he was having a 'rabid attack of writing music' whilst working in Brinkwells on
the Violin Sonata which he completed in a month.

Reed's description here was perceptive – Elgar's methods were unusual.
In his introduction to the score of his elaboration of Elgar's Third Symphony
Anthony Payne makes a similar point. He writes: 'The composer had an

* Written to the Windflower on 11 September 1918 of the middle movement of the work which later
still he made a symbol of his devotion to Vera Hockman with whom he played it. See Allen, p. 37.
† Reed, *Elgar as I Knew Him*, p. 24.

extraordinary way of working, jumping from movement to movement as the spirit took him. It was as if he was shaping the various pieces of a jigsaw, before fitting them all together. Ideas sometimes came to him outside the context of a tempo, for instance, and one, clearly marked 'scherzo', eventually ended up in the slow movement.' Here too one can make an analogy between Elgar's fluid, rapid, and seemingly disconnected methods of assembling works with the divergent thought processes and the fast, easy movement from idea to idea that can characterise manic episodes. It is the closeness between artistic inspiration and the 'high' of the bi-polar state which is of interest in this case.

In a sense, whether or not a consultant psychiatrist makes a formal diagnosis of manic-depression is secondary to the question of whether the depressive episodes can be 'cured' or mitigated by appropriate drug therapy for an artist without adversely affecting the natural creative 'high' of inspiration. Faced also with a range of bewildering *physical* symptoms Elgar's doctors tended to prescribe more tobacco smoking – Elgar's solace being his pipe (which he found soothed his nerves). 'Lady Nicotine' is now recognised as a remarkable drug if it can be isolated from the other toxic ingredients of tobacco smoke. In fact, Elgar was probably blissfully oblivious of the damage being done to his heart and lungs. It is only relatively recently that the connection between tobacco smoking and cancer has been securely established to the satisfaction of even the tobacco companies.

During the 1920s the physician Dr Arthur Peregrine Thomson * treated Elgar in Birmingham and came to the conclusion that he was a neurotic who needed constant reassurance, saying that he would brighten up considerably once this had happened. But this had been a characteristic throughout his creative life and it was perhaps the dichotomy between his belief in his music and his periods of depression that made for such an uncomfortable existence. As Marcel Proust, who should know, pointed out in *Le Cote de Guermantes* (1920-1): 'Everything we think of as 'great' has come to us from neurotics. It is they, and they alone, who found religions and create works of art. The world will never realise how much it owes to them, and what they have suffered in order to bestow their gifts on it.'

Elgar also undoubtedly had some serious physical illnesses at various times in his life, one of the most painful and trying emanating from badly infected tonsils which plagued him with symptoms for many years. They were subsequently removed in 1918 at a comparatively advanced age. But even after this there is evidence of the constant need for medical reassurance. Alice did not seem to hesitate to summon a stream of eminent consultants to the Elgar residence when she thought her husband needed medical attention. (For more detail see Appendix 4.) At less critical moments she herself administered aids and comforts – she travelled with them to various concert and conducting venues – including at one point supplying seven hot water bottles for Elgar's bed when he complained of being cold.

---

* See Appendix 4.

Objections to Elgar

Elgar's music has not always enjoyed the sympathetic response that it now usually evokes. In 1934 Constant Lambert wrote: 'Much of Elgar's music, through no fault of its own, has for the present generation an almost intolerable air of smugness, self-assurance and autocratic benevolence.'

Some other critics, particularly in the 1930s, accused Elgar of a pervasive jingoism, an unpleasant 'musical imperialism' which is intrinsic in all his work, however abstract it may apparently be. The distinguished conductor Sir Colin Davis has commented:

> Today we are far enough away from the time in which Elgar lived that we can listen to his music with completely different ears from his contemporaries and not be side-tracked by talk of empires and jingoism. It is wonderful to go back to these pieces now – for instance Falstaff which is so ingenious and charming. There is something so like Falstaff about Elgar himself. He was a big, bluff man who loved his walks by the river, with his dog, just plucking melodies out of the air. Then he also had great and real melancholy, and I think this combination of opposite characteristics is so appealing. He was such a brilliant musician. Take a score like the 2nd Symphony – it's wild and so original. [*]

As to the two boo-words, 'jingoism' and 'imperialism', some of the verse he set, not infrequently as a war-time patriotic duty, is particularly embarrassing when seen through 21st-century spectacles. But as products of their time they are a great deal more understandable. Despite the view of an older generation of critics that these factors 'contaminated' the rest of Elgar's output – Cecil Gray finding, for instance, the last section of the Enigma Variations full of 'undiluted jingoism' – these factors too are really totally irrelevant when assessing Elgar's best work, including the four master works produced at Brinkwells. [†]

Vulgarity

There is also a long-standing criticism that his music is 'vulgar' (or probably worse, 'velgar'). But what does 'vulgar' mean in this context? If it is taken to refer to Elgar's choice of words for his music, then it has to be admitted that some of his word-settings are better than others and the sentimentalism of some of them clearly affects also the quality of the music, as David Willcocks rightly points out above. But here we have also to remember that Elgar himself often set 'second rank' poetry, claiming that great poetry was already music in its own right. In other cases the v-word is applied to some of Elgar's salon pieces or Pomp and Circumstance Marches. To take the latter case, people can experience for themselves on the last night of the Proms, year after year,

---

[*] See J. Tolansky, 'Elgar and the LSO', LSO programme note, 1998.
[†] We will leave sceptics to peruse Bernard Porter's demolition of much of this 'undiluted jingoism' theory in his essay 'Elgar and Empire – Music, Nationalism and the War' in Foreman (ed.), *Oh, My Horses*, ch. 4 (Elgar Editions, 2001).

the continuing popularity of the Land of Hope and Glory trio section of the March No. 1. The predominately young audience is not put off by allegations of vulgarity in the face of a very good tune (which it is often overlooked came <u>before</u> a usually somnolent king suggested – as the composer subsequently asserted in correspondence – that suitable words be added by someone else). *
The tune is inherently well-structured and only equalled as a patriotic icon, perhaps, by Parry's inspired setting of Blake's Jerusalem. Undoubtedly some musicians are affronted by the seemingly brash tastelessness of this flag-waving ceremony – and to judge from Elgar's own reaction to conducting the massed bands and choir assembled at Wembley for the British Empire Exhibition in 1924 – 'no soul & no romance & no imagination' – the composer himself might well be among the sceptics.

A similar defence can be made of a number of Elgar's earlier 'salon' pieces. Salut d'Amour which quite a short time ago was almost universally condemned by anyone wishing to retain credentials as a serious musician has now been substantially reinstated. The climate has in fact completely changed and a well-shaped piece with a fine melodic basis, such as this, will be unashamedly applauded. So whilst the charge of vulgarity may still occasionally be appropriate, it should never be accepted uncritically. Elgar sometimes miscalculated, but not nearly as frequently as his critics have suggested.

The only sin that such an audience distinctly disapproves of is the deadly one of dullness. Elgar was an uneven composer and some of his work, often taken from much earlier drafts, seems so lacking in inspiration that it is in danger of boring its listeners. Some of this material is incidental music, explicitly not written for occasions when the listener's undivided attention is expected, and dating from a period before writing for films was developed by Walton and others into a more arresting art. And writing boring music is not the same as writing vulgar music. Elgar himself admitted that he found it difficult to write to order and needed to be 'lit up', to use Alice's expression, by his work.

Emotion

Audiences today react sympathetically to far more emotionally expressive performances than was hitherto the case, for example the famous one of the Cello Concerto by Jacqueline Du Pré (with Barbirolli) or the 16-year-old Menuhin's recorded Violin Concerto under the composer's baton (found to be too emotional by some at the time). In spite of Elgar's carefully adopted stiff-upper lip and military posture he was driven by his emotion rather than his reason. His instruction to performers was to find the spirit of the music and on occasion he conducted his own works with tears running down his face. His performances were controlled, often brisk by modern standards, but they were highly charged within the parameters of what was acceptable at the time. The

---

* Or did Clara Butt make this suggestion? See Yvonne M. Ward, 'Edward Elgar, A. C. Benson etc' (2004), *Elgar Soc. Jo.*, Vol 13, No. 5, pp. 13-37.

critic of the *Nottingham Daily Express*, for example, writing of a performance of The Kingdom in 1909 with the composer conducting, noted how 'his orchestral renderings are marked by waves of emotion'.* In fact Elgar's music was often intentionally emotional: '… it's good! awfully emotional! too emotional but I love it …' he said of the Violin Concerto.

Nevertheless the emotionalism of his work was significantly different, for example, from that of Mahler. It is salutary to recall that within the living memory of the older generation of music-lovers in England a performance of a Mahler symphony was a rarity. His music was regarded as neurotic in the extreme and something that only a foreigner, and an Eastern European one to boot, could or should produce. Now Mahler is likely to fill the English concert hall more certainly than most composers and if the aim is to leave the performers and audience emotionally exhausted this is often achieved. Elgar's emotionalism operated in a different way, despite the efforts of some conductors (such as the late Leonard Bernstein) to conflate the two. There is little evidence of neuroticism in Elgar. There is an English restraint about his music – yet it can be intensely moving.

Auto-didacticism

Another frequently voiced criticism was that Elgar was 'self-taught' and there-fore, one assumes, not academically competent to write music of any com-plexity. In the present era where many people have received their higher education through the wonderful achievements of the Open University, or by other 'distance learning', without relinquishing their ordinary work, we take a different attitude to the need in all cases for residential, institution-based study. For being in this sense 'self-taught' is no longer a handicap.

In this connection, Elgar had the supreme ability to learn quickly and thoroughly from his father, his friends and his musical surroundings (including the scores and primers available in the family business) all that he needed. Despite his own patent insecurity he was quite the equal of his more 'academic' colleagues on all matters theoretical, including in particular the difficult art of orchestration. Nor was he in this unique – William Walton in the next generation of composers achieved a similar feat. In fact it is worth considering the happily purely academic question of whether the 'soul' in either composer might have been irrevocably destroyed by the teaching available at the time in the UK's universities and conservatoires. 'The letter killeth', as Hardy's *Jude the Obscure* tragically found out. Elgar, though, must have missed the company of bright and like-minded students, often in retrospect the most valuable part of formal tertiary education.

---

* Moore, *A Creative Life*, p. 556.

Discrimination

There is now a fair degree of consensus amongst Elgar scholars that the insecurity which underlies much of Elgar's creative life stemmed at least in part from his position as an 'outsider' in social terms. He was brought up as a Roman Catholic in a family where his father retained strong 'free-thinking' (rather than, as some maintain, specifically Protestant) views. His father wrote to his Dover home when his wife decided to convert to Catholicism some four years after their marriage, referring to various churches in the following almost Humeian terms: '... the absurd superstition and playhouse mummery of the Papist; the cold and formal ceremonies

6 *Alice in Court Dress in 1912*

of the Church of England; or the bigotry and rank hypocrisy of the Wesleyan.' *
Catholics were still a small minority much distrusted in some circles, partly as a result of the then current Irish nationalist agitation and partly because of the constitutional history of Britain from Henry VIII's break with Rome onwards. 'No popery' was a familiar street cry to most Englishmen. So apart from any family tensions there may have been, Elgar felt discriminated against in the job market, particularly in his younger days.

He was also the son of a mere tradesman, ie of a lower 'class' (formally 'lower middle class') than the numerous rich business people, professionals and even royalty with whom he and Alice subsequently liked to mix. There was too a distinct class gap in their own union, Alice being the daughter of a distinguished and knighted Major General. On top of all this there was his lack of a university academic education, alluded to above, to hold against him. He was also nine years younger than his bride-to-be. Little wonder, then, that Alice's family were opposed to their marriage in 1889. The couple's future must have looked very unpromising.

Academic Attitudes

A good summary of contemporary academic attitudes, particularly in Cambridge, was Professor E.J. Dent's renowned entry about Elgar in the influential *Handbuch der Musikgeschichte*, edited by Guido Adler (1924). It neatly sums up the objections to Elgar's music by a number of critics and runs in translation:

> Elgar entered musical life later than the others and surprised his hearers by the unusual splendour of his orchestration and the ardent sensibility of his music ... He was a professional violinist and studied the works of Liszt, which were an

---

*   Moore, *Spirit of England*, p. 6.

abomination to conservative academic musicians. He was moreover a Catholic and more or less a self-taught man who had little of the literary education of Stanford or Parry ... To English ears Elgar's music is over-emotional and not entirely free from vulgarity. His orchestral works ... are lively in colour, but pompous in style, and with a knightly chivalric flavour about the expression. [*] His most beautiful orchestral work is the symphonic poem Falstaff which, though weakened by an excessively close dependence on its programme, is certainly a work of great originality and power. His chamber music ... is dry and academic. [†]

Before leaving Dent's masterpiece of damnation with faint praise, we should note that he was present at early performances of the Quartet and Quintet and afterwards wrote to Elgar to say how deeply impressed he was. As Robert Anderson dryly remarks, 'He seems later to have changed his mind somewhat'. [‡] Furthermore this attack on Elgar's status and musicianship caused a number of the more distinguished younger generation of composers and performers in Britain (such as John Ireland, E. J. Moeran, Philip Heseltine (Peter Warlock), Beatrice Harrison and William Walton) to draft a widely distributed circular letter to refute these aspersions. Dent's attack thus proved counter-productive. [§]

The suffocation wrought by the British class system is well known in many other contexts and perhaps only in the new millennium can its influence in some respects seem to be on the wane. Elgar's supposedly defective education has been for present purposes sufficiently defended above. But running as a corrosive thread throughout his adult life was a further factor, his constant inability either actually to earn enough money from his composing to keep his family and himself in the style to which he aspired, or, if in fact his income in later life from composing, conducting and royalties etc was sufficient, to bring himself to acknowledge it. The shadow of poverty was perceived by Elgar always to hang over him. This did nothing to assuage his melancholia and led to a purported dislike and distrust of the music business generally.

There is a startling example of this attitude of mind in his Will made on 2 January 1932 which cuts out former legacies to lifelong friends. 'Owing to the sudden collapse of everything artistic and commercial ... I leave nothing to any Charity as I have given everything possible during my life and I much regret that it is now necessary to cancel the legacies which it had been my purpose to leave to servants and friends and institutions.' Nowhere is it explained what the nature of this 'sudden collapse' was, nor did subsequent events, in terms of royalties and other intellectual property, in any way justify Elgar's pessimistic outlook.

---

[*] The German text is 'einer gesuchten Ritterlichkeit des Ausdrucks'.
[†] For an in-depth analysis of this article, see Trowell, 'Elgar's Use of Literature' in *Edward Elgar, Music and Literature*, ed. Monk, p. 286.
[‡] Anderson, *Elgar*, p. 138.
[§] Moore, *A Creative Life*, p. 790.

Elgar's God

Elgar's religious beliefs have been analysed by Elgar scholars, whether in the context of his deeply felt affection for Newman's poem 'The Dream of Gerontius' or generally. [*] In fact it was reasonably common knowledge amongst Elgar's contemporaries that Elgar lost any enthusiasm for his faith towards the end of his life. Some have attributed this to the influence of George Bernard Shaw, and this appears to have been his daughter Carice's view. Others, such as Rosa Burley, would say perspicaciously that at no time did he get any real comfort from his religion, whatever he actually believed.

There are many instances which reveal Elgar's disillusionment with a personal God. For example Elgar's remarks in a letter to his friend Frank Schuster dated 25 August 1914, included the passage:

> Concerning the war I say nothing – the only thing that rings my heart and soul is the thought of the horses – oh! my beloved animals – the men and women can go to hell – but my horses; – I walk round and round the room cursing God for allowing dumb animals to be tortured – let him kill his human beings but HOW CAN HE? Oh, my horses.

(In Elgar's defence, his love of animals is well known and the slaughter of human beings wreaked in that war had then hardly begun.)

Or, writing to Sir Ivor Atkins on 30 December 1922 about memories of his much earlier King Olaf:

> It sweeps me off my feet: it seems strange that the strong (it is <u>that</u>) characteristic stuff has been conceived & written (by a poor wretch teaching all day) with a splitting headache after dinner at odd, sustained moments – but the spirit and will was there in spite of the malevolence of the Creator of all things … But through it all shines the radiant mind and soul of my dearest departed one: she travelled to London (I was grinding at the High School) and became bound for one hundred pounds so that my work might be printed – bless her! You, who like some of my work, must thank <u>her</u> for all of it, not me. I shd. have destroyed it all and joined Job's wife in the congenial task of cursing God. [†]

The extract to Atkins in 1922, above, should be read as a deeply felt statement of his immense debt to his wife, but also as an illustration of his attitude towards his God – unusual for a Roman Catholic, and undoubtedly blasphemous to theists. Again, Elgar, understandably upset after the first disastrous performance of his Gerontius, came out with a similar statement in a letter to his friend Jaeger about God's failure to understand creative artists, 'I always said God was against art and I still believe it'. [‡] At this stage in his life (1900) Elgar appears to have had a vision of a very personal God in which there was a considerable element of projection.

---

[*] See Geoffrey Hodgkins, 'Providence and Art – A Study in Elgar's Religious Beliefs' (2002).
[†] Moore, *A Creative Life*, pp. 761-2.
[‡] *Ibid*, pp. 334-5.

Certainly after Alice's death there is little suggestion that he was sustained by his beliefs. In a letter to Sidney Colvin from Brinkwells in 1920 Elgar wrote:

> I find everything as usual but sad, sad, and sad beyond words: inscrutable nature goes relentlessly on, birds, flowers, everything as of old. But I could not see the beauty in it. … I wander about aimlessly like a lost – no, there are no souls – dog is good enough. [*]

Whilst these are private expressions of his religious anguish, part of his public persona was that of a composer and conductor of sacred music and he was very conscious of his reputation in this respect. After the first performance of Gerontius, he soon recovered from his over-reaction, helped no doubt by the subsequent enthusiastic acceptance of the work, particularly in Germany where it prompted Richard Strauss to hail Elgar as the 'first English progressivist'. By 1902 it was on the Worcester Three Choirs Festival menu subject to its text being 'bowdlerised' to make it more compatible with Anglican doctrine – a proposal which obtained the reluctant consent of the executors of Cardinal Newman. The bowdlerisation worried Elgar too but he seems to have been able to live with this provided the music was not affected. In fact with its essentially non-biblical basis Newman's poem was repellent to many staunch Protestants at the time, and for many years afterwards it was not eligible for performance at most public schools founded in the Church of England tradition, despite the widespread recognition that the work contained outstanding music. [†]

Views differ on how Elgar regarded his next mighty project, the planned trilogy which eventually resulted in The Apostles and The Kingdom. Some think that Elgar had an almost messianic urge to write a great non-sectarian Christian saga and was surprised when even this proved controversial. But it is quite clear that to within about ten years of his death he was still actively considering the composition of the missing third part. In the end fragments of it finished up in other works (including the uncompleted Third Symphony), a victim of Elgar's lack of creative motivation.

It may have been significant that in his later years Elgar did not usually accompany his wife and daughter to Sunday worship in their chosen Catholic church. But he retained many friends working in the Protestant cathedrals and churches of England, and particularly in Worcester itself. Moreover, his widespread conducting engagements for performances of his later oratorios plus the royalty streams that Gerontius in particular increasingly engendered must have strongly indicated that discretion was the better part of valour. There is, however, an amusing incident narrated by Vera Hockman when in about 1931 she was going to enjoy a performance of Gerontius with her daughter and happened to meet the composer. 'You poor things,' said Elgar, 'an evening of Gerry's nightmare! I am going to the Windmill.' [‡]

---

[*] EBM, Letter no. 3511.
[†] Dr Douglas Fox, Clifton, in conversation, c.1953.
[‡] Allen, *Elgar in Love*, p. 80.

As has been pointed out already, it was undoubtedly the case that Elgar also felt discriminated against economically because of his Catholicism. As Rosa Burley related in her book: 'He told me of post after post which would have been open to him but for the prejudice against his religion, of golden opportunities snatched from his grasp by inferior men of more acceptable views. It was a subject on which he evidently felt very bitter for he embroidered it at great length.' [*] It is, of course, impossible now to say how far this embroidery went. His bitterness, like his neurosis over money, may in part have been fuelled by depression.

It is, however, clear that Elgar's religious convictions underwent considerable changes as he got older. In part, they, like other aspects of his character, were bound closely to the cyclic nature of his depressions. With setbacks and disappointments he would rail against God and this was intimately connected with the artistic discontent that was part of his nature. Moreover, as in other outlooks and opinions, Elgar was never consistent. But the War made him question his beliefs. Writing to Binyon in answer to a request to write music for a 'Peace Ode' in November 1918, Elgar refuses, saying that as much as he admired the poem he regretted 'the appeal to the Heavenly Spirit which is cruelly obtuse to the individual sorrow and sacrifice – a cruelty I resent bitterly and disappointedly.' [†] It is the word 'disappointedly' which tells us most here – speaking of a sense of loss – a sense of being let down. This idea is enforced later in the letter to Ivor Atkins dated 30 December 1922 (above) in which he talks of 'the malevolence of the Creator of all things'.

In later years he appeared to move away from conventional Christianity – his use of a quotation from Walt Whitman for his 1929 Christmas card is a case in point. This included the words: 'I think I could turn and live with animals … They do not make me sick discussing their duty to God …'. He could also take an almost tongue-in-cheek attitude to the doctrinal niceties of the established church, for example in suggesting settings of two very 'pagan' poems by Shelley in 1928 for performance at Worcester Cathedral which were unacceptable to the Dean.

Elgar and Pantheism

Part of the thesis of this book is that the Brinkwells experience gave rise to a new type of inspiration in the elderly composer, and this has a great deal in common with the inspiration which also characterises much of the creative work of the artist Rex Vicat Cole and the author Algernon Blackwood. Clearly this motivating power is closely associated with 'nature', its forms and elemental forces generally and, in the case of these three, trees specifically, and it is easy to call the movement an aspect of 'panthesim'. But this is a slippery word and may wrongly suggest either that Elgar was flirting with paganism or some variety of

---

[*] Burley, *Record of a Friendship*, p. 26.
[†] Anderson, *Elgar*, pp. 135-6.

7 *Rex Vicat Cole,*
Boughs of an
Old Spanish
Chestnut

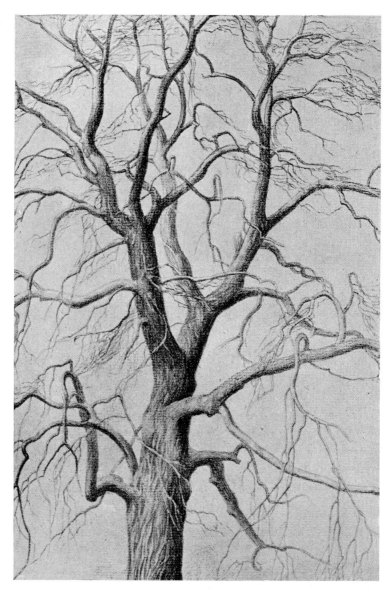

polytheism, or that any of the three had ideas based on the putative centrality of a numinous deity.

Pantheism, from the Greek 'Pan' – 'all', 'Theos' – 'God', can be taken to mean God is within all that lives from the amoeba to man; and that every living feature of the environment without which nothing else could live, and which necessarily, therefore, has a symbiotic relationship with other living things, is a manifestation of God. But this idea can be expanded further to include phenomena such as rivers, mountains and stones, particularly in the poetic sense. It then ceases to be a God-centred belief and can develop into a form of animism where every natural feature develops a 'soul' of its own.

Shelley was one of Elgar's most revered poets and was prone to express this type of feeling. From *Adonais*, an elegy on the death of Keats (1821), comes:

> He is made one with Nature: there is heard
> His voice in all her music, from the moan
> Of thunder, to the song of night's sweet bird;
> He is a presence to be felt and known
> In darkness and in light, from herb and stone,
> Spreading itself where'er that Power may move
> Which has withdrawn his being to its own;
> Which wields the world with never wearied love,
> Sustains it from beneath, and kindles it above.
>
> (Stanza XLII)

Elgar was not alone at that time in reflecting in his music his 'awe of nature', as good a definition as any of Elgar's variety of 'pantheism'. Arnold Bax, for instance, recaptures the rugged spirit of Tintagel in Cornwall in masterly fashion in his tone poem of that title; and it is not difficult to imagine Sibelius, another fine violinist who at an early point in his career intended to become a soloist, wandering in the forests of Finland with his violin, summoning the powerful spirits of the woodland in the contemporary Tapiola.

As we shall see the intensity of Elgar's response to the natural world had also an element of identification with the moods and aspects of nature – a feeling that his own mercurial personality was mirrored by the outside world – nature in some ways becoming a kindred spirit.

At the very end of his life, Elgar told the doctors treating him for his terminal cancer that he had no faith whatever in an afterlife and that he believed there was nothing after death but complete oblivion.[*] During his last days he also requested that he should be cremated and that his ashes should be scattered at the confluence of the Rivers Teme and Severn, in the country which he had loved since childhood. But in the end family wishes prevailed and this did not happen. He was given the last rites and buried beside Alice at the Catholic church in Little Malvern.

Summary

In summary then, we have attempted to outline the complexities of Elgar's personality and the conflicting impressions that he gave to his friends and acquaintances. On the face of it he was a typical English gentleman of military bearing right up to his last years. Underneath the carapace was a highly, almost neurotically, sensitive musician suffering from disabling bouts of depression

---

[*] Moore, *A Creative Life*, p. 818. See also *Elgar Soc. Jo.* (November 2006), vol. 14, no. 6, p. 14, where Dr Moore details the great care that he took to ensure the accuracy of this report. The consultant physician in question was Sir Arthur Peregrine Thomason – see Appendix A.

which were in danger of stultifying his output altogether. Between the two, there was the genial, good humoured and kindly Elgar who loved jokes and japes and had the capacity for child-like enjoyment of games and hobbies. He had a great talent for friendship and for eliciting friendship from others as we shall see below. But to those less close to him the discrepancies between his projected image and his music were disconcerting. Listening to Elgar play the piano and lunching with him in 1924 Siegfried Sassoon came to the conclusion that there was a real Elgar and another, different, man. He wrote that seeing him play made him forget the 'other' Elgar who came across as a typical club bore who told long-winded anecdotes about himself. 'The real Elgar', Sassoon concluded, 'was left in the music room.' * Even this conclusion is too simplistic, for there were many Elgars, but only those closest to him knew them all.

Elgar himself was reluctant to enlarge on his sources of inspiration, or discuss his music in any serious way. But he never made any secret of his feeling for the power of nature. He loved his native 'sweet borderland' of the Three Choirs counties, where he was born and where eventually, full of temporal honours, he died. How was it, then, that in the apparently antipathetic dog-days of the Great War, far from his beloved Worcestershire and with the bombardment in France sometimes actually audible, he found in a primitive but atmospheric cottage in the depths of Sussex his last real surge of inspiration? At Brinkwells he wrote what are now recognised by most music-lovers as four masterpieces. We now explore the possible answers to this question.

---

* Anderson, *Elgar*, p. 155.

CHAPTER THREE

'I Long for the Country'

The Home Front

The early years of the war saw an increasing burden of pressure, ill-health and worry settle on Elgar. In one respect he was lucky; he had no sons to be broken on the insatiable wheel of trench warfare. His immediate family unit remained intact. But there were other pressures no less real which added to the general discomfort of wartime living experienced by everyone. They occasioned in Elgar, increasingly as the war progressed, a restlessness and need for escape, answered in 1917 by finding his Sussex retreat and finally resolved by his extended stay at Brinkwells in 1918.

When war was declared on 4 August 1914, the Elgars were in Scotland where they had been holidaying at Gairloch. Elgar had fished and Alice had accompanied him (and had confided to her diary that she found fishing rather monotonous). The declaration of war brought such simple pleasures to an end and the family tried to return to London as quickly as possible – a journey made difficult by troop movements, the commandeering of transport and a lack of change for English five pound notes. (This was not a phenomenon limited to Scotland. The days before the war were marked by the withdrawal of gold from banks by private investors and fear of national bankruptcy. The eminent polymath and diarist Edward Heron-Allen describes how, in London, on 5 August it was impossible to cash small cheques or to get change and that people were buying sovereigns by cheque for £1 2s. 6d.) [*] The Elgars were also desperate for news which had been hard to come by in Scotland.

Both Alice and Elgar had a deep attachment to Germany, its people and music, which they had regarded as part of their cultural heritage. Germany had often been the destination for their holidays together, Alice spoke German fluently and it had been the country in which Elgar's music had first been properly recognised. It is understandable that when Rosa Burley visited them at Severn House at the beginning of the war she found them 'in the depths of despair'. However, in spite of this they threw themselves behind the war effort. Elgar announced that he would serve in any capacity, writing to Alice Stuart-Wortley from Scotland that 'I am returning to London as soon as possible to offer myself for any service that may be possible – I *wish* I could go to the front

---

[*] *Edward Heron-Allen's Journal of the Great War*, ed. Harvey and Fitzgerald, p. 5.

but they may find some menial occupation for a worthless person.' [*] He was by then 57 years old.

In the event on 17 August he enrolled as a special constable in the Hampstead Division (an organisation intended to release policemen for war service), whilst Carice found work with the Navy League and the Red Cross. Billy Reed voiced misgivings at this development and these must have been shared by most of his friends. He wrote that Elgar was very excited by joining the special constables and that he

> donned armlet, belt, and hat; he also had a truncheon, which he handled rather gingerly, I thought … I trembled as I thought of him going out to perambulate the streets at any hour of day or night and in any weather, firmly grasping his truncheon and looking about for German spies and dynamitards with whom our imagination peopled every dark corner, characters whom I prayed he might never meet. [†]

Far from being absurd, these fears were very widespread at the time for a wave of spy fever gripped the nation during the first months of the conflict and some 8,000 'spy cases' were investigated. Reed expressed his relief when Elgar resigned the following February. Yet even then he continued with public service by joining the Hampstead Volunteer Reserve where he had to practise rifle drill and shooting – something at which he became very good according to Alice, although it did make his hand shake afterwards.

War Music

But all of this was, of course, a diversion from what people, both his friends and the public, saw as Elgar's real role in the war. And that was to create patriotic music. After all, how could the composer of the Pomp and Circumstance March No 1, which had so excited the public, or of The Coronation Ode, which had encapsulated a great public ceremony, not have something pertinent and uplifting to say to a nation at war?

Immediately on return from Scotland Elgar had attended a concert of his music given at the Queen's Hall on 15 August 1914. Alice recorded the wonderful response to Land of Hope and Glory at which the enormous audience rose to its feet and shouted. He had, on first gaining some success in 1896, confided to Rosa Burley that 'truly success is harder to bear than adversity' [‡] and perhaps he found an echo of this belief later in the war. At the beginning of hostilities, the public mood was one of eagerness for the fight and men rushed to enlist. Elgar, like the rest of the British public, was eager to play his part and moved by the plight of the Belgians during the invasion of their country. He was also moved to tears by the poem written by the Belgian writer Emile Cammaerts

---

[*] Moore, *The Windflower Letters*, p. 136.
[†] Reed, *Elgar as I Knew Him*, p. 54.
[‡] Burley, *Record of a Friendship*, p. 91.

commemorating the fall of Belgium which had been translated into English by his wife Tita Brand Cammaerts. The result was the first of his significant war works, Carillon, in which the poem was recited against a background of Elgar's music. The work was premiered on 7 December 1914 and caught the public imagination with its impassioned, emotional character. There followed more pieces: Polonia in aid of the Polish Relief Fund, Une Voix dans le Désert and Le Drapeau Belge, again settings of Cammaerts' poems, and the hugely popular, nautical shanties the Fringes of the Fleet which set poems by Rudyard Kipling in what Elgar described as a 'broad salt-water style'. Between composing Elgar undertook countrywide conducting tours as well as conducting and arranging in London. It was an exhausting schedule.

Later in the war, when the certainties that many people had felt began to fall away, Elgar's tone of heroic sorrow and pity for the fallen again caught the public mood. This was particularly so with his greatest piece instigated by the war, The Spirit of England. It was written against a background of a worsening situation on the Western Front with unimaginable numbers killed or wounded. The piece set three poems by Laurence Binyon that had been published in his collection The Winnowing Fan in December 1914. Although begun in 1915, the work was not completed and performed until 1917. It was not a piece of national triumphalism; it had, rather, the tone of a requiem and a statement about the horror and waste of war – and again he caught the public mood. But not everyone was impressed. Parry found it 'Very poor stuff for the most part … Like a sentimental part-song.'[*] Yet this judgement fails to recognise how it found an echo in the hearts of the audience. It was certainly emotional and for certain listeners the emotional charge of the work, coming as it did with the war still being fought, was almost too moving. Rosa Burley remembered the first performance:

> This was an almost harrowing experience and I remember that Gervase Elwes, who had taken part, told me that he hardly knew how they had all got through it. The war casualities at that time were heartrending and almost every member of the choir must have lost a close relative or a friend. [†]

For Elgar too, the work marked a turning point. In a letter to Ernest Newman dated 17 June 1917 he described the way that he had treated the Binyon text, adding at the close: 'And this ends, as far as I can see, my contribution to war music.' By its very nature Elgar's war music could not be 'absolute' music. There was no great 'war symphony', much as Alice would have loved him to write one. Instead he had chosen to write pieces and to set verse which were particular to contemporary events and which closely reflected the war and people's reaction to it at the time. This in part explains why they disappeared from the repertoire with peace. Even The Spirit of England which more than any other war piece of his does transcend the period is now heard only rarely. It deserves to be heard

---

[*] Martin Bird, 'An Elgarian Wartime Chronology', in Foreman (ed.), *Oh, My Horses!*, p. 436.
[†] Burley, *Record of a Friendship*, p. 199.

more, but perhaps still needs a degree of historical awareness and sympathy from the listener. (See also, for another view, an interview with the conductor David Lloyd-Jones in 2003 where he describes himself as 'surprised and saddened' by its infrequent performance and states that he prefers this work to The Music Makers.) [*] With the end of his war music and the beginning of his Brinkwells period, Elgar retreated into himself, away from the public statements he had been making and towards an intimate expression of his innermost emotions.

Blackwood's Fairyland

There were, however, even in the war years some chances of musical escape from the ever-present reality of the conflict. Two pieces in particular represent sheer escapism in the face of the horrors of warfare. These were the music for the ballet The Sanguine Fan and the incidental music for Starlight Express. Of the two the latter was by far the more important for Elgar. It was in dimension a major piece of writing which on completion ran to over an hour's music and was achieved in little over a month between November and December 1915. But it also brought him into contact with Algernon Blackwood, an unusual and charismatic character who was quickly to become a firm favourite with both Elgar and his wife (they called him 'Starlight'). Starlight Express was a stage adaptation of Blackwood's book *A Prisoner in Fairy Land*, a story about fairy enchantment and the healing power of human sympathy. The theme appealed to Elgar both in its sentiments and in its setting which recalled for him incidents in his own youth. It did, moreover, extol the virtues of childhood and there was still much of the child in Elgar.

The idea for the play enchanted him – and his music for the production which had been described by the producer as 'half reality and half fairyland' was both light and captivating – particularly in the midst of London at war. He wrote to Sidney Colvin in December 1915: '… it has been a real joy to have something so pure and simple to do …'. [†] Billy Reed recalled that it occupied him 'practically the whole of the time he could spare from his duties in the Hampstead Volunteer Reserve'. [‡] Elgar was certainly totally consumed with writing; Alice's diary for 7 December reads: 'E. not out all day – absorbed in his 'Starlight'. Mr Blackwood to dine – very pleasant and interesting. E. told him many stories. Blackwood entranced with E.'s music.'

But even this delight was not without problems for Elgar. Both he and Blackwood thoroughly disapproved of the stage designs and the costumes for the piece which Blackwood characterised as 'suburban, Arts & Crafts rubbish' and which Elgar believed ruined any chance of success the play might have had, asserting that the designer should be put in a 'Home'. Moreover, to add to his concerns, Alice was involved in a worrying accident in a London taxicab

---

[*] *Elgar Society Newsletter*, November 2003, p. 14.
[†] EBM , letter no. 3459.
[‡] Bird, *op. cit.*, p. 408.

8 Elgar and Algernon Blackwood in 1916

just before the opening which kept her at home whilst she recovered from concussion. The production had only a short run but which was not entirely without success, opening on 29 December 1915 at the Kingsway Theatre and closing on 29 January 1916. Critics liked the music but some found the play self-indulgent, 'preachy and pretentious'. Both men, according to Alice, 'felt the closing of the Starlight very much'.[*]

It had in many ways been an escape for Elgar but that did not mean that the exercise was an irrelevance. Once again, Elgar seems to have connected with a more widespread need that was shared by the public at home and the men serving in the unimaginable world of the trenches. A letter from Captain J. Lawrence Fry, serving at the Front, explained to Elgar what the Starlight Express music meant to his Mess. He wrote: 'We possess a fairly good gramophone in our Mess, and I have bought your record Starlight Express … It is being played for the twelfth time over.' He goes on to describe the gramophone, and Elgar's music, as 'the only means of bringing back to us the days that are gone, and helping one through the Ivory gate that leads to fairyland, or Heaven, whatever one likes to call it.'[†]

Captain Fry's letter illuminates the reasons why this music should have captured the public imagination. For not only was it nostalgic for earlier years, and childhood with its innocence and purity, but it was also optimistic in its belief

---

[*] Alice Elgar's Diary, 30 January 1916.
[†] Bird, *op. cit.*, p. 434.

in humanity. It reflected too a current interest which whilst apparently directed at children had also a more serious 'adult' meaning involving a preoccupation with fairies. Blackwood's *A Prisoner in Fairyland* certainly shared this concern, and it was perhaps the reason why the critics had found the Starlight Express play too moralising. Blackwood's fairyland was seen by him as an essential part of humanity. One of his characters laments the fact that the world no longer believed in fairyland and that even the children have become scientific. He goes on to suggest that 'Perhaps it's only buried though. The two ought to run in harness really – opposite interpretations of the universe. One might revive it – here and there perhaps. Without it, all the tenderness seems leaking out of life.' *

Contemporaneous with this, a similar vein of seriousness could be detected behind the artist and illustrator Arthur Rackham's delight in fairy tales which he described at the end of the war as 'general truths, rather than particular truths. True to human nature and human ways of considering human experience, sifted and transmuted till they become truer than truth, essence.' † Rackham's wartime work included contributions to many patriotic publications including, like Elgar, *King Albert's Book* (1914), and in 1916 *The Allies' Fairy Book* which gathered fairy tales from each of the allied nations in a collection that aimed to delight rather than terrify (the editors obviously thinking that real life was terrifying enough at that time). Rackham, like Elgar, took inspiration from the West Sussex countryside around Arundel, and, as it happens, was a fellow member of the Hampstead Volunteer Reserve. Perhaps if this preoccupation with fairies seems bizarre to the modern reader we only need to recall the huge success of J.M. Barrie's *Peter Pan* (1906) which played then mainly to adult audiences and which still enchants today.

Medical Problems

Musical problems were only one of the things that Elgar had to contend with at this period. Another was his rapidly declining health both physically and psychologically. Alice's diary records a succession of minor ailments, psychosomatic symptoms and physical symptoms which often interfered with his punishing schedule. Many of the symptoms were long-standing ones which had dogged his early years – headaches – eye problems – throat problems – frequent colds and infections – in fact her diary during the war years begins most entries with two things: the state of Elgar's health and the weather (the latter sometimes seeming to affect the former).

Some of these afflictions appear now to have been the result of stress. In earlier years the alleviation of the stress was sometimes enough to bring about a cure, as with his earlier decision not to proceed with his lectures at Birmingham University, and Carice's observation that his headaches would often disappear if he became interested in something sufficiently absorbing. But during the war

---

* Blackwood, *A Prisoner in Fairyland*, p. 59.
† Hudson, *Arthur Rackham*, p. 154.

years his problems became less easily dealt with and towards the end of the conflict there was, clearly, a serious physical condition. The resolution of this, as we shall see, had an almost cathartic effect on the composer.

Elgar had complained of noises in his ear before the outbreak of war – and in 1912, with increasing symptoms of giddiness, he had been diagnosed as suffering from 'gout' in his eyes and head by the eminent physician Victor Horsley.* The noises continued into March of that year and Elgar turned to Sir Maurice Abbott Anderson for help. He was a physician who was thereafter frequently in attendance – often dispensing necessary reassurance – and who quickly became Elgar's first port of call if there were any doubt about his state of health. It was feared that he was suffering from Menières Disease, a syndrome that is characterised by the flooding of the labyrinth of the ear and resulting 'cluster' attacks of vertigo, tinnitus and bouts of sickness. Menières is, moreover, a disease that re-occurs after periods of remission – sometimes prolonged ones – and which, eventually, can result in deafness.

The problem re-emerged in April 1916 when, on the way to visit his sister Pollie Grafton at Stoke Prior, Elgar was taken ill on the train. Alice, who never accompanied Elgar to his sister's home, was meanwhile in London suffering from flu. Her diary, however, records her distress at the news and also conveys her sense of guilt that she had encouraged him to leave even although he had complained of being giddy. She felt compelled to write down her excuses: she was ill and their large London house was cold and she had hoped the change would do him good. Alice immediately 'phoned Sir Maurice so he telephoned the home and gave directions'. On Elgar's return to London three days later on 11 April, Alice expressed her hope that it was more to do with influenza than his 'former illness'. But doubts remained and by 2 May Elgar still needed reassurance from the obliging Sir Maurice that he would be well enough to fulfil a conducting engagement. Thereafter Alice's diary for 1916 has the recurrent thread running through it: 'E. not very well.' Another visit to Stoke Prior had to be delayed in June because of his health.

Although Elgar continued to suffer from bouts of giddiness, some medical opinion now favours a diagnosis of stress rather than Menières. There is no mention of frequent attacks of sickness in the diaries or from his doctors, and although he would complain at times of noises in his ears, he did not seem to have suffered from the continuing tinnitus which afflicts the Menières sufferer even after the vertigo attacks have subsided. Neither is there any evidence of increasing deafness later in life. Certainly his giddiness tended to appear at times of significant stress, when, for example, in 1917 Kipling objected to 'The Fringes of the Fleet' poems being performed, and also after Alice's death in 1920.

The ear problem may also have been exacerbated by a very real physical problem that grew increasingly apparent during 1916 and 1917. Sir Maurice had treated a throat infection in August 1916 with electric cautery and although it appeared to respond, the condition returned and was treated again on the

---

* For information on Elgar's doctors, see Appendix 4.

5th and 10th of the following January. Thereafter Alice's diary records constant infections and headaches when Elgar sometimes stayed in bed and sometimes got up (appearing downstairs in his fur coat when the house got too cold). They relied heavily on Sir Maurice to say whether Elgar was well enough to go to concerts or rehearsals. By December 1917, his condition was causing great worry. Sir Maurice called on 3 December with 'admirable medicines' but Elgar was still feeling ill at Christmas and Sir Maurice was called out again on Christmas Eve to give a new prescription. On Christmas Day Carice went to collect the new medicine and Alice rather tersely wrote in her diary: 'very quiet day – rather depressing.'

The new medicine did not seem to be effective and on 27 December Sir Maurice was back, returning two days later with Dr Hale-White, in Alice's words 'a tummy specialist', to give a second opinion. He could find no organic trouble and recommended smoking, golf, and change. But Elgar was clearly unwell whatever the diagnosis may be – and he knew it. In a postscript added to Alice's letter to the Windflower dated 29 December 1917 he wrote, 'The Doctors say nothing the matter: but I am not well.'[*] Elgar's sole diary entry for 4 January sees him conforming to Dr Hale White's recommendation: 'smoked a cigar', he recorded bleakly – but it was to do him no good.

Eventually Sir Maurice decided that an x-ray was in order but the results were negative, and, after another examination this time by Dr Stanley Melville, the diagnosis of a 'dropped stomach' was made with the promise that Elgar would soon be better. But Elgar continued to be ill. At one stage his teeth were suspected and Sir Maurice met him at the dentist to see what could be done, but it was not until March that Elgar saw a throat surgeon: 'E. to Mr Tilley with Sir Maurice. Tonsils condemned', Elgar recorded tersely in his diary for 6 March 1918. The operation to remove his tonsils was carried out by Mr Tilley on 15 March and it was discovered that one tonsil in particular was badly infected 'all over abscess matter and a black stone, pea size in it' as Alice's diary records. (See Appendix 4.) It was a considerable operation for someone of his age, and painful too. In a letter dated 5 April 1918 to Ivor Atkins Elgar wrote: 'I have had a bad winter, one illness after another and the entertainment culminated in a throat operation (vilely painful) and a spell in a nursing home, which was not cheering. I have been home for more than a week now and things are settling down but I am not yet strong by a long way.'[†] In fact his infected tonsils may well have explained his long history of throat problems and recurrent infections and may have exacerbated complaints in his ears.

It is hardly surprising that these medical problems did little to lighten Elgar's depressive tendencies. His unhappiness is evident in a letter written to Alice Stuart Wortley in December 1916: 'Everything pleasant and promising in my life is dead' he asserted:

---

[*] Moore, *The Windflower Letters*, p. 196.
[†] Atkins, *The Elgar-Atkins Friendship*, p. 287.

I have the happiness of my friends to console me as I had fifty years ago. I feel that life has gone back so far when I was alone & there was no one to stand between me & disaster – health or finance – now that has come back & I am more alone & the prey of circumstances than ever before. *

Finances and Severn House

If health were a constant worry, then so were the Elgars' finances. In the first month of the war Elgar had announced that he, Alice and Carice were financially ruined, and whatever the truth about this it revealed Elgar's continual worry over money. However, 'ruined' or not, they continued to entertain throughout the war in London, Alice having instigated a Sunday afternoon 'at home' to attract interesting and stimulating company for Elgar and on one occasion these Sunday guests numbered over twenty. Alice and Elgar had knowingly extended themselves financially with the purchase of their London house in December 1911. Severn House, as they named it, was a formidable edifice which had been designed by Norman Shaw for the painter and Royal Academician Edwin Long in the 1880s. Alice had wanted a house that would reflect Elgar's eminent position; indeed Elgar was keen to have the house too, and it certainly fulfilled Alice's criteria, being designed for formality and effect rather than comfort.

They had bought it with difficulty, Alice having to break the conditions of the trust that held her capital, and as the house had been standing empty for a few years, there was much work to be done on it, and money to be spent. It was the only house that they were to buy as a married couple. The impressive entrance to Severn House through high front doors of beaten brass designed by Long set the tone for the rest of their home. There were three floors, the first two devoted to 'public' rooms, large spaces and a grand staircase. There was a 60ft picture gallery and upstairs on the first floor a grandly proportioned painting room, which became Elgar's music room. On the third floor there were eight bedrooms to house the family and staff. Everything was heated by a complicated heating system that Elgar took some time to master.

It was a grand home, but it was not necessarily a convenient one. Carice described it as 'by no means everybody's house' explaining that it would only accommodate a small family as domestic convenience had been sacrificed to the long stately corridor and the large music room and annexe, a large dining room and large basement. She adds that there were 'two large bedrooms and three quite small ones, and three even smaller for the staff'. †

At first Elgar was happy there and Alice threw herself into the job of creating a fit background for his genius. The scale and distinction of the house was even noted by the press who singled out Elgar's billiards room and the Blue Study (which Alice had decorated entirely in shades of deep blue – even to

9 *Severn House*

the bindings of the books) for particular mention.* It was not made public knowledge, however, that Elgar had chosen to sell his valuable Gagliano violin in order to buy the specially designed billiards table (valued at £110 in 1913) – something which upset Alice deeply – especially as she was the one to take it to Hill's (the world-renowned violin dealers and makers of Wardour Street) to be sold.

But there were two inherent problems with the house. The first of these was that whereas it fulfilled one side of Elgar's personality – his desire for recognition and honours – it did less for the 'escapist' Elgar – the one that liked to disappear on to the Malvern Hills or listen to the wind in the trees.

Rosa Burley had a presentiment that Elgar too recognised something of this when he showed her round the house before the purchase. In her memoirs she wrote how Elgar had taken her to Hampstead to see the house before he bought it. She described it as a 'very impressive' building standing half-way up the hill of Netherhall Gardens and wrote how she realised as they walked through the empty rooms that Elgar meant to buy it, although she doubted whether this was a financial possibility. She considered this visit as 'one of the strangest afternoons we ever spent together and I have never known the duality of his character so strongly marked as it was that day.' She could see how the grandeur of the house with its fine aspects and long music room attracted him whilst at the same time he went out of his way to stress that his success was unimportant to him. So on one hand he drew her attention to the beauties of the house whilst on the other he confessed to her that he felt there was always some lovely thing in life which had somehow escaped him. Rosa Burley then added 'he also told me that the only part of his life that had ever been happy was the period of struggle at Malvern and that even now he never conducted his music without

---

* Moore, *A Creative Life*, p. 631.

*10 The Billiards
Room, Severn
House*

finding his mind had slipped back to summer days on the Malvern Hills, to
Birchwood or to the drowsy peace of Longdon Marsh.'*

Elgar's habit of finding happiness in the past (whether it existed then or not)
is evident here, but more important is his continuing association of his music
with landscape. In his former houses there had always been an escape route
into deep, isolated landscape: an easy walk on to the hills, into the Hereford
countryside or a stay at his cottage, Birchwood, a short journey from Malvern.
In spite of the proximity of the Heath, Severn House was a more serious
proposition – a more urban proposition – expanding one side of his life but at
the risk of contracting another. Elgar had attempted to modify the atmosphere
a little with the purchase of a puppy in November 1912 but, whilst he and
Carice loved dogs, Alice did not. The first candidate was deemed by her to
be untrustworthy and in a contest between the expensive new carpets and an
untrained dog, the carpets won. Another experiment two months later saw the
acquisition of an Aberdeen terrier puppy which simply disappeared and could
not be found the next day by Elgar even at the Battersea Dogs' Home. In the
event Severn House remained a home without dogs.

Once Elgar had experienced a lengthy stay at Brinkwells and, deep in the
country, had become immersed in his highly personal, emotionally revealing
chamber works, he became convinced of the unsuitability of London for
composing. In letters to Alice Stuart Wortley in October 1918 Elgar confessed
that the thought of 'town life' made him feel 'just as limp as before the nursing
home episode' and that in London he felt that the air did not agree with him
and he 'longed to get back to his quiet woods'. [†] And two months later he made

---

* Burley, *Record of a Friendship*, pp. 191-2.
† Moore, *The Windflower Letters*, pp. 213-4.

the point again in a letter to Schuster, writing that if there was a return to Severn House from the country 'music is off'. *

The second drawback to Severn House became apparent because of the war. It was in those circumstances too large, too expensive, too cold and required a number of domestic staff who became increasingly difficult to find – a situation that was apparent to many house owners even after the Armistice. As early as 25 August 1914 Elgar was telling Sidney Colvin that they had reduced their staff at Severn House, and thereafter Alice's diary records the comings and goings of various domestics, some of whom stayed only for a few days before they were replaced by someone else. Not only were men of suitable age enlisting for service but women were being encouraged to take jobs which hitherto had been filled by men. This for former domestic servants meant the opportunity of a higher wage and the sense that they were engaged in meaningful war work. Many women also joined the Red Cross, the Women's Army Ancillary Corps or the Women's Royal Air Force. In his War Journal Edward Heron-Allen, Elgar's virtual contemporary, described the shrinkage in his household which, with the departure of the cook and the housemaid to be Wrens, left him with one housemaid and a 'tweenie' by May 1918 which meant that his wife had to do the cooking. †

With the growing strictures of DORA (The Defence of the Realm Acts) and a shortage of coal which had been apparent early in the war, the heating of Severn House became a real problem. Householders had to submit forms for their coal allocation in 1917 and were encouraged to use gas or coke instead, but a coal and lighting crisis continued into 1918 with some London houses being kept in semi-darkness as a result. Entries in Alice's diary reflect the growing problem: she records no coke and a frighteningly cold house in April 1916 (at a period when Elgar was unwell). The next winter was also intensely bitter and Alice records a cold house in January again at a time when Elgar was suffering and her relief at the arrival of some fuel in the middle of a hard spell of weather. By February 1919 Alice had had enough and went down to the Town Hall to remonstrate about the coal allowance. She painted a picture of 'Sir Edward' sitting in a cold studio with no food. She was successful and noted in her diary that by the evening an augmented allowance was notified. However, notification was one thing, delivery was another, and by the middle of February she was again complaining of a cold house and no coke. By 4 March she writes that no coal or coke had arrived and that they had heating enough only for one day – although nothing came the next day either and the complaint was repeated in the middle of the month. This was not an unusual experience. Even by 1917 not only had the price of coal soared but it had become extraordinarily difficult to get it delivered and some Londoners took to collecting their sacks of coal from the coal yards in taxis (and were charged heavily for the privilege).

---

* Moore, *A Creative Life*, p. 732.
† *Edward Heron-Allen's Journal of the Great War*, ed. Harvey and Fitzgerald, p. 189.

Escape from the City

During the war years Elgar made a habit of leaving London as often as he could to stay with family or friends in the countryside. This was not the case with Alice who spent a far greater amount of time at Severn House. The war was brought home to Londoners by the growing number of Zeppelin and aircraft attacks on the capital. Raids had started at the beginning of 1915 with a Zeppelin attack on the East Coast of England and by September they had reached central London causing considerable damage to property and loss of life. By November 1916 enemy planes were reaching London and these bombing raids continued despite the established air defences and the adoption of 'barrage fire' to bring them down. Between 1914 and 1918 over 8,000 bombs were dropped from Zeppelins or aircraft and the total number of people killed or injured was believed to have been nearly 5,000, London accounting for about half this number.

The air raids and the resulting damage stimulated much curiosity and Alice's diary for 4 September 1915 records how she and Elgar had taken the omnibus to Leyton to see the damage from a Zeppelin raid there, whilst a few days later Alice and Carice watched a raid from Severn House, ignoring Elgar's advice to go down to the basement; 'Could not leave this extraordinary sight', wrote Alice. The following day, 8 September, she watched from the windows of Severn House and described the scene in her diary: 'The sky was lit by flying searchlights – part of Zeppelin visible like a gilt box, and star-like shells bursting more or less near it, and the boom of guns sounding!' Later in the war, when Elgar was touring outside London with the Fringes of the Fleet, both he and Alice experienced very close bombing at Chatham at a time when Elgar was also far from well. In a letter to Alice Stuart Wortley he gives his account of the experience: 'Alice and I are here – no performance last night – terrible gun firing – raid etc etc: they expect one every night. I am not well as the place is so noisy and I do not sleep – the guns are the quietest things here. I long for the country and Stoke. I think all the time of it – and you … '.[*]

As well as the danger from enemy bombs, there was too the inconvenience of the blackout – but Elgar confessed that he rather liked the darkness of the streets and the atmosphere this created – like Alice, he could react to the visual changes that the war brought and see some beauty in them. In a letter to the Windflower he wrote:

> How beautiful it is in the still quiet streets without the trying brilliant lights: it all seems so muffled – a muted life to me and so sweet & pure; I do not like the idea of garishly lit roads & streets again – I love them so much, so much as they are. [†]

To explain Elgar's escapes into the country solely in terms of the war would be misleading. Certainly the war made London dangerous but Elgar had

---

[*] Moore, *The Windflower Letters*, p. 191.
[†] *Ibid.*, p. 141.

always needed the country. However, the war did have the effect of making the country seem of even greater value to him. In a letter to Ivor Atkins dated 26 October 1914 and addressed from the Special Constabulary, Hampstead South Division, Elgar wrote:

> ... here I feel as if you in the country were doing something, but altho' I am busy from morning till night the <u>houses</u> seem to choke it all off. We are fighting for the <u>country</u> & I wish I could <u>see</u> it ... ..If it is sunny just go round to the W. end [of the cathedral] and look over the valley towards Malvern – bless my beloved country for me – & send me a p.c. saying you have done so. [*]

It is clear that in Elgar's mind, it was not the Country, not London, but the *countryside* for which he was fighting.

His wartime escapes began in 1914 with a visit to his sister Pollie and these continued, although as we have seen above he was prevented on some occasions because of ill health. Pollie had been born in 1854, the third of Ann Elgar's five children and her relationship with Elgar was a close one. She had married William Grafton in 1879, they had acted as witnesses at Elgar's marriage to Alice, and it was to their house at Stoke Prior that Elgar made frequent trips. It is fortunate that in 1915 Pollie had a new housemaid, Ellen, who remembered Elgar's visits and told an acquaintance about them. From her we get a picture of a relaxed Elgar, walking the dogs, playing the piano and sitting in the garden in the afternoon 'immaculately dressed as usual in open-necked shirt with a stock at the throat and Norfolk jacket' listening to the birds with his eyes closed – 'a most wonderful symphony', he called it. She remembered him as a gently-spoken, reserved man with a Worcestershire accent who had a keen sense of humour and who one day played the piano just for her whilst she sat at his side. [†]

What Pollie and her family offered Elgar was a retreat from London and from pressure – and the kind of relaxed family life in the midst of nephews and nieces that was unlike his own. Ellen, curious that Lady Elgar never visited with her husband, asked Pollie the reason and was told that 'she does not care for travel'. This clearly was not the case as on one occasion in 1916, having been in Worcester together, Elgar then travelled on to Stoke Prior to stay with Pollie whilst Alice visited friends at Broadway, and some other explanation must be found. Certainly there was one side of Alice that saw leaving London in the war as a sort of 'running away', but she went with Elgar to the Lake District to stay with the Stuart Wortleys, and to Frank Schuster's house in Maidenhead, and on other excursions as well, so this cannot explain her absence from Elgar's family at Stoke Prior.

She had never been close to his family: they were not of her social class and perhaps she thought that this was one part of his life in which she did not fit. Also, as intent as Alice was to protect and shield Elgar from anything unpleasant, she

---

[*] Atkins, *The Elgar-Atkins Friendship*, p. 265.
[†] Moore, *A Creative Life*, pp. 685-6.

was not possessive. She knew that she did not answer all his requirements and that his many-sided personality needed input from others in order to be happy. Wulstan Atkins remembered the relationship between Elgar and his sister and described her as being 'almost like a mother to him' – a description that could also fit Elgar's relationship with Alice. Perhaps Alice was happy to hand over the responsibility for a time. She knew that Elgar was safe at Stoke Prior and there is little doubt that Pollie was good for him. They had, according to Wulstan Atkins, 'a wonderful understanding and brought out the very best in each other. There were lovely little touches of humour and twinkling of eyes.'*

As well as the house at Stoke Prior there were other destinations where Elgar was among understanding friends away from the noise and distractions of London. There was Frank Schuster's house on the Thames at Maidenhead, 'The Hut'; there was Edward and Antonia Speyer's house 'Ridgehurst' in Hertfordshire; and there were opportunities to see the Stuart Wortleys in the Lake District where they holidayed at Walls (a house belonging to Charles Stuart Wortley's cousin Lord Muncaster). Elgar also visited the Berkeleys at Spetchley Park, which brought back memories of his childhood in Worcestershire.

Finding Brinkwells

During the war Elgar exploited all these opportunities for escape. These breaks became very frequent in the summer of 1916. Elgar stayed at Stoke Prior between 3 and 15 June and then at Ridgehurst between 24 and 26 of the month. After a weekend at The Hut in Maidenhead Alice wrote in her diary on 12 July that Elgar was out a great deal and longing for the country and by 15 July he was again at Stoke Prior. Alice became worried that he had been away so long and confided in her diary that she was missing him dreadfully. Then on 29 July she wrote that he was going from Stoke Prior to Stratford 'all by himself'. At the beginning of the next month Alice met Elgar at Bridgnorth and on 2 August they decided to go to the Lake District the next day where they stayed for nearly two weeks. September continued for Elgar with visits to Ridgehurst, Spetchley Park, Stoke Prior and to Holmbury St Mary to stay with Lalla Vandervelde.

Alice wrote in her diary that he returned looking better for these holidays, but they didn't really answer the need that he had for his own isolated retreat in which he could concentrate on music. Elgar's restlessness would reassert itself often only days after his return to London and so in July 1916 Alice started looking for their own country cottage, beginning her search at Penshurst. They had decided on Sussex for compelling reasons. Elgar needed somewhere that was easily reachable from London – and Sussex had good rail connections from Victoria. Moreover, they both liked the county and had pleasant memories of it.

Their association had started in 1894 with a golfing holiday for Elgar in Littlehampton when he and Alice had visited Chichester and Arundel. Then in 1915 they had been lent 'Hooklands' in Midhurst by Admiral Caulfield and his

* Atkins, *The Elgar-Atkins Friendship*, p. 429.

11 Brinkwells (c.1920); photograph possibly by John Vicat Cole

family with whom Rosa Burley was staying. After a day's visit to the house there on 20 July, Alice decided to take up the Caulfields' offer, writing in her diary in a somewhat desperate tone: 'Felt we must go there … .E. wanting change.' The stay was obviously a great success although initially Elgar had seemed reluctant and had, according to Alice, become tired on the journey and had wanted to turn round and go home. Once there, however, Elgar bonded with the Caulfield's dog, who, according to Elgar 'has adopted me and takes me for walks in the wildest places – he knows them all & I tell him everything!'*

Hooklands was set in woods and on seeing it Elgar had thought it beautiful and Alice's diary noted gratefully that the house was 'left so nice & ready & all welcomy and pleasant.' They stayed there between 16-30 August but the day after their return, Alice wrote that Elgar was restless and wanted to go away again. Rosa Burley commented that the beauty of West Sussex had made a deep impression on him and so, when in May 1916 Elgar was, according to Alice, 'tired and very anxious to get away', Alice decided on Sussex again, this time Eastbourne in East Sussex.

Eastbourne itself was not a success. Alice, who was intolerant of anything provincial, wrote that Eastbourne was 'like Hampstead Heath on a Sunday –

---

* Moore, *The Windflower Letters*, p. 151.

horrid place!' Elgar also disliked the town, but both of them agreed that the air was lovely and when they hired a car and toured the surrounding countryside, Sussex again rose in their esteem. They drove to Pevensey (where Elgar fell asleep in the castle grounds) and Herstmonceux (having tea at what Alice called 'a wretched little inn') and enjoyed the drive, the flowers, the birds and the interesting churches. Back home at Severn House on 23 May Alice wrote that 'E. seemed so much better' but then a day later she wrote that he was not very well again.

Continuing her search for a retreat, Alice made another exploratory journey to Sussex with Carice on 2 May 1917 whilst Elgar was visiting Pollie at Stoke Prior. This time she was successful. Her diary entry describes her first sight of Brinkwells.

> A. & C. to Fittleworth to see a cottage – a 2 seater met them but after arriving at the inn preferred to walk – <u>Lovely</u> place, sat in lovely wood & heard a nightingale, turtoo doves, and many other dicksies & saw lizards and heard Tuckoo first time. Also saw swallows. Lovely <u>hot hot</u> day. A. much perplexed as cottage is so very cottagy but large studio and <u>lovely</u> view & woods, dear place – finally took it for June – Lovely walk thro' woods & by primroses to station …

Alice and Carice returned via Horsham (where they had to wait for 45 minutes) but found that they were not tired by their long walks. In the event they were there again before June and Elgar had found his retreat.

Some years before, in 1908, Elgar had written to August Jaeger bemoaning the fact that he could not afford to get 'a <u>quiet</u> studio' where he could work. But in 1917 he found, or rather Alice found, exactly that: a quiet, affordable studio surrounded only by the sounds of nature and by the beautiful hills and forests of the West Sussex countryside where he could write new music undisturbed.

CHAPTER FOUR

'Remote from the Spoor of Man'

To Let

The cottage of Brinkwells is situated about a mile and a half north of the village of Fittleworth and surrounded by sweet chestnut woods. The cottage itself and the land around it belongs to the Stopham Estate which was, and still is, owned by the ancient Barttelot family whose history can be traced back to the time of William the Conqueror. The estate has been in possession of the family since the 14th century and the present owner, Colonel Sir Brian Barttelot Bt, says that Brinkwells has belonged to his family for at least 150 years and possibly for longer. [*] The name of the cottage could have originated from that of the first settler there, 'Brynca', who may also have owned Brinksole and Brinkhurst Furze.

The cottage is deep in countryside and difficult to locate and it would have been almost impossible for Alice to 'find' it by chance. She must have had prior knowledge but it is now impossible to say exactly how this was obtained. It is most likely that she heard of Brinkwells from Sidney and Frances Colvin, who had rented E.V. Lucas's cottage at Tillington, near Petworth, for the summer. Or, it is possible that the then tenant, wishing to sub-let, may have advertised. The tenant was the painter Rex Vicat Cole, who had first rented the cottage in 1905. With the outbreak of the War and his own entry into the Bedham division of the Civil Guard and later into the United Arts Rifles, Vicat Cole could no longer make use of the cottage. He was, moreover, in need of more income for his wife, Hannah, and his two sons who were left in London in 1917 when he was posted to training camp at Beccles. It was therefore Hannah who dealt with the business of letting the cottage although on two subsequent occasions Rex Vicat Cole himself was involved.

It is clear from Alice's diary that Hannah would sometimes visit Severn House to fix the details of the lettings, which were on a short-term basis, a little time before the Elgars departed for Sussex. On at least one occasion, Alice also wrote to her to ask whether they could make some changes in the garden. [†] For their second stay, in August 1917, Alice wrote in her diary that she had heard they could have the cottage for a fortnight '& took it' a week before their departure – an arrangement made by post as Alice was away in Hereford at

---

[*] Letter to the authors 21 April 2003.
[†] For a more extended discussion of the letting terms and legal situation surrounding Brinkwells see Appendix 3.

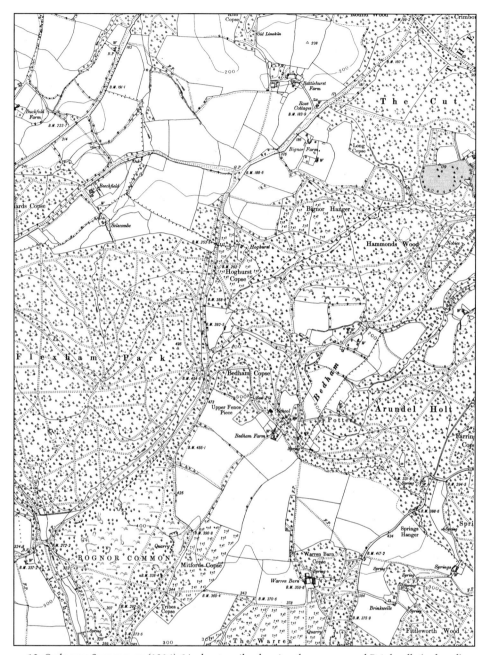

12 Ordnance Survey map (1914) 6 inches to mile, showing the area around Brinkwells (reduced)

the time. Later that year, in November, Hannah and one of her boys went to tea at Severn House where she would have met Algernon Blackwood, another Sunday visitor.

The following year, prior to the Elgars' departure for Sussex on what was going to be their most extended stay at Brinkwells, there was a flurry of arrangements with the Coles. Alice went to see Hannah Vicat Cole about details of the stay on 26 April, and then two days later both Rex and Hannah paid a visit to Severn House for tea – an occasion noted in Elgar's diary and the only evidence of any meeting between him and Rex.

In 1919 there is further evidence of the relationship between Alice and the Vicat Coles as Alice attended an exhibition arranged by Rex in London in March.* A month later, Hannah again took one of her sons to tea at Severn House for Alice's Sunday afternoon 'at home'. Hannah was also there on 10 June, along with the Windflower and Billy Reed, three days before Alice and Elgar left again for Brinkwells. With the Elgars' friends, Sidney and Frances Colvin, installed in temporary accommodation at Campden Hill Square in 1919, there might well have been further contact as the Cole's home was also nearby. †

A few months before her death, and aware of the necessity of selling Severn House, Alice tried to negotiate the purchase of the Brinkwells lease. Her diary for 10 December 1919 runs: 'Mr V. Cole in afternoon & had tea – serious conversation re Brinkwells. Whether they w'd give it up – Do hope so.' But this attempt, carried on by Elgar and Carice after Alice's death, was, as we shall see, ultimately unsuccessful. The Elgars had fallen in love with the cottage but the Vicat Coles' association with the place went back much further and their feelings for it ran very deep.

A Divine Woodland Place

Their enthusiasm for the cottage is understandable. Brinkwells sits on high ground, reached by a road that winds uphill from Fittleworth towards Bedham and which passes through extraordinarily beautiful woods. These are the remains of the ancient hunting forests of Sir William de Alta Ripa whose ancestors had been granted land by William the Conqueror. When Elgar first saw the cottage, it was reached by an unmade-up track and he was disappointed when, after the war, a road was made, feeling that it spoilt the remoteness that he had so loved. But even so, the cottage still has to be approached down a farm track from the very narrow road. This track must be just as it was in the early years of the 20th century. It runs slightly downhill to the cottage, which is on the left as you walk down, and then continues as a footpath. Ordnance Survey maps of the period show that opposite the cottage on the other side of the track there were some structures – most probably the thatched barns and farm out-buildings which appear in Rex Vicat Cole's *Down the Green Lane* (1906). These have since disappeared although some foundations are still visible.

Billy Reed gives us a good idea of what the approach to Brinkwells was like in Elgar's time. He wrote:

---

* This was most probably the Memorial Exhibition for Byam Shaw organised by Rex Vicat Cole.
† Alice Elgar's diary records visits to the Colvins at Campden Hill Square on 4 and 5 September 1919.

13 The Track down to Brinkwells (c.1910); photograph by Rex Vicat Cole.

When I arrived, Mr Aylwin, a neighbouring farmer, met me at the station with a pony and trap, it being rather a long way to Brinkwells and difficult to find unless one was acquainted with the district; also I had a bag and a fiddle-case. We jogged along through some wonderfully wooded country, along a road which twisted and turned continually, until at last we came to about half a mile of straight road rising up a fairly steep hill, with chestnut plantations on either side. [*]

It was this remoteness that so enchanted Elgar – as it had Rex Vicat Cole who described his life at Brinkwells as an ideal isolation from the world. In a letter to Ivor Atkins Elgar enthused, 'The cottage is in Sussex … it is a divine woodland place and remote from the spoor of man.' [†] His enthusiasm had been evident from the start and, writing to the Windflower at the beginning of their first stay in the cottage on 26 May 1917, Alice expressed her relief that her choice had been so appropriate. 'I am delighted to tell you', she wrote, 'that Edward's first exclamation was "It is too lovely for words" & he was quite pleased with the house & has loved every minute since we came – So you may think how relieved & pleased I felt. I am in the garden & before my eyes lies a wonderful deep wood & low hills beyond & then the downs …' [‡]

'Cottagy' had been Alice's assessment of Brinkwells and it certainly fitted this description. Its origins probably go back to about 1600 – although some marks

---

[*] Reed, *Elgar as I Knew Him*, p. 56.
[†] Atkins, *The Elgar-Atkins Friendship*, p. 288.
[‡] Moore, *The Windflower Letters*, p. 183.

on the beams suggest that they could have had a previous existance as ships' timbers. [*] Its position in the woods suggests that it was connected either with charcoal burning or the making of wooden barrel hoops. Elgar found the cottage solidly built of stone with a thatched roof and on one side a wooden extension with a row of leaded windows on each floor (fire destroyed some of the top floor and the roof area in 1976 but it was subsequently rebuilt with minor alterations). [†] There were two half-timbered rooms downstairs with an open inglenook fireplace in the sitting room and a bread oven, and three rooms upstairs – two bedrooms with a small 'mezzanine' room on a half landing probably used as a maid's room. During the 1970s this became a bathroom. [‡] When the Elgars took the cottage, they obviously found it somewhat spartan and, as we shall see, set about making it more comfortable. It had been furnished with solid wooden furniture by their artist landlord Rex

14 *Rex Vicat Cole,* Down the Green Lane, *oil painting (1906)*

Vicat Cole, who had also decorated the interior with painted wooden panels of flowers and leaves. [§] A series of unique photographs taken by him about 1910 gives us the clearest idea of the cottage, the studio and its surroundings as it was at this period, and as it was when the Elgars stayed there.

There was a rudimentary kitchen area which Alice found inadequate and also two wooden lean-to buildings against the exterior wall. The most open aspects of the cottage faced part of the garden and the track back up to the road rather than the view (unlike the studio) and some of the rooms must have been dark. There was an earth closet in the garden some fifteen or twenty yards from the house near the studio and water was taken by pump from the well close to the cottage. [¶] So, conditions were fairly basic although this seems not to have affected Elgar's feelings for the place – in fact he seems to have revelled in the simplicity of life there.

Outside things were more expansive. There was a large garden with space enough for flowers, vegetables, hens, a tennis lawn (overgrown, but cleared by Elgar), a 'wild garden', and fruit trees – including one very prolific greengage tree. Writing to Frank Schuster on 7 June 1917, Elgar declared: 'It is divine: simple thatched cottage & a (soiled) studio with wonderful view: large garden

---

[*] Robert Walker in conversation, August 2004.
[†] Collett, *Elgar Lived Here*, pp. 83-4.
[‡] Robert Walker in conversation, August 2004.
[§] Barringer, *The Cole Family*, p. 127.
[¶] Sir Brian Barttelot in conversation.

15 The Interior of Brinkwells (c.1910); photograph by Rex Vicat Cole.

unweeded, a task for 40 men' – a verdict which irritated the Vicat Cole family when they learnt of it as they had worked hard on the garden. Something of the charm of the place can be ascribed to the way that it blended with its surroundings – the cottage seemed to be part of the garden and part of the landscape – an impression which was certainly felt by Cole's wife, Hannah, when she wrote: 'It looks like a dwelling that has been dropped bodily, garden and all into an enchanted wood. You wouldn't believe how beautiful it all is unless you could see it.' *

The Studio

From the garden there was a wonderful view across the Arun valley to the Downs – a view that was shared by the studio. Contemporary maps show the studio to have been a large structure with a floor space almost as big as that of the cottage. The studio was originally built by Rex Vicat Cole when he began to rent the cottage as his summer retreat in 1905 and was partly constructed from the timbers of a disused railway carriage. It was placed in the north-east corner of the garden at some distance from the house. According to Billy Reed it had a very large window on one side overlooking a stretch of garden that sloped away from it and beyond that there was an extensive view. The studio may well have been divided into a workshop area and a painting area, for Alice's diary for 19 August 1918 records that when Elgar's piano arrived it was carried 'thro'

---

* Barringer, *The Cole Family*, p. 126.

16 Hannah Vicat Cole in the Garden at Brinkwells (c.1910); photograph by Rex Vicat Cole

garden & workshop & to nice position in studio'. (This area was probably where Elgar indulged in his woodwork.) At some stage, most probably after the studio had been moved from Brinkwells to Bedham, the interior acquired wooden panelling to waist height which may have come from Petworth House. *

In the following years, when Rex Vicat Cole's lease had expired, the studio was transported up the hill to the hamlet of Bedham where it was installed in the garden of the cottage once occupied by the author Ford Madox Ford – then known as Coopers Cottage. † According to a long-standing resident of Bedham this happened in 1926 when the (presumably dismantled) studio was put on a farm cart. This would also accord with Rex Vicat Cole having taken a 21-year lease – a conventional period for a short lease. Once the studio was established at Bedham it sprouted some additions and improvements, but the original studio section is still clearly discernible.

There can be little doubt that the studio, which was to become the centre of Elgar's life in Sussex, proved to be the environment for which he had been searching. Once his creative strength had been revived and his thoughts turned to music late in the summer of 1918, he set about turning the 'studio' into a 'music room' and found in it the perfect environment for artistic work. Its sense of space, its distance from the house and the peace which surrounded it made it singularly appropriate. It had, after all, been built and conceived by an artist whose intensity of feeling for the exquisite countryside in which it was set

---

* Paul Yule in conversation.
† The studio was then incorporated into a house by the addition of wings at either end.

17 Rex Vicat Cole's sons, John and George, outside the Studio at Brinkwells (c.1910); photograph by Rex Vicat Cole

was clear in his paintings. The depth of Elgar's own feelings about Brinkwells was to be mirrored in his disappointment when attempts to buy the lease for Brinkwells failed. But this was not a one-sided affair – in just the same way the Vicat Coles love of the place was reflected in their two young sons' antagonism towards the Elgars for robbing them of their woodland retreat.

The Natural World

A little way from the garden, in the woods, there was what Billy Reed described as a 'primitive shack' around which Elgar could work on cutting chestnut poles and making barrel hoops. So the house, through its studio and outbuildings, extended its arms into the woods echoing the intimate relationship that both Elgar and Vicat Cole enjoyed with the natural world that surrounded them. It is this harmony between Brinkwells, its surrounding trees, and the life lived there which runs through both the paintings and the music that issued from the garden studio. And this sense of unity marks these works as particular and distinctive in the oeuvres of both Elgar and Vicat Cole.

The nearest habitation to the cottage is Springs Farm which sits on higher ground clear of the woods a quarter of a mile or so to the north-east. Part of the Stopham Estate, it was named after the numerous natural springs which arise in the area and it is reached from Brinkwells by a footpath through the northern end of Fittleworth Wood. During Elgar's time at Brinkwells its tenant was Thomas Aylwin who farmed there with his wife Ellen and his sons, his youngest boy, Arthur, having been killed in the Great War in 1916. Mr Aylwin provided a crucial local service, fetching and carrying with his pony cart and wagon. To the due south of Brinkwells a large arable field (then farmed by Aylwin) is edged by the southern mass of Fittleworth Wood. There are still many paths through this wood down to the village of Fittleworth and the Elgars explored these – although the topography was far from clear and more than one guest at Brinkwells got lost. Billy Reed, for whom Elgar had drawn a map showing how to find the cottage from Pulborough, relates how, on this visit to the cottage on 28 May 1921 with Percy Hull, the complexities of the woodland paths proved too much. Hull, who was determined to walk back to the station on his own, departed confidently enough having

18 *Thomas Aylwin of Springs Farm*

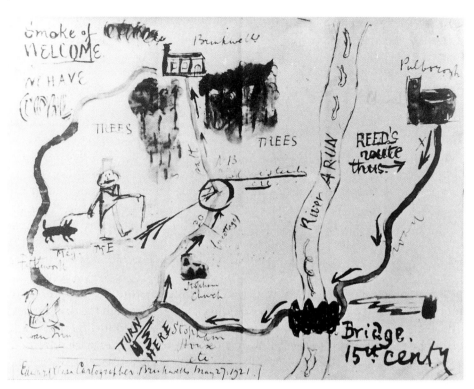

19 *Elgar's map of the way to Brinkwells from Pulborough drawn for Billy Reed on 27 May 1921*

been primed by Elgar with complex directions. To everyone's surprise an hour later, having walked energetically in what he thought was the right direction, Hull found himself back where he had started. Reed recalled that the look of astonishment on his face was indescribable.

Bedham

About a mile and a half to the north-west of the cottage over the hill and on higher ground is the small hamlet of Bedham. Set deep in beech and chestnut woods, it was originally the site of charcoal burners' huts. The author Rhoda Leigh, who lived there a little after Elgar's time, wrote an atmospheric account of the place and its inhabitants in her book, *Past and Passing. Tales from remote Sussex* (1932). On her first introduction to the place, she was struck by the marvellous view that unfolded as she climbed the road up from Fittleworth to Bedham – the view that was shared in part by Cole's studio. She wrote:

> In a field on the crest of this hill we paused for breath and looked back. An amazing view lay before us – a glimpse of the sea in the distance, the range of the South Downs, with Chanctonbury Clump standing sentinel over Steyning and Washington, Amberley chalk-pits gleaming in the sunshine, Arundel gap

displaying a square space of sky between the trees in the park at the top of
Bury Hill.

She also found the woods so vast and the paths so numerous that she was often
lost and, although the landowners employed men in the woods to clear the
ground and paths, rarely did she meet anyone.

In Elgar's time Bedham consisted of a farm (Bedham Farm), a few cottages
and, rather surprisingly, a chapel school. The building, with its consecrated
sanctuary, was erected in 1880, the pews doubling as school desks for the
children of the charcoal burners who still inhabited the woods at the turn of
the century – one well-known family of burners living in a mud hut in the
vicinity. It was run as a Dame School until 1925 and used to take up to 40 pupils.
However, after the school had closed the building was still used as a church
until 1959.* It was the bell of Bedham Chapel that Alice heard from Brinkwells
celebrating the signing of peace on 28 June 1919. She wrote: 'About 10.30 we
were upstairs – suddenly heard Bedham Chapel School bell ring – it went for
nearly an hour.' She found the sound 'very touching' and the next day she heard
more bells after the Sunday service 'sounding so sweet through the summer air'.
The chapel school can still be seen at the bottom of a steep incline to the side
of the Bedham Road – but it is now a roofless ruin closely encircled by trees
which even on the brightest of days give it a melancholy and eerie atmosphere.
It was the great wind of October 1987 that finally ruined the building which
had, prior to that, been used off and on by local residents. Beyond the chapel
and the cottages lie Bedham Copse and Flexham Park, heavily wooded areas
which became favourite destinations for walks from Brinkwells and a source of
inspiration for Elgar.

All around the district there were also signs and reminders of older
occupations – the making of Sussex bricks which were wood-fired and esteemed
for their mellow colour – glass-making, the result of which was often used for
local cottage windows – as well as stone quarrying and iron making. But the
main character of the environment around Brinkwells and Bedham was rural
– deep woods and long paths – and everywhere wild flowers.

Fittleworth

Fittleworth, a mile and a half to the south, was in the early years of the 20th
century a small Sussex village of just over 600 inhabitants which could trace
its origins back to the 12th century. It was decidedly rural but it was the
nearest port of call for the Elgars to get provisions, their post and news of the
war. Writing in his book *Highways and Byways of Sussex* (1904), E.V. Lucas
described how the village had a dual character – in the south being low and
dominated by the river, whilst in the north there was high ground with gorse-
covered commons, fir trees and woods. There were in fact two commons and as

---

* *Sussex County Magazine*, Vol. XXIX, Jan-Dec 1955, p. 203.

20 Horses working in the Woods near Bedham (c.1910); photograph by Louis Paul

21 Bedham Chapel as it is now

usual at that period they were roamed by geese. In *The Story of Fittleworth* the Hon. Lady Maxse recalled how

> The advent of the motor car has put an end to the geese and has thus destroyed a typical feature of Sussex commons and roadsides. As a child I recollect the flocks of grey geese who pastured on the broad margins of the roads … Fittleworth with its stretches of common land was a paradise for geese … The geese were a prolific source of food.

The geese were still there in 1910 according to a handwritten account of life in the village by two elderly residents. They described a way of life that would change little before the Elgars knew the place and explained how the children all collected firewood from the commons and coppicing and fence-making provided local employment. They went on to say how the Bedham carrier and Mrs Puttick at Egdean used a donkey and cart, but most local transport was horse-drawn. The village folk walked everywhere (as did the Elgars whilst they were there), and people would think nothing of travelling miles to work or to school along the footpaths and lanes. At that time cattle and sheep were driven daily through the village, families kept their own chickens and a pig and there were geese on the common. [*]

This sense of rural simplicity was echoed by Rex Vicat Cole in 1938 when he gave his memories of the area which had so enchanted him to a reporter for a local Sussex newspaper. The reporter wrote how Cole had 'made his home in a little thatched cottage near Fittleworth where he and his family lived for 15 years. Their neighbours were Sussex labourers and they lived a primitive country life, baking their own bread and chopping their own wood.' He then goes on to quote Rex: 'There were no cars in those days … My two sons had to travel by pony and trap each day to the nearest village, where they had lessons with an old parson. The labourers used to drop in and have a glass of cider with us …' [†]

Fittleworth was also famed for its inn, the *Swan*, parts of which were 500 years old and which was described by Lucas as a 'venerable and rambling building … in which one stumbles up or down into every room, and where eggs and bacon have an appropriateness that makes them a more desirable food than ambrosia.' [‡] However, its reputation rested not only on its bacon, but also on its role as a mecca for artists. In fact, as we shall see, Fittleworth's reputation as an artistic centre predated both Rex Vicat Cole and Elgar.

During the Great War, 143 Fittleworth men joined up to fight; 21 never returned. The work of the village was carried on by older men and women, whilst some of the younger women joined the VAD nurses at Bignor Park where the large house was turned into a hospital for war wounded. As the invalids improved they would take the short walk to the village school where they were

---

[*] See Gil Saunders, 'Fittleworth, Village of the Artists', at www.sussexlife.com/gils_guide.
[†] *Sussex Daily News*, 2 February 1938 (Cole Papers).
[‡] Lucas, *Highways & Byways of Sussex*, pp. 95-6.

entertained by the children.*
The war was brought home
too by the sound of the guns
of the Western front that could
be heard on occasion. Lady
Maxse recalled the sound as 'a
dull flat thud' which was more
audible in some places than in
others, and Alice also wrote
of the noise in her diary on 20
and 30 May 1918, describing
the sound at the cottage as
'incessant gun fire (distant
cannon)'.

22 The Swan Inn *as it is now*

Within easy walking distance of the cottage to the south-east was Stopham,
seat of the Barttelot family. Placed at the junction between the Rivers Rother
and Arun, Stopham boasts a fine bridge which was built in 1423 and has been
called one of the most beautiful structures of the county. Alice was much
impressed by the place, writing of it as 'the most exquisite spot' and exclaiming
over the wonderful brass monuments in the church. The Elgars walked there
often, taking guests to see the bridge and the church.

Another destination for their walks was Petworth which they could reach
across the fields to the west. Called a 'paradise of old-fashioned architecture' by
E.V. Lucas in 1904, he declared, however, that he would not like to live there,
explaining himself in this way: 'Petworth must be the very home of low-pulsed
peace; and yet a little oppressive too, with the great house and its traditions at
the top of the town – like a weight on the forehead.' As a result of this feeling,
perhaps, Lucas himself had a cottage at Tillington, a mile or so to the west of
town, which he later let to friends of the Elgars, Sidney and Frances Colvin.

'The Dear Wood Folk'

These, then, were the immediate surroundings of Brinkwells and the places
which were to become so familiar to the Elgars. But a place and its character
are determined by more than physical surroundings; they are also conditioned
by its people and their beliefs. There can be little doubt that Elgar and Alice
grew to have great affection for their neighbours at Brinkwells – 'the dear wood
folk' as Elgar was to call them – and that this affection had been shared also by
the Vicat Coles. Compared with many of the people with whom they mixed
in London, the inhabitants of Fittleworth and Bedham had a simplicity and
strength of tradition which made them appear old-fashioned even then. Rhoda
Leigh confirmed that this was still the case in the early 1930s and reckoned that
the country people there lived a life of forty years past. She wrote:

---

* Pentecost, *A Shepherd's Daughter*, p. 35.

We are less than sixty miles from London, yet many of the folk in our hamlet have never been in a train. Many of the older people can neither read nor write; they are contented with the simple country routine, a journey to Pulborough or Petworth in a farm cart on market-days constituting their only dissipation. *

With this reluctance to change came the persistence of old beliefs. The area had a long tradition of myths, traditions and superstitions some of which continue to this day. Moreover, Petworth and its surrounding villages had been a place of pilgrimage for centuries and writing in the early 1930s Lady Maxse recorded the existence of 'a Holy Well between Petworth and Fittleworth which is still held locally to possess healing qualities.' She suggested that the healing reputation of this water could have dated from pre-Christian times.

As with many locations in West Sussex, Fittleworth superstitions included the legend of a great snake which would rush out of the bushes and scare people – a legend that still lingered in the later years of the 19th century – and also the regular sighting of witches. One hill in particular, Wyncombe Hill, was called Witches Hill topped by three pine trees. The various tales of witches and hauntings that surrounded it meant that the area was shunned by people after dark. The hill, still topped by pines, can be seen on the Pulborough Road just to the east of Fittleworth. Interestingly, the authors were told by a Petworth resident that something of that reluctance remains today in the more remote, wooded areas. The woods also were held to be the home of apparitions – some seen by the keepers who worked for the Barttelot family – and some still seen by residents of Bedham. One resident told the authors that her husband would think her mad but she regularly saw the (benevolent) ghosts of former villagers walking in procession across their garden – as had a recently visiting child. John Ireland (1879-1962), a next-generation composer who lived for many years in West Sussex at Washington under Chanctonbury Ring, reported a similar experience involving the ghosts of dancing children to the novelist Arthur Machen. His reply to Ireland was, 'So, you've seen them too!'.

The area around Brinkwells was therefore one that was steeped in history and legend and it is not surprising that, like Vicat Cole, Elgar was struck by the atmosphere of the woods and the mysterious, sometimes sinister appearance of groups of trees. When the Elgars had visitors from London often their response to the place was that it was 'magical', something with which the local 'wood folk' would have wholeheartedly agreed – as did the painter Rex Vicat Cole whose paintings and books about trees capture the timeless essence of the woods.

---

* Leigh, *Past and Passing*, p. 14.

CHAPTER FIVE

'Wild and Free' – Alice and Elgar at Brinkwells

Domesticity

Writing to Alice Stuart Wortley on 12 May 1918 from Brinkwells, Elgar tried to give her an idea of what he did in the country. He wrote:

> I rise about seven – work till 8.15 – then dress. Breakfast – pipe (I smoke again all day!) work till 12.30 lunch (pipe) – rest an hour – work till tea (pipe) – then work till 7.30 – change – dinner at 8. Bed at 10.0 – every day practically goes thus – of course instead of work, which means carpentering of the roughest kind, sawing wood, repairing furniture etc etc and weeding, we go lovely walks – the loveliest walks really – ... [*]

He paints an attractive picture of himself and of his pursuits in anticipation of the Windflower's visit. But, whilst this tells us something of what he did and how he saw himself, it does not tell us what life was like at Brinkwells. As a description it also represents the tip of a domestic iceberg the weight of which was carried in the main by Alice. Things were to change later that year for him, of course, with the return of his creative drive and his renewed concentration on music but in reality that would mean the substitution of one type of 'work' for another within the same pattern. For Alice his return to music must have justified their life at the cottage which, although Arcadian in some respects, was not without difficulties for her.

After two short stays during 1917, the Elgars spent prolonged periods in West Sussex in 1918 and 1919, staying until December in 1918 and October in 1919. [†] Given the basic nature of the cottage they did well to stay as late in the year as that. It is little wonder that Rex Vicat Cole writing to his wife during the war congratulated her specifically on finding someone to take the cottage for the winter. Brinkwells was at its best as a place at which most of the time was spent outside – or in the large studio which was lighter than the cottage and had the best view.

Much has been made of Alice's dislike of being there and Elgar certainly attested both to Schuster ('Poor dear A. is not well & of course is bored to death here while I am in the seventh heaven of delight') [‡] and to Alice Stuart Wortley

---

[*] Moore, *The Windflower Letters*, p. 203.
[†] After Alice's death Elgar also stayed there with Carice in 1920 and 1921. See Appendix 1.
[‡] Elgar letter to Schuster 3/12/1918.

that Alice 'does not enjoy life here as I do', but both these comments were written at a time when Alice had been unwell and Brinkwells was no place to be ill. When she was in better health she felt differently and this point is made clear in a letter written by Elgar to Sidney Colvin on 21 November 1918 from Brinkwells reporting that 'Alice is better now and finds the place divine still'. * At such times, as we shall see, she enjoyed the beauty of the surroundings and the extensive walks that she and Elgar took.

It is in the details of the Elgars' time at the cottage that we begin to see what life must actually have been like for them. As in all their other house-moves (and there had been many) the logistics of departure and arrival were left entirely to Alice who often saw to it that Elgar was safely away with friends whilst she got on with arrangements. On leaving London for Sussex not only had she to supervise the closing of Severn House for a period and see that Brinkwells was ready for their arrival but also to manage staff arrangements and deal with the bureaucratic demands of official food rationing which began early in 1918. (Meat, butter and margarine were officially rationed at the end of February and householders had to register for their rations – something which caused confusion amongst those who had more than one residence. †)

Carice leaves us some idea of what this process involved for Alice on their departure for Brinkwells in May 1918. Whilst Elgar's contribution amounted to choosing the tools that he would need for woodwork and buying a map of the Brinkwells area, Alice, who described herself as 'very very busy' three days before departure, tried to think of what would be needed in the country where, according to Carice, 'there was a scarcity of furniture and comforts'. ‡ Some of her packages which were sent by train, moreover, on this occasion went missing between London and Pulborough.

On their return to London a similar scenario was played in reverse. Elgar, in a letter to Alice Stuart Wortley dated 27 December 1918, explained how he would go to Ridgehurst whilst Alice and the servants returned to Hampstead. Alice, who had been unwell, was faced once again on return with the task of cleaning and opening the house, which had been closed up for some time, and unpacking. Her diary gives us the sense of someone struggling under these domestic burdens. She wrote on 1 January 1919 with exactly one week to go before a party at Severn House for a performance of the Quartet and Violin Sonata that she was: 'Trying to unpack and settle things a little – the house so lovely but very dirty of course.' The next day she was 'struggling on' with only two staff and on the fourth she describes how she phoned Frank Schuster and said that she 'seemed always to be having to do impossibilities'. If she was seeking some release from her burdens, she didn't succeed. 'But you always achieve them', Frank replied.

* Quoted in Young, *Letters of Edward Elgar*, p. 247.
† Harvey & Fitzgerald, *Edward Heron-Allen*, p. 176.
‡ Young, *Alice Elgar*, p. 179.

Communications

The actual journey down to Sussex was usually by train from Victoria – a less than comfortable experience during the war with Alice recording on one occasion as many as thirteen to a carriage. There were also no porters to carry luggage and Alice describes Elgar carrying heavy bags along the platform in 1919, both of them making an 'exhausting walk to the tube with heavy things to carry'. The journey from London was made via Horsham and then to Pulborough where there was the option of a branch line service to Fittleworth Station. It was, moreover, possible to do the return journey in one day, as Alice did when Severn House was burgled in 1918, leaving Brinkwells in the dark at 6 o'clock on a December morning. The service was good but during the war overcrowding meant that visitors did not always manage to get on the appointed train and that in itself posed problems for the last stages of the journey that were usually made by Mr Aylwin's pony cart or waggon.

Thomas Aylwin lived at Springs Farm which was within walking distance of Brinkwells. (See ch. 4.) His were the fields that surrounded the cottage and which Alice and Elgar looked out on with such delight as the seasons changed. Often, when he met the Elgars from the train at Pulborough or Fittleworth, he would take the luggage up to the cottage while they walked and was always 'delighted' to see them. Occasionally he would also collect goods for the Elgars that had been sent by train or bought in Petersfield. He was much in demand and he had to be 'booked' in advance – so it was not always possible to get him.

The train strikes of 1918 and 1919 made a great impact for not only were there no newspapers or post but the Elgars found themselves virtually cut off. The strikers of 1919 aroused Alice's fury: 'wicked and traitorous ... Worse than the worst enemies – they have no excuse' she thundered in her diary, concluding that they ought to be shot. [*] A week later, on 3 October, Elgar wrote to Sidney Colvin about the strike: 'We have been cut off entirely here and still partly so as there are no trains on this branch line ... I fear our move to town would be difficult ... letters are beginning to get through ...'. [†]

After the war, in May 1919 they made the journey by car but returned in the usual way by pony cart and train. The car journey was a success, in spite of Elgar becoming, according to Alice, 'rather worried as to the road' . They lunched in Horsham, decided that they should perhaps have taken another route, but nevertheless ended up safely at Brinkwells where they found 'the house all open and ready'. The car experiment was repeated in June, this time via Billingshurst, Wisborough Green and Bedham.

Enchantment

Once safely at Brinkwells it is clear that both Elgar and Alice were enchanted by the place. Their descriptions of the cottage, its garden and the surrounding

---

[*] Alice Elgar's diary 26 and 27 September 1919.
[†] EBM, letter no. 3487.

23 Rex Vicat Cole, Study of Broken Sunlight

woods give us a clear idea of why they became so attached to life there despite its shortcomings. The pictures they paint are of an area abounding with flowers, birds and trees and their initial responses in 1917 reflect their wonder at the seemingly endless beauty around them. Their descriptions, in fact, echo those of Hannah Vicat Cole as does their intensity of feeling about their surroundings. A few days after their first arrival at Brinkwells, Elgar records the 'wonderfully beautiful daffodils just over in woods – but primroses, bluebells etc'. and writes to Alice Stuart Wortley of the 'really divine country place' that they find themselves in. Alice too is struck by the abundance of flowers in the woods, describing in her diary the 'great gardens and borders of flowers' growing there and tells Alice Stuart Wortley that it is the most extraordinarily lovely spot with 'endless walks and paths in the woods'. * In her account of Bedham life, Rhoda Leigh also describes the carpets of flowers which covered the region: 'As far as the eye could see,' she wrote, 'the woods were carpeted with pale yellow.' She relates how one local tradition centred around the wild daffodils which could be picked by the residents of the estate on 'Staters' Sunday' in March and used to decorate their cottages, or to be sent to the local hospital or placed on every grave in the churchyard that had no flowers so that no one there should be left out. †

The Elgars' delighted reaction was shared by many who knew the area. Stella Bowen, who lived nearby first at Scammel's Farm and then at Cooper's Cottage

* Moore, *The Windflower Letters*, p. 183.
† Leigh, *Past and Passing*, p. 89.

at Bedham with the author Ford Madox Ford between 1919 and 1921, described Bedham as 'an extravagantly beautiful and quite inaccessible spot … There was an immense view, and lonely paths winding through beechwoods over the hillside'. She too remembered the wild daffodils and bluebells that surrounded their house.[*] They, like the Elgars, grew to love the place but eventually were driven out by the mud, the damp and the darkness in the winter of 1921/22.

Birdsong

The woods were full of birds, and observing them was an enthusiasm which Elgar and Alice shared. Alice did not have time for domestic animals, liking neither dogs nor cats, and when on their arrival at the cottage in August 1917 they found five kittens 'frolicking about' in the garden Alice made it very clear that they were not welcome guests. 'Not wanted by A.' she wrote firmly in her diary, underlining the 'not' for good measure. But she was very fond of birds. Mrs Richard Powell (Dorabella) remembered that when Alice and Elgar were living in Hereford at Plas Gwyn she turned two sides of the veranda which ran around the house into a sort of 'birds hotel and restaurant' where they fed, watered and roosted in the honeysuckle, becoming as a result very tame.[†] She was therefore in her element at Brinkwells. Both Alice and Elgar noted the birds that they saw around the house and in the woods in their diaries and the picture that emerges is one of extraordinarily lively bird life. On 16 May 1918 Alice described the air as 'vibrating with song of birds … Nightingales also pouring out their song' and the next day Elgar's diary records how warm it was and how they had sat outside until eleven in the evening watching nightingales and owls under a moon. Flexham Park to the north-west of the cottage, at that time completely wooded, was full of owls and at the beginning of the 20th century Sussex was known to be good nightingale country, welcoming birds in April as they concluded their flight and made their homes in the woods. A century later nightingales are still to be heard in the woods there serenading the residents after dark.

Elgar and Alice also saw nightjars in the woods, tom tits, chaffinches, blackbirds, hawks, larks and cuckoos and time after time heard the singing of nightingales. For Elgar this in particular must have reawakened memories of Birchwood, his cottage near the Malvern Hills which had been surrounded with woods full of birds and wild flowers. He had always turned to nature for inspiration and comfort – not only the countryside, but also his 'beloved wild creatures' – these, he explained in a letter to Jaeger of 1903, helped him to get 'heartened up' and gave him general inspiration.[‡]

---

[*] Judd, *Ford Madox Ford*, p. 328.
[†] Powell, *Memories of a Variation*, p.8.
[‡] Moore, *A Creative Life*, p. 58.

The Changing Seasons

There was certainly plenty of wild life around the cottage. Rabbits, squirrels and butterflies, cockchafer beetles and a wild cat; fish in the ponds and rivers; wasps and snakes. Elgar and Alice noted them all in their diaries – he conscientiously measuring some of the adders (after he had killed them of course) and finding some full-grown adults well over two feet long. They noted the effects of harvesting on the animals (on one occasion the machine revealing one lone mouse in the centre of the field) and recorded the whole slow round of the harvest in their diaries – the cutting of the wheat fields, the barley and the clover that belonged to Mr Aylwin – enjoying the changing scents and colours of the seasons – sitting in the fields – and helping with the harvest when they could. Their help was probably appreciated in days when most of the able-bodied men of Fittleworth and Bedham were fighting and harvests were the work of older men, young boys and the women. In her reminiscences of a childhood in West Sussex, close to Fittleworth, during the Great War Evelyn Pentecost recalls how children were allowed to leave school at twelve so that they could work in place of those who had joined up to fight. [*] Elgar's diary for 9 August 1918 explains that he and Alice helped with stooking in the cut wheatfield whilst Alice gives a slightly fuller account, writing that Elgar worked hard in the field after tea (this in spite of her belief that he was not very well) with her help, although she admitted that she found the sheaves heavy. In this, as in many of the aspects of their Brinkwells life, one has to admire Alice and her commitment to making Elgar's life happy. She was by then nearly 70 years old and yet threw herself into the active and physically challenging life of Brinkwells, always putting Elgar's wishes first.

As the year progressed and the weather deteriorated, both Alice and Elgar complained of the cold. The bitter winds gave Elgar neuralgia or earache and in November 1918 Alice, herself unwell, was 'frightened that the cold would hurt him'. Yet even bad weather failed wholly to extinguish their appreciation of the place. Elgar walked the wet woods in oilskins and navy boots originally used on stage in The Fringes of the Fleet; when it was too cold he wore his fur coat outside (on one occasion in June); Alice might complain of the wind or of the wet; but underlying all this was a sense of freedom and of communication with nature. So, in spite of neuralgia Elgar writes to the Windflower of the ravishing colours in the autumn woods. Later, on 10 December 1918, when they had doubts as to how much longer they could manage at the cottage because of the cold, Alice's diary includes a rhapsodic eulogy to their surroundings. 'Wet morning – brilliant later. A. to PO – a wonderful walk – unsurpassed clearness & marvellous colouring – Fittleworth Lower Common shining gold – lovely golden clouds.'

---

[*] Pentecost, *A Shepherd's Daughter*, p. 35.

Violent Gardening

From their first arrival at Brinkwells in May 1917, both Alice and Elgar threw themselves into improving both the cottage and the garden. Work in the garden fell to Elgar, who was helped by Carice when she was staying, and in this he had the assistance of the gardener/handyman Mark Holden who, as we shall see later, played an important part in their domestic arrangements. Frequently Alice's diary records whole days spent by Elgar working on the weeding or the fruit and vegetables. 'E. gardening violently' she wrote three days after their arrival in 1917 and a few days later – 'E. would not leave the garden all day'. As they were there infrequently in 1917, he found that the garden became terribly wild in their absences and on 31 August, after an absence of nearly three months, he wrote to Carice that he had literally hewed a way through the overgrown paths and that the weeds were 50,000 times worse than when she had been there. 'The whole place', he continued, 'is an impenetrable jungle.' * His commitment to the garden continued throughout their time at Brinkwells not only in maintaining what was already there but also in making improvements. He erected the sundial which they had had in their garden in Plas Gwyn which had been a present from Schuster, fixing it with the help of a compass that had been sent to him by Alice Stuart Wortley. In July 1918 he began work on the wild garden which was close to the studio, making steps and opening up vistas and clearing a view. 'E. very tired – heavy work', he wrote on 25 July, but the next morning he was hard at work there again. Visitors too were sometimes impressed to help. Alice Stuart Wortley helped Elgar in the garden on her stay in May 1918. 'She worked quite hard', Alice conceded in her diary – but she knew that Elgar had the knack of making his friends work for him.

A Man about the House

It was not only the garden that needed Elgar's attention, however. He also carried out numerous small jobs around the house and, writing to Carice on 13 May 1918, he described his work: 'I have done heaps of things: we sorted and dusted all the oddments in the workshop, I've set up the sundial which is a great joy when there's any sun … Everything is getting tidied up except (as you will well guess) this writing table, which is a scandal.' † He put up a bedstead in the studio – a useful addition to the limited space in the cottage – made a screen for the corner near the front door, white-washed the garden house and built a shelter for Alice to sit in so she would be protected from the wind (which was unfortunately blown over in a night of strong gales in September 1918). He also tackled the fowl pen, working on it for a number of days and letting in more light by getting Mark, Elgar's 'factotum' (whose role is described later), to cut down the hedge above it, and removed some wire by the gate after he had seen a hawk become entangled in it. (In fact the

---

* EBM, letter no.580.
† Bird, 'An Elgarian Wartime Chronology', in Foreman (ed.), *Oh, My Horses!*, p. 442.

24 Hannah Vicat Cole and her sons in the Garden at Brinkwells, the studio in the background (c.1910)

Elgars wrote to Hannah Vicat Cole about the wire and whether they should remove it on 28 May 1918. But by 30 May Alice wrote in her diary that Elgar was determined to take it down and did so with Mark – but she omitted to say whether they had got permission or not.) The arrival of roofing felt, noted in Elgar's diary for 14 September 1918, suggests further work on the cottage or the studio. Meanwhile Alice too was busy. She put up new blue curtains in Elgar's room and tidied up the interior, moving the old bread tub to a corner near the front door where it looked decorative and generally working to make the place more attractive and suitable for visitors.

Woodwork

During their first visits in 1917 and for the first three months of their 1918 visit Elgar wrote little music and his energies were thrown into the garden and particularly into his woodwork. But so great was his enthusiasm for this hobby

25 Brinkwells Garden (c.1910); photograph by Rex Vicat Cole

that he continued to work at it even when he started writing chamber music in September 1918.

He took to his woodwork from the first moment they arrived and on 26 May 1917 Alice wrote to the Windflower describing the house and adding 'There is also a Carpenter's bench & tools etc & E. has already made me 2 rustic footstools'.* In fact rustic footstools became something of a speciality – Elgar making at least seven as well as a large garden seat for the upper lawn, a birch broom (which proved to be too heavy), two tables – one for the guest room and one for the studio on which he eventually wrote the Violin Sonata, a music stand for Billy Reed when he visited, a stand for a coffee pot, a candlestick, a door stop, a shelf for the outside WC, walking sticks, a pen holder etc etc. It had always been the case that when he took up a hobby Elgar tended to get carried away by it. And his hobbies were numerous and diverse.

A list of those pastimes which Elgar took up (and then put down again) during his life would have to run the whole gamut through chem-

26.   *Traditional barrel making in the woods near Brinkwells (c.1910)*

istry and kite flying, golf and microscopy, boomerangs and heraldry, cycling and going to the races, literary research and billiards, and many more. But in Brinkwells they took on a special character because they were so intimately connected with his environment, and looking at his time there one has to say that his domestic life was directed and fashioned by the woods that surrounded him. When he turned to his music there, the same thing applied. His domestic situation, his music and his hobbies were united in Brinkwells by the all pervading cycle of nature and in that environment the dichotomy between his projected image and his inner creative life ceased to operate.

This is made clear by the extension of his love of woodwork and gardening into working outside in the woods. He had from the beginning shown a great interest in the traditional skills of the area and had noted in his diary when he observed someone making hurdles or when he had bought working wood from Mark in the form of 'hoop-tops' and 'splits'. The logical outcome of this interest was his purchase of one and a half acres of underwood – that is, the right to cut any wood except forest trees such as oaks, beech and elms – from the wood reeve for the Stopham Estate. The purchase took place on 16 September 1918 and cost him £3. At that time he had already begun to write music again and one might have expected all his energies to have been directed there. But that

---

* Moore, *The Windflower Letters*, p. 183.

27 *Working in the woods near Brinkwells (c.1910)*

was not the case and, having bought the underwood, on the same day Elgar immediately started work by cutting a boundary. Alice recorded his delight in this development in her diary writing that Elgar was 'very excited and pleased & took chopper & worked hard clearing path. A. helped.' The next day she joined Elgar's two preoccupations in a way that would encapsulate the subsequent time at Brinkwells when she wrote 'E. absorbed in his music & delighted with the wood – much walking in it & chopping & clearing'.

We get one of the clearest pictures of Elgar the woodman from Billy Reed who visited Brinkwells a day later. As he was driven up the track from Fittleworth to the cottage by Mr Aylwin he saw at the top of a hill 'looming on the sky-line' what he took to be a statue but which in fact turned out to be Elgar leaning on his long-handled axe. Reed wrote:

> The picture was perfect and the pose magnificent. It was Sir Edward himself, who had come to the top of the hill to meet me, and placed himself there leaning on his axe and fitting in exactly with the surroundings. He did these things without knowing it, by pure instinct.

Even given that we are hearing this from someone who was in thrall to the great man, Reed's descriptions ring true – particularly in his account of Elgar's enthusiasm for the woods. Without waiting for Reed to reach the cottage, Elgar takes him off into the trees to show him what he had been up to. Reed continued:

> Chemistry, physics, billiards, and music were abandoned and forgotten: nothing remained but an ardent woodman-cooper.
> We soon came to a primitive kind of shack, round which were piled numbers of newly cut chestnut-poles. In it were contrivances for stripping and splitting these poles, making hoops for barrels, and doing all sorts of things in the craft of which I could make nothing. Sir Edward had picked it all up, and was now bubbling over with excitement as he explained it to me. [*]

It is no surprise that after tea Elgar encouraged Reed to help with cutting the low chestnut brushwood with axes and hauling it back to the tool shed. Visits to Elgar at Brinkwells tended to be taxing for his guests.

---

[*] Reed, *Elgar as I Knew Him*, pp. 56-7.

Servants

Yet however industrious Alice was on the distaff side, and however active Elgar was in making refinements for the cottage and working on its surroundings, their life could not run smoothly without servants. They had always relied on staff – maids and cooks in particular – as did every household of the middle and upper classes of the time. Alice was particular about maids and neither she nor Elgar could cook. When they had retreated to their Malvern cottage, Birchwood, they had taken a maid with them, and they went to Brinkwells with the same expectations. In some respects the staff situation was easier there during the war than it had been at Severn House as there were available local residents who carried out the necessary tasks. One, in particular, Mark Holden, was a fixture from the start. According to Reed he 'went with the house, like the tool shed or the chestnut wood' and had worked for the Vicat Coles before Elgar, becoming something of a favourite with their sons. Reed believed that Mark had spent the whole of his life within five or six miles of Fittleworth and at the time of the Elgars' residence he lived at Targrove – about half a mile from Brinkwells down the hill towards Fittleworth. Mark looked after the garden and the wood and did odd jobs about the house; he emptied the waste-paper baskets, helped guests with their luggage, and did any really heavy task (such as helping to carry the piano into the studio when it arrived).

He was a taciturn man, 'unimpressionable' was the word that Reed used to describe him, and his short, monosyllabic replies became a delight for Elgar. He remained as completely untouched by the stream of well-known visitors to Brinkwells as he was by the results of Elgar's woodwork. Yet in spite of his somewhat distant manner there seems to have been genuine affection for the Elgars and this was reciprocated. Once, in the very hot summer of 1919 when the countryside became parched and burnt, Elgar saw Mark working in the fields and took him his old panama hat to wear. 'He seemed so pleased', Alice wrote in her diary for 14 August, '& put it on at once & looked like a Moroni picture of an Italian gentleman.'

In the house their needs were met initially by Mrs Hewitt who cooked and 'did' for them. She was a local lady whose husband was serving in France. It appears that it was through her as well that Alice found a cook for their London house – Rose Elliot from Bedham, Mrs Hewitt's niece, went to Severn House in February 1918. On their arrival at Brinkwells the Elgars would find everything prepared for them – thanks to Mrs Hewitt – and on one occasion when Alice and Carice paid a day's visit she had the lunch and the vegetables on ready.

Both Alice and Elgar recorded the comings and goings of their domestic help in their diaries and we can see from their entries the difference that this help made. When Mrs Hewitt was ill or away – on several occasions because her husband was on leave – she found the Elgars a deputy, to Alice's obvious relief. Her diary for 28 May 1917 runs: 'Mrs Hewitt (cook etc) heard her husband had leave before going to France – found a deputy to our relief – a farm daughter, married, with large farm to run in Canada (but husband left all & joined the Red Cross).' This was Mrs Haggis who was according to Alice a 'wonderfully nice woman … also a perfect cook'. Alice went to call on Mrs Haggis and her people, 'very nice and friendly' she noted in her diary, and on their return to Canada in December 1918 Mrs Haggis and her husband called at Brinkwells to say goodbye.

When neither cook was available, things got difficult. Alice's diary entry for 19 May when Mrs Haggis was out and the maid also absent records a 'rather laborious evening' and her entry for 14 July 1918 expresses something of the Elgars' helplessness in the face of cooking for themselves. It reads: 'Very wet and misty – most unpleasant day – Mrs Hewitt away. E. & A. did breakfast, Mrs Haggis came for lunch, E. & A. did dinner. Very trying here with the hateful back premises – quite different at home.' E.'s diary is terser but even so records the getting of breakfast as a significant event: 'A. & E. alone. Got breakfast', it reads. Did the Elgars continue to change for dinner even when they got it themselves? Probably. It would make sense after a day in the woods. But whether they went to the extent of evening dress, as Ford Madox Ford did in the wilds of Bedham, resorting to a very ancient dinner-jacket in the evenings, is uncertain.

In June 1918, Grace, the maid from Severn House, arrived at Brinkwells to work for Alice there. Later that summer Sarah Allen, Alice's old maid from her days at Hazeldine House, also arrived. She had originally entered domestic service as a young girl working for Alice's mother Lady Roberts. She then stayed on to look after Alice but by the time she stayed at Brinkwells she was elderly and eventually died in 1923. This relationship illustrates the bond and the responsibility that Alice felt towards her domestic helps – a responsibility that, as we shall see, was expressed by the small gifts that Elgar distributed after her death to those who had helped them at Brinkwells.

When in 1919 Alice and Elgar travelled down to Sussex by car having sent Elsie the cook and Grace the maid in advance to get things ready (Grace returning by the car to London), they also took their butler, C.F. Byard. He was a recent acquisition to the household and one of Alice's rather less successful domestic experiments. He had been recommended by a friend as a deserving case (one of many such after the war) and Alice had taken him on. He proved to be a disaster and the final scene of his short engagement was played out at Brinkwells where he immediately began to cause discord. Alice's diary initially calls him 'unsatisfactory' but then a day later adds that that he 'did almost nothing & all wrong & disagreeable. E. could not bear it – A. hated it.'

On the following day, 18 June, Elgar found fault with Byard who retaliated by threatening to fight him. Alice wrote that they told him to leave at once and then she, followed by Elgar, dashed all the way up through the woods to Mr Aylwin's farm to see whether he could take the offending butler and his luggage to the train in his cart immediately. They were in luck. She continued in her diary: 'So thankful that he could – A. terrified for E. when out of her sight. Disagreeable leave taking – he rather threatened A. & his eyes looked most forbidding. Such a relief when he had gone, inexpressible.' The affair gave Elgar a bad headache the next day and also a bad mood – but he knew where to lay the blame: 'An end of A.'s experiment. An entire and utter failure & lamentable expense. Entirely A.'s doing', he concluded. [*]

For the most part, however, they were lucky with their help. There were times when they had to juggle guests, staff and staff holidays. But on the whole it worked well. The employment they offered also meant that they were drawn into the community of Fittleworth and Bedham and, in spite of their relatively short stay there, they found that they had struck very deep roots.

War Privations

Most of their time at Brinkwells was spent in an era of food shortages, rationing and general privations caused by the war which affected people across the social board. Even after the end of the war rationing and shortages prevailed. So how did they fare? To start with the cottage itself was productive – there were hens, a large vegetable garden, fruit trees, a strawberry bed, and Mark could be counted on to provide the odd addition to their diet – but at a price (pigeon 6d. – rabbit 1s.). In a letter to Carice dated 31 August 1917, [†] Elgar described the enormous potato crop (cultivated perhaps as a result of the food scare earlier that year when a potato famine was predicted and there was talk of rationing) and the laden greengage tree in the garden. Later on in 1918 his diary mentions lettuce and tomatoes from the garden as well. When Elgar began fishing, trout was added to the menu although not often, as most of his catches were small and thrown back. There were also abundant blackberries – Carice once recording a haul of 14 pounds picked in an evening.

Groceries could be bought at Fittleworth where there were two shops selling a wide range of goods from bread and groceries (delivered by hand cart or horse and van) to boots, shoes, hardware and sweets. There were also shops at Petworth and Pulborough – the latter having, according to Alice, three shopping centres. Whilst Alice used Fittleworth for the Post Office and to get news, many of their purchases were from the other two towns. Oliver's Stores in Pulborough sold practically everything that they might have wanted – even furniture and drapery as well as paraffin, groceries and wines – and Mr Aylwin's services were called upon to transport them, and their purchases, there and back. The Elgars' stocks were also augmented both by provisions that they brought down with them from London and by gifts from friends.

When the Windflower anticipated a visit in May 1918, she asked what she could bring in the way of food. Elgar answered her: 'We get on well with the provisions generally; you need bring very little of anything but if quite convenient some dry biscuits might be a joy – as the stock in these villages (& towns, e.g. Petworth) has run out for days … .' [‡]

[*] Quoted in Young, *Alice Elgar*, p. 195.
[†] EBM, letter no. 580.
[‡] Moore, *The Windflower Letters*, p. 203.

For Elgar's birthday in June 1918 his friends sent food – a most welcome gift at that period. (Heron-Allen's mother recalled her delight in receiving a half pound of Devonshire butter as one birthday present in 1918.) But Elgar's friends were more generous: Rosa Burley sent asparagus, there was a large parcel from Fortnums from Marie Joshua and a few days later a present from the Windflower which provoked Alice to a paean of praise: 'The jam is hailed with real joy! & will be most valuable, & the delicious dates & chocolate, & supply of tea & biscts. but those you really are too spoiling to send. E. so enjoyed some of that gigantic lobster – says it is the best he ever tasted.'

There seemed also to be a plentiful supply of beer and cider – obtained from the *Swan* in Fittleworth and put down in the cellar of Brinkwells. Whisky and wine were also sent for and delivered. 'Food good and plentiful – much beer!', Elgar wrote to the Windflower in May 1918 and, despite Alice's complaint that there was a shortage of materials to provide adequate tea for guests in 1919, on the whole they seemed to have managed relatively well. To put their situation in context, a little way south-west of them in Chichester in February 1918 volunteers had to be called out to guard the provision shops from the threatening attitude of the population who were fearful of food shortages. [*]

Other goods also came from Petworth and Pulborough, Elgar sometimes joining in the expedition when he was in need of tobacco, tools or razor blades. In this last item he seems too to have adopted a wartime attitude of stringency, noting in his diary that he had used the same razor blade from 9 May until 22 July 1918. When he began composing, his MS paper was sent from Novello, but writing paper and ink were sometimes in short supply.

Occasionally the Elgars would attend an auction to look for useful objects and in September 1918, with the onset of autumn and colder evenings, they went to a sale at Lee Farm, hoping to acquire a stove, but they were unlucky. The cottage was heated by open fires and oil or paraffin stoves and in May 1918 they seemed to have been using coal for the fires as Elgar's diary records the difficulty in obtaining any. Later this problem was solved when he bought the underwood and in a letter to Sidney Colvin dated 8 October 1919 he wrote that the evenings were cold but that they had 'more wood to burn than we can ever consume'. [†] Fires were started in the downstairs rooms by late September 1919 and reading lamps were needed in the evenings by August 1918. Casks of paraffin for these lamps and the stoves came from Petersfield or Pulborough via Mr Aylwin but their use was not always straightforward as Elgar found out to his cost. His diary for 25 November 1918 reveals how he had lit the paraffin stove in his room without closing it and had returned to find 'everything covered with dense black smuts' which necessitated a 'great cleaning of rooms' the next day. Unlike Rex Vicat Cole, Elgar does not seem to have been worried by the possibility of a fire. The cottage, which was thatched and filled with wooden furniture, was very combustible – a fact that was driven home in the 1970s when a fire there destroyed some of the first floor.

---

[*] Harvey and Fitzgerald, *Edward Heron-Allen*, p.139.
[†] EBM, letter no. 3492.

The Colvins

Isolated as the cottage may have been, the Elgars quickly established a social round that did not wholly rely on visitors from London, although these too were a frequent part of their Brinkwells life. The range of this local socialising changed slightly between 1917 and 1919 as they got to know a wider circle of people in the countryside and because one of their most frequent visitors and friends in 1917 and 1918, Sidney Colvin and his wife Frances (who were to be the dedicatees of the Cello Concerto), did not spend the summer of 1919 in Sussex.

Sidney Colvin had already played a significant part in Elgar's musical and social life in
London before they met again at Brinkwells
on 31 August 1917. The Colvins, at Tillington
for the summer, were therefore within walking
distance of the Elgars – Tillington being a
mile the other side of Petworth and Petworth
being one hour and ten minutes on foot from
Brinkwells (as timed by Alice and Carice).
They were older than the Elgars – and, like
Alice, Lady Colvin was older than her husband
having been born in 1839, whilst Sidney was
born six years later in 1845. Although Colvin
had been Director of the Fitzwilliam Museum,
Cambridge, and Keeper of Prints and Drawings
at the British Museum, a post from which he
retired in 1912, his tastes were literary rather
than artistic. E.V. Lucas described him as a

28 Sidney Colvin in 1921

platonic lover of painting rather than a passionate one and Sir Martin Conway, who had been one of his pupils at Cambridge, wrote that Colvin 'often said to me that Art was not his chief interest; that was literature. Art provided his bread and butter, first at Cambridge, afterwards at the British Museum, but all the time he was looking forward to the day when he could lay it aside and write the life of Keats'. [*]

His taste for literature and his wide knowledge appealed immensely both to Elgar and Alice, and in 1917, when they met at Brinkwells, he had just completed one of his major pieces of writing, his *Life of Keats* – a book which Elgar was to describe as 'new and first class'. Colvin had known many of the great literary figures of the age: George Eliot and Browning, Robert Louis Stevenson, Tennyson and Pater, Henry James and Conrad, amongst others. He was Treasurer and then President of the Literary Society (resigning from the Presidency in 1921) and Elgar was delighted when in 1920 he proposed that Elgar should become a member. Colvin was known for his traditional outlook

---

[*] Lucas, *The Colvins and Their Friends*, p. 29.

and at his death in 1927 his friend J.L. Garvin wrote a personal note for the *Observer* in which he celebrated the memory of his friend, who, he wrote, 'meant to live for chivalry and the sense of beauty'. There were other reasons, too, why the friendship between the Colvins and the Elgars, begun in London, should have continued in the country. Colvin's family had had Indian connections, as had Alice's, and Frances Colvin's unhappy first marriage had taken her to India as well. She had been married at 16 to the Rev. Albert Sitwell and there was no formal end to the union which produced two sons until Albert's death in 1894. Colvin and Elgar, moreover, shared a strong traditional regard for social distinctions and honours, as did Alice.

Frances Colvin was by all accounts the most sympathetic of women, something which Elgar in particular appreciated, and tributes to her after her death in 1924 praised her youthful spirit, her capacity for helping others and her 'sibylline beauty'. Colvin himself wrote a memorial for her in which he recalled her beautiful singing voice which transported listeners and expressed the full richness of her spirit. But time and time again it was to her judgement and sympathy that her friends paid tribute. One of the most moving was written by the novelist Hugh Walpole who, after describing the way that they complemented each other as a couple, wrote of her that her greatest quality of all was her tenderness, adding 'she loved without selfishness, was intelligent without preciousness, laughed at life without cruelty and had great principles of conduct without priggishness.'[*] It is not surprising that Elgar had chosen to write to her on 3 May 1910 about the death of Carice's pet rabbit, Pietro d'Alba, to whom he had been much attached. He knew that he could touch her heart. 'You are always so very lenient to me in my foolishness,' he wrote, 'so I write to tell you how very sad we are today ...'.[†] She was, Elgar wrote, one of only two people who would understand his grief.

Frances Colvin was something of an invalid by the time she was at Tillington (she was then 78 years old and quickly became the recipient of one of Elgar's footstools). She did not often stray far from her cottage. Although she did visit Brinkwells courtesy of Lady Leconfield's carriage, the usual practice was for the Elgars to visit her. Elgar also had limited faith in Colvin's constitution – 'he is rather a weakling alas!', he wrote somewhat less than charitably to the Windflower in July 1918. He did, however, rely on him for local knowledge when he was suffering from blepheritis. In an (undated) letter to Sidney Colvin addressed from Brinkwells, Elgar wrote:

> Alice wants me to ask you to send me the name of the best doctor in Petworth – in case the eye gives further trouble ... Alice has been in nervous fits over my prettily swelled lid; purple, look you & what nicer colour is there in the rainbow? And still she grumbles at it.[‡]

---

* Lucas, *The Colvins and Their Friends*, pp. 350-53.
† Quoted in Anderson, *Elgar and Chivalry*, p. 361.
‡ EBM, letter no. 3470.

A few days after their initial contact at
Brinkwells, on 3 September Colvin invited the
Elgars to see their cottage at Tillington. They
made a day out of it, first going to Petworth
where they walked around the town, lunched
at the *Swan*, and went into Petworth Park
where Elgar fell asleep under a tree. 'Very
uninteresting' was Alice's verdict on the whole
experience. But then things improved. 'Then
walked to Tillington', Alice wrote in her diary,
'Sidney Colvin took us both to E. V. Lucas'
house which they have. Very pretty houses
in village – lovely views of downs & "The
Cottage" charming as a house – but much too
residential'. The theme was taken up by Elgar
two days later in a letter to the Windflower:
'We went over to see the Colvins on Monday &
I found them well & rejoicing in the weather,

29 *Mrs Sitwell, later Lady Colvin*

which has become good at last. They are in a highly civilised (<u>residential</u> I shd.
think) village, quite lovely for them but I shd. die of it – here we are <u>quite</u> wild
and free.'[*]

Was Alice echoing Elgar's opinions about the over-civilised nature of the
Colvin's cottage in her diary, expressed by him perhaps on the long walk back
in the evening? (They had got lost and it had taken them longer than expected
so that Elgar was worried that they were out so late.) Or did she really prefer
their freedom in spite of their own 'hateful back premises'? It is impossible to
say with any certainty but loyalty to Elgar shines from her diary throughout
her life and probably colours her reaction here. Just as interesting is Elgar's
interpretation of their life: 'wild and free', he writes to the Windflower – partly,
perhaps, to paint an attractive picture for her and partly in recognition of just
how far he was from his life in London.

After their initial socialising with the Colvins in Sussex, there were regular
visits between them. Either Sidney Colvin would walk up, or drive over, and
then walk in the woods and have tea. When the Elgars visited Tillington there
was always a warm welcome and sometimes the discussion turned to poetry
– on one occasion Colvin reading them a Clough poem and on another visit
one of his own translations – Homer's Hymn to Demeter. He also brought E.V.
Lucas to tea at Brinkwells in August, 'a delightful visit' according to Elgar's
diary (which resulted in a gift of bowls for the Brinkwells lawn from Lucas) and
three days later both Sidney and Frances Colvin arrived by carriage and had
tea at the *Swan* with the Elgars. In early September 1918, the Colvins returned
to London and, although they were eager to rent somewhere near Fittleworth
for the next summer, nothing seems to have come of it. The affection in which

---

[*] Moore, *The Windflower Letters*, p. 190.

Elgar held both Frances and Sidney Colvin is reflected in the letter he sent asking their permission to dedicate the Cello Concerto to them. He wrote: 'Your friendship is such a real and precious thing that I should like to leave some record of it; I cannot say the music is worthy of you both (or either!) but our three names would be in print together even if the music is dull & of the kind which perisheth.'*

The Social Round

Another local luminary was Sir Julian Corbett (1854-1922), the naval historian who was a supporter of Admiral Fisher's reforms of the Royal Navy and is best remembered for his major work on naval theory, *Some Principles of Maritime Strategy* (1911). He was also, like Colvin, a member of the Literary Society. Sir Julian lived with his family at Stopham, a short walk towards the south-east across the fields from Brinkwells. They called on the Elgars on 11 September 1918 and five days later Alice and Elgar visited the Manor Farm. Alice was delighted with the whole occasion: 'To tea at Stopham Manor Farm', she wrote, 'very pleasant – tea in old panelled room … E. very genial – all hung on his words.' The visit was reciprocated after a few days on 21 September when Sir Julian went to tea at Brinkwells and walked through the woods with Elgar to Flexham Park. Five days later he again went to tea, this time with Lady Corbett. This socialising continued into 1919. On one occasion on 16 August when Elgar was fishing, Sir Julian happened to pass him in a boat at the very moment when the great composer stepped on a wasps' nest. Sir Julian told Alice about it who faithfully transcribed it into her diary, adding, 'Sir Julian said he only heard words that sounded like "dear me!"'

Between 1918 and 1919 the Elgars clearly established themselves within the social circle of the district. They called on the local historian, the Hon Lady Maxse, who took tea at the cottage. She lived at Little Bognor with her husband General Sir Ivor Maxse K.C.B. and was the elder daughter of the 2nd Baron Leconfield. They were also drawn briefly, and not very satisfactorily, into the social ambit of Lady Leconfield of Petworth House who, as Beatrice Violet Rawson, had married the 3rd Baron in 1911. She called, unexpectedly, on 2 October 1919 and stayed for tea – 'a long visit' was how Alice described it. The result was an invitation for the Elgars to lunch at Petworth on 7 October and to see its famous collection of paintings. She offered to send the carriage, which Elgar and Alice gladly accepted.

The Petworth collection was well-known and famous for its masterpieces which included examples from Italian and Dutch painting as well as the canvases by Turner. It was open to the public on certain days during the week when visitors would be shown round by one of the staff. According to E.V. Lucas writing in 1904, however, the lighting was bad and the conditions poor for the appreciation of great art.

---

* Letter to Sidney Colvin dated 26 June 1919 quoted in Kennedy, *Portrait of Elgar* (1982), p. 279.

The Elgars were honoured in having a private viewing but Alice's diary shows that Elgar did not enjoy himself. They started off on foot and met the carriage at the quarry just below Brinkwells before proceeding to Petworth. At lunch, Alice had a 'nice talk' with Lady Leconfield and Lady Cunliffe, whom she liked very much, but Elgar complained that he found no 'warming spark' in the conversation which he thought dull. Things did not improve when they moved on to see the paintings for, although Lady Leconfield lit them up so they could see them, she, according to Alice, 'appeared bored over it'. The day reached its unsatisfactory conclusion when, after seeing the Turners, Alice and Elgar were left to find their own way out: 'we sd. goodbye & found ourselves in the hall with no one to show us out', Alice wrote later, 'E. rang & a butler & footman appeared.' She does not say whether they had to walk home as well.

A much warmer relationship was established in 1919 with Lady Gladys Barttelot whose family owned the Stopham Estate and Brinkwells. Alice had called on her for tea on 16 August whilst Elgar was busy fishing and had had a delightful visit which Lady Barttelot had reciprocated the next day by visiting with her younger son who helped Alice make the tea. Elgar too seems to have been charmed and gave her a piece of the Sonata sketches.(Brian Trowell suggests that this was probably the violin part for the unrevised finale which is no longer traceable.) * Four days later there was another visit which Alice recorded in her diary: 'The youthful Sir V. Barttelot rode up with a note on a beautiful chestnut with a beautiful red setter and looked so typically English' – and all this on a busy day for Alice when the Corbetts with their daughter were there for tea and the Windflower was staying.

Two days after their unhappy experiences at Petworth House, Lady Barttelot called again and this time they accompanied her some of the way back after tea. Alice's diary captured the emotion and beauty of the evening: 'it was wonderful to see, golden and crimson sky & pearl downs & brilliant moon – she loves it all so'. After the Elgars had returned to London, on 9 December 1919 Lady Barttelot visited them at Severn House when Alice was unwell and had been unable to leave the house since the middle of November.

There was also some contact between the Elgars and other members of the Cole family, who, like Rex and Hannah, rented cottages in the woods around Fittleworth. On Saturday 8 June 1918 Alice recorded a visit to one of Rex Vicat Cole's sisters, Maud. She wrote – 'A & C for a very hot walk to 'Fowlers' to call on Mrs Cargill. Tiny cottage, Mrs C making gooseberry jam, seemed so cheerful with all the work. Very isolated cottage in fields' – an attractive picture of industrious rural life. (Maud Cargill, Rex Vicat Cole's elder sister, was a musician who taught piano, it is thought at the Royal College of Music. She had the reputation in the family of being 'rather ferocious'.) The visit was reciprocated a few weeks later when both Mr and Mrs Cargill called in at Brinkwells – a visit that was rather too late in the day according to Elgar. †

---

* Trowell, 'The Road to Brinkwells' in Foreman (ed.), *Oh, My Horses!*, p.384.
† See Elgar's diary, 21 August 1918.

One bonus for Alice was the existence of the Newburys at the Rectory as Mr Newbury's sisters were living at Alice's family house where she had been brought up, Hazeldine House at Redmarley D'Abitot, now in Gloucestershire, and he could give her news about her old home. That this was particularly pleasing to her comes over in her diary when she writes how she went to the Rectory and had a 'pleasant talk about Hazeldine to Mr Newbury. He loves it – & thinks it's the most beautiful place for its size that he knows'. At other times there were the usual tea time visits when Mr and Mrs Newbury would tell stories of 'homely Bedham proceedings' and on one occasion a concert which Elgar obviously took in the right spirit: '(Concert! at Rectory)' he wrote in his diary.

Whilst there is no evidence that Elgar ever attended church whilst at Brinkwells, local rumour is that he played the organ occasionally at Fittleworth Church. Alice could walk into Petworth to the Roman Catholic church there, which she certainly did with Carice, and sometimes Carice would cycle in on her own.

Walking in the Woods

Whilst socialising and improvements at the cottage took some of their time, both Alice and Elgar spent hours walking in the woods and countryside. Elgar had loved walking as a young man and walking had also been part of their early married life together. On their visits to Germany early on in their marriage they had set off with rucksacks to explore the countryside and in Malvern they had adopted the habit of walking to meet guests or accompanying them part of the way back, something which they continued in Brinkwells. During their first stay there between 24 May and 4 June 1917, they explored extensively in the immediate vicinity of Brinkwells, walking down to Stopham ('the most exquisite spot', Alice writes) and up the hill to Bedham where they exclaimed over the lovely beech trees and the view. Alice, ever conscious of social conventions, carefully noted in her diary how Bedham was correctly pronounced: 'Care must be taken', she wrote, 'to pronounce the last syllable clearly'. They wandered the wood paths and Carice, who was down with them, found a wonderful place where foxgloves would flower. On the following visit that year they walked to Bognor Common which much impressed Alice, 'lovely, a really fairy place – long vistas under arched trees' and went back to look at Stopham Bridge. By 7 September 1917 they had already found and indentified the 'sinister trees' by Bedham that were to act on Elgar's imagination when a year later he turned to his chamber music. But at that stage they were just that – 'sinister trees' – and there was no mention of any local legends surrounding them. (See chapters 7 and 9.)

Walks to Fittleworth (where Alice went regularly for the post, news and provisions), to Bedham and Stopham became part of their daily lives. When they had visitors they, too, would be taken to see the pine walk, the sinister trees, the 'octopus' beech tree, the glades around Flexham Park, and the hamlet of Bedham. The walk up to Springs Farm where Thomas and Ellen Aylwin lived was frequently made, particularly by Alice, to enjoy the view or call into the farm. Sometimes they walked together, sometimes separately, and they became known by sight to the few people they met. In her reminiscences of childhood in Fittleworth in 1918 (*A Miller's Daughter*), Phyllis Catt recalled how she would occasionally see Elgar striding past Fittleworth Mill on his walks always looking, to her eyes, very serious.

In 1918 the Elgars' walks became more extensive and they would go to Petworth or to Pulborough to have lunch and shop. As we have seen, they would sometimes walk

30 Rex Vicat Cole, Trees Crowded in a Wood

on from Petworth to Tillington – on some occasions covering about seven miles on foot after which Alice admitted to feeling tired. They walked to their limit – one day in 1919 after walking to Pulborough, going round the town, having lunch and walking back, Alice wrote in her diary, 'E. very tired and lagged behind much coming back'. Yet even when they had walked a long way, the next day they would often walk again, finding new paths and routes in the seemingly endless woods. On Christmas Day 1918, still at Brinkwells despite the cold, the day was spent walking in the woods which Alice described as 'a wonderful grey-bronze colour'.

Fishing

Fishing was the other occupation that kept Elgar outside. He applied for a permit to fish two rivers (the Rother and the Arun) and also made regular fishing trips for trout to Bognor Pond which they had found on a visit to see Lady Maxse at Little Bognor – the pond lying almost directly on the footpath walk from Brinkwells. Elgar saw it as a possibility for fishing but Alice thought the site 'sombre and dreary'. The pond, now improved as part of the Leconfield Estate, is still fished for trout and something of its remote, wooded atmosphere remains. During the First World War, however, with few men available to work the woods, its aspect must have been much darker and wilder.

With the arrival of his permit on 11 June 1918, Elgar took up fishing with the enthusiasm with which he had pursued all his hobbies. Guests were inveigled to join him, Alice, too (despite her deep-seated belief that fishing

31 Bognor Pond as it is now

was monotonous), gamely accompanied him – on some occasions helping with the landing net.

Initially he was lacking suitable equipment and wrote to the Windflower on 17 June:

> … on Saturday for the first time went to the pond & landed two trouts! We ate them for dinner – or rather at dinner – although one was quite a good sized fish. I did not like to say anything about tackle to you so I have sent to the A & N Stores & I know what they send will be dull!

A few days later he takes up the theme again:

> I think I have everything now for this rough fishing but if you saw a cheap knife <u>with scissors</u> (fisherman's) I sh. like it but I <u>must pay</u> for it. I wd. not mention it but all my men friends are gone & there is no list to be had to order from, a bit of <u>tying</u> silk and some <u>india rubber</u> float caps wd. be a joy but I have 'substitutes' which do for everything except Windflowers for which no substitutes are to be had. [*]

The Windflower obliged and by the beginning of July Elgar was fully kitted out for his fishing expeditions with the articles that she had sent and the tackle and landing net from the Army and Navy Stores.

Sometimes he and Alice would leave the cottage very early before breakfast to go to the pond or river – but this was not unusual behaviour for Elgar as, according to Carice, he was always an early riser. [†] The day after Elgar wrote to thank the Windflower for his knife, silk and float caps, 2 July 1918, he and Alice were up at ten past five for a fishing expedition to Bognor Pond. They returned to Brinkwells by nine o'clock proudly carrying three fish – Alice having helped with the landing net – and this must have been the feat celebrated in

---

[*] Moore, *The Windflower Letters*, pp. 205-6.
[†] Interview with Carice Elgar Blake, BBC Light Programme, 24 July 1957 (EBM).

Elgar's (undated) letter to Sidney Colvin. 'Plundered three decent fish, 2½ lbs the three', Elgar enthused after telling Colvin how they had started at five am. 'Oh I wish you were a mile this side of Petworth', he continued, ' I should have descended on you with a shower of trout this morning.'[*] Two days later, obviously encouraged by their success, they left at half past four in the morning but this time only netted one fish. At other times they would go out in the evening – even if it meant warming up their own dinner on return.

Elgar became as absorbed in his fishing as in his woodwork. Everyone who visited the cottage got drawn into the activity. Lalla Vandervelde, who had gone down to Brinkwells to recuperate after exhausting war work and about whom Elgar had written rather sharply to the Windflower on 14 July 1918 that during her visit 'she was lying about here all day and rather(!) incommoded us', had, in fact, joined Elgar fishing both at Bognor Pond and the river. Even Felix Salmond, who went down to Brinkwells in August 1919 to play the Cello Concerto for Elgar, found himself on a fishing expedition. The visit provoked Mark into a 'Markism' that delighted Elgar and which Billy Reed faithfully recorded. Mark had helped Salmond with his cello case, and, later, 'Sir Edward said to him, "Mark, that gentleman who came today with the big case is a very famous musician, a great 'cellist, a very important person, you know."

'"Well, I suppose," said Mark, to console him, "it takes some of all sorts to make up the world."'[†]

On two occasions at least, Elgar was so carried away with his hobby and stayed out so long by himself that Alice got worried and went out to look for him. Of course, both times she found him quite safe and happily fishing, but unfortunately doesn't record whether he was pleased to have had his reverie interrupted. But this does illustrate one of the overriding concerns in their relationship: Alice worried about Elgar – and worried obsessively. Carice wrote about her mother that, when Elgar was away

> One could hardly get an answer about anything and until a telegram came saying he was safely in London – or wherever it was – she was terribly on edge, and seemed to think that one was very unfeeling if one did not appear to be worried about the journey. If she ever allowed herself to throw off this terrible worrying, she could be the most delightful companion, but unfortunately this did not very often happen.[‡]

It seems that this worrying was not only about the longer journeys of Elgar's life but also about a few hours by the river.

Elgar took his fishing quite seriously and at the end of his diary for 1918, on the page entitled 'Cash Account', he crossed out the word 'cash' and substituted 'fish', listing underneath all the fish he had caught at Bognor Pond between June and August. A total of 12 (large and small) and two returned.

---

[*] EBM, letter no. 3471.
[†] Reed, *Elgar as I Knew Him*, p. 62.
[‡] Young, *Alice Elgar*, p. 149.

32 *Rex Vicat Cole,* Brinkwells at Night, *charcoal on paper*

Elgar's diary for 30 August 1918, a day when Billy Reed was visiting, captures something of his Brinkwells life when he writes 'fiddled, fished & fooled walked to river no fish cut sticks etc lovely day'. And with such diversions around the cottage it is hardly surprising that the Elgars, while they were there, hardly ever left the immediate vicinity. There was a one day-trip to Chichester – mainly to get medication for Elgar's eye – on 16 July 1918, although he got a haircut as well. Alice, whose appreciation of Sussex towns was not marked, described Chichester as 'such a dull little town. So glad to escape'.

The other occasion was, uncharacteristically, a day out for Alice and Carice, leaving Elgar hard at work at the cottage. On 29 September 1919 they set out in Mr Aylwin's pony cart and, as the weather started to improve becoming hot and sunny, they proceeded via Pulborough to Storrington and then to Findon. At Findon they found an omnibus going to Worthing and, faced with this temptation, they abandoned their original plans of going to Cissbury Camp,* boarded the bus and made for the seaside. 'So hot & lovely', Alice enthused in her diary, '& <u>blue</u> sea.' Although she found the sea lovely, rather predictably she

---

* Alice wrote 'Sisbury' in her diary perhaps having heard the name but not seen it written.

hated the town and it was added to the litany of disappointing Sussex venues: Eastbourne – horrid, Petworth – uninteresting, Chichester – dull, and now, Worthing – hideous.

But they enjoyed themselves despite the 'hideous' environment and eventually made their way back on a crowded omnibus, thankful that the conductor made a seat for Alice in a niche. When they got back to Brinkwells she wrote with relief in her diary that Elgar was all safe. It was the only day that Alice had 'off duty' during their time at Brinkwells.

As the days shortened with the approach of winter and the evenings grew dark, they were driven inside more and would spend their evenings reading or playing cribbage by the light of their lamps. Elgar's diary for 10 September 1918 reads: 'Autumn really here – all these evenings cribbage (!) after dinner.' Once Elgar had turned again to composing there were also evenings in the studio when he would play through his new work for guests – and there was always the gramophone to entertain them. But in the summer the woods held sway until it was dark – and sometimes later than that with the attraction of the moon, owls, nightjars and nightingales.

CHAPTER SIX

A Loving Acquaintance with Trees –
Rex Vicat Cole and Brinkwells

Elgar's Art

Writing to Troyte Griffith from London four days after returning from his first stay at the cottage in June 1917, Elgar expressed his interest in the work of his 'landlord', Rex Vicat Cole. He wrote:

> I am so dreadfully disappointed that you can't come to Brinkwells you wd. have loved it & (it's Vicat Cole's) there are many sketches & pictures which wd. [have] formed a text for much expounding of miracles on your part I know – I shd. have something to say also on British R. Academic art – no Art. Gosh! [*]

Elgar was obviously impressed by the work that he found at Brinkwells and whilst neither he nor Alice might have put art at the very top of their list of interests – that place probably being taken by literature – they were nevertheless keen and knowledgeable gallery visitors and would have been acquainted with Rex Vicat Cole's name from the Royal Academy where he had regularly exhibited since 1896. (One of his paintings, *Hollies Weird and Flowers of Spring* (1901), was exhibited at the Worcester Victoria Institute in 1901 which Elgar may also have visited.) Early on in their marriage, during their unsuccessful period in London, they found that their house in Upper Norwood was convenient for the Dulwich Picture Gallery and at this period they started to make a list of their favourite artists. Then the house that they found in Malvern was called Forli, and they found the association between the name and the Renaissance painter Melozzo de Forli (1438-94) a happy coincidence. [†] Their tastes were further developed by visits to the great galleries in Munich in 1892 and in later years by their travels in Italy which reinforced their knowledge and love of Italian Renaissance art. When it came to their own collection of art at Severn House, they displayed their love of prints rather than paintings – although this may well have been the result of financial constraints. Photos and framed prints decorated many of the rooms with only a handful of relatively undistinguished oils and some watercolours – several of these by Troyte Griffith. However, their awareness of art in general sometimes filtered into their descriptions of the

---

[*] Quoted in Young, *Letters of Edward Elgar*, p. 231.
[†] A painter connected with Piero della Francesca who used extreme foreshortening in his work.

world around them, Elgar finding a particularly beautiful view at Brinkwells like a Turner or contrasting his chamber music with Cubism; and Alice finding that Mark in an old panama reminded her of a Moroni portrait.

At Severn House it was often Alice who proved to be the more assiduous exhibition visitor during the war years, attending contemporary exhibitions of war paintings including the Belgian Exhibition 'Art at the Front' of 1917. Her diary records her attendance at the Grafton Galleries and her visits to see the 'wild animal pictures' of John Guille Millais (1865-1931) in Bond Street in 1919. He was the son of Sir John Everett Millais, and Alice Stuart Wortley's brother and he not only painted animals and birds but produced books on natural history as well. Alice also viewed the work of the landscapist Lindsay MacArthur, fl. 1890-1930, who exhibited at the RA and produced landscapes of the Cotswolds. Alice's taste in this respect may have been driven in part by her social milieu but she also turned to painters who in some way depicted the nobility that she sought in the world. One of these was Watts, another Burne-Jones, and in an essay entitled 'The Ideal in the Present', written in the 1890s, she had described these artists as 'painters of the absolute ideal'.

Elgar shared his wife's tastes but added to it preferences of his own: he esteemed the work of Paul Sandby (1725-1809) and the prints of Giovanni Battista Piranesi (1720-78), both artists in whose work there is obvious skill, detailed workmanship and an eye for atmospheric effects – and also the strong sense of a particular place. Elgar liked things to be well made and in this respect the intricacies of print-making appealed, and he and Alice followed up this interest by subscribing to the Medici Society's Renaissance prints. Whilst he also understood as a professional creative artist himself the difficulties in making something to the highest standard, he knew how that skill must be aligned to something higher. This is what in particular he found in Piranesi whose prints turned him away from the ephemeral and insignificant and towards the great things of life. In short, they were inspirational.

Whilst there is a strong vein of conservatism running through Elgar's taste in art (he could not, for example, warm to the modernistic primitivism of Roger Fry's designs), there is no doubt that he could be strongly affected by art on an emotional level. Pictures could impinge on his consciousness – and he had the habit of turning pictures to the wall or covering them up in houses that he rented so that they would not disturb him. * He had also used the painting of *Christ in the Wilderness* by the Russian artist Ivan Nikolaevich Kramskoi (1837-87) as a source of inspiration for The Apostles, describing it as 'my ideal picture of the lonely Christ'. It was hardly a great painting – but its sentiment touched some chord in Elgar's spirit.

It would be out of character to find consistency in Elgar's choice of art when he showed so much inconsistency elsewhere in his life. So it is not surprising that when he tried his hand at oil painting in 1905 (another one of those hobbies that was taken up and then dropped) the resulting work should not be a meticulous,

---

* Powell, *Memories of a Variation*, p. 93.

Piranesian exercise in tonal control and atmosphere, or an elegant Sandby-inspired landscape, but something which, according to Alice, reminded her of William Blake (1757-1827), the visionary poet and artist, Giovanni Segantini (1858-99), the Italian Divisionist painter and member of the Vienna Secession, and Arnold Boecklin (1827-1901) who evolved a personal symbolic and sombre style which, he believed, should pervade the soul in the same way as music. [*] Alice described Elgar's paintings to Jaeger as 'strange symbolic pictures' adding that 'He certainly has a power of representing a scene from his imagination.' [†] Alice's choice of comparisons suggests also that Elgar was working in strong colour and in a visionary, imaginative mode. It is perhaps the inner, wild Elgar that comes to the surface in his own painting, as in his music – while his 'tastes' in art represent more the conventional, outer man. Unfortunately none of Elgars attempts at oil painting seems to have survived. However some of his quick, caricature-like drawings have, and they reflect his lively sense of fun as well as an ability to capture an idea with a few expressive lines.

Rex Vicat Cole – the Painter

What, then, in the studio at Brinkwells, persuaded him to accord the many pictures and sketches that he saw there by Rex Vicat Cole the capital 'A' in

Art? Cole's work was neither symbolic nor wild. It did not reach for the imaginative atmosphere of Piranesi or espouse the topographical tradition of Sandby but it did touch one quality that went deep into Elgar's psyche – a profound love and knowledge of the countryside and the ability directly to transform the experience of a particular landscape into art. It is in their response to the countryside around Brinkwells that Elgar and Vicat Cole share common ground – and in particular their response to the woods that surrounded the cottage which played such a major role in the work they

33 *Portrait of Rex (Reginald) Vicat Cole (1898) by John Byam Liston Shaw*

---

[*] His best known work, 'The Isle of the Dead', inspired Rachmaninov's 1909 work of the same name.
[†] Moore, *A Creative Life*, p. 456.

produced there. In tracing the influence of Brinkwells on Vicat Cole's work we can more fully understand the experience that Elgar had there and what his surroundings must have meant to him.

Vicat Cole, like Elgar, came to Sussex searching for a landscape that would replace an earlier affection – in his case, Yorkshire – and, like Elgar, he found in Sussex what he described as 'ideal isolation from the world'. Reginald (known as Rex) Vicat Cole came from an artistic background; he was the third generation of a family of painters. * His grandfather, George Cole (1810-83) had first exhibited in London in 1838, initially choosing a wide variety of subject matter from portraits to animal studies before concentrating more on landscape. His works sold well and his major landscapes, particularly those of Hampshire and of harvest scenes, united a sense of arcadian vision with his love of a particular place. He sketched outside in order to prepare for his paintings, and this commitment to working from the landscape was carried on by his son, Rex's father, George Vicat Cole.

George Vicat Cole (1833-93) was influenced in his turn by the contemporary developments in British painting, in particular Pre-Raphaelitism, and his paintings demonstrated a love of detail and high colour with carefully observed and finished foreground scenes. He also worked direct from nature, intent on capturing a detailed account of what he saw. He became attached, as his son would, to particular landscapes and in the 1870s, when his style was becoming broader, he began to paint in West Sussex in the area around the River Arun. His love of trees, and the care with which he depicted them can be seen both in his large oil works and in watercolours. He was a popular artist and his works brought high prices, so much so that the family were able to live in some style in Kensington and as a boy Rex was sent to Eton. George Vicat Cole tended to work on certain themes or in series – in one of these he explored and recorded different aspects of the Thames with the intention of producing a book of engravings – and this thoroughness of approach was again something that was passed on to the next generation where it became even more marked in Rex's oeuvre.

This, then, was the background to Rex Vicat Cole's career. Initially his father had intended him to become an engineer but he was convinced otherwise by Rex's passion for art and by his obvious talent. Unlike Elgar Rex emerged from his privileged background with a secure sense of his social standing. He was brought up in an artistic household in which he had to contend with the considerable success and status of his father and to make his own way in the art world in his own right in spite of this. In some ways this was hard – his father had become one of the best known landscapists in the Royal Academy where he had been elected an Associate in 1870, the year of Rex's birth, and a Royal Academician ten years later. This was a distinction that Rex never achieved – although many in the art world felt that he should have done. Whilst he exhibited

---

* George Cole (1810-83), George Vicat Cole (1833-93), Rex Vicat Cole (1870-1940) and John Cole (1903-75). See Barringer, *The Cole Family.*

regularly at the Academy, his works never attained the peaks of popularity reached by those of his father. He was consistently undervalued during his life and had to rely on teaching and writing to make a decent living.

But Rex Vicat Cole had great strengths – amongst them intellectual curiosity and energy, the ability to inspire others through teaching and writing, and an enduring honesty and balance of vision that was to underpin all his work. These qualities were recognised in an article written about the artist in 1910 by Austin Chester. He wrote: 'there is an intellectual integrity and an individuality about Mr Rex Vicat Cole's work which emancipates him from any suspicion of imitating that of his father'. * It is equally clear, looking at the body of Rex Vicat Cole's paintings, that over and above everything else was an approach to nature which united a deep understanding of how things grew and developed with an expression of mood.

Rex Vicat Cole had disliked Eton and gave it little credit for his education apart from the help that he had received there from the art master, the watercolour painter Samuel Evans (1829-1904). Thereafter, between 1888 and 1890, he trained at the St John's Wood School of Art, an independent institution which had been founded in 1878 by A.A. Calderon and which enjoyed a high success rate in preparing students for the Royal Academy Schools. † The St John's Wood school was open to both men and women and the students could follow courses in painting, composition, anatomy, perspective, wall painting, commercial art, animal painting and working from nature. The regime was strict; pupils were expected to be punctual, to work at the School between 10 a.m and 5 p.m., and to work in silence. Rex Vicat Cole called it 'incessant drudgery' and saw it as a way of testing an artist's commitment to his subject. One benefit, however, over and above any artistic skills that were taught there, was his friendship with his fellow student John Byam Liston Shaw (1872-1919) with whom he was to found The Byam Shaw and Vicat Cole School of Art in 1910.

Rex failed to gain admission to the Royal Academy Schools but before he was let loose on the world as a landscape painter, he spent two years working with his father and helping him with his increasing burden of work. There is no doubt that he valued the time so spent and admired his father's commitment to landscape painting and his understanding of trees – a subject that Rex was to make truly his own.

He had begun to exhibit in London in 1890, but like his father and his grandfather he needed an inspirational landscape. He found what he was searching for in Yorkshire and the countryside around Wharfedale formed the subject for many of his oil paintings of the 1890s. He made repeated journeys to the area around Bolton Abbey, making his base New Hall Farm which belonged to the Gill family. It was their beautiful younger daughter, Hannah, whom he married in 1901. The Yorkshire paintings, with subjects such as *A Winding of the*

---

* Chester, 'The Art of Mr Rex Vicat Cole', *The Windsor Magazine*, July 1910, pp. 369-82.
† The provision of a school to train artists was part of the original Instrument of Foundation of the Royal Academy in 1768.

Wharfe (exhibited at the R.A. in 1896) and *Haytime in Wharfedale* (exhibited at the R.B.A. in 1900) show Rex's growing independence from his father's style in their broader treatment and more direct informality of vision. Yet whilst there is a greater sense of the realities of the country in these works, they are also imbued with poetic mood, intensity of feeling and a celebration of the light and atmosphere of a particular place. All these characteristics are apparent in even his most informal sketches made quickly outside. One such sketch is the rapidly-painted small painting of the moors near Bolton Abbey with its scudding clouds, brilliant patches of blue sky and purple heather-covered hills (see plate III). His works are not topographical 'views' but records of the countryside and some of his smaller paintings done at the beginning of his career were almost domestic in their depiction of fields and hedges. His understanding of a particular landscape was one of the qualities that struck contemporary critics and after his exhibition at the Dowdeswell Gallery in London in 1900 of 48 canvases of Yorkshire subjects painted in the neighbourhood of Bolton Abbey, one reviewer remarked specifically on his understanding of the moods and tempers of that countryside. This exhibition was itself ordered by months – pictures starting in the spring and following the changing seasons and sometimes introduced by a piece of poetry in the catalogue. In one annotated copy of the exhibition catalogue, now in the British Art Library, we get some idea of how the public reacted to these pictures: 'delicate' and 'tender' are amongst the words used as well as favourable comments on Cole's use of colour. The same sensitivity of vision coloured his paintings from other parts of the country. His very early small painting of Kent fields near Headcorn entitled *Under the Lilac Hedge* (see plate II) shows that even at the very beginning of his career he could evoke a wonderfully naturalistic representation of spring with golden-coloured fields edged with lilac trees.

Hannah and Rex Vicat Cole settled in London in 1901. Rex continued to exhibit at the Royal Academy and at the Suffolk Street Galleries of the Royal Society of British Artists of which he had been elected a member in 1900.* He spent as much time as possible in Yorkshire at the studio he had built himself at New Hall Farm, but he had other, growing commitments as he developed his ability as a teacher in a post at King's College, University of London Women's Department. This position involved teaching landscape drawing and he would regularly take parties of his young lady students up to Yorkshire for six weeks of sketching tuition in the countryside he loved so much.

His qualities as a teacher were quickly apparent. He established his role at King's College where he worked alongside Byam Shaw by becoming co-principal of the art department. An article about his teaching appeared in *The Studio* in 1900 but by the end of that decade it was clear that the committee of

---

* The Royal Society of British Artists was founded in 1823 by artists who wished to distance themselves from the Royal Academy. Under the presidency of Whistler the status of the Society grew and it was constituted 'Royal' in 1887. Their annual exhibitions were originally held at Suffolk Street.

King's College did not have the same aspirations for the department as he had. As a result Rex Vicat Cole and Byam Shaw decided to form their own school of art, which still exists today. * Opened in 1910, The Byam Shaw and Vicat Cole School of Art occupied purpose-built premises in Kensington and received the support of a number of eminent artists.

One of Cole's prime motivations as a teacher was to instil in his students an almost reverential attitude to nature: 'Be absolutely truthful', he wrote, 'yet not mechanical in everything you paint from nature' – and again he drove home the point – 'worship of nature, together with enthusiasm for art, are our only guides, but the love of truth should help to check excesses.' † He believed that once students had the right reverential approach they would then only wish to represent nature in the best possible way of which they were capable. He makes it clear in his writings that verisimilitude was not enough and that the artist should strive to capture the sentiment and the idea suggested by nature. In this as in other aspects of his art he may have been influenced by his father who, according to his biographer, sought to express 'the ideal through the real'. ‡

The business of running an art school in London fully engaged him and he found teaching an engrossing occupation. Both he and Hannah established an easy, almost paternalistic relationship with their students and by the beginning of the Great War the school had firmly established itself as an institution which successfully prepared its students for the Royal Academy Schools. The war, of course, interrupted this development and the school's reputation had to be re-established at the end of the conflict but this time without the help of Byam Shaw who died in 1919 at the age of forty-six.

Rex Vicat Cole's career in London, both as a painter and as a teacher, meant that he had increasingly less time to spend in Yorkshire. But his need remained for an inspirational landscape that he could come to know fully. So, as his father and grandfather had done, he turned to Sussex, and, like them, explored the area around Fittleworth and the River Arun. He already knew something of its magical beauty and, as the Elgars would realise some years later, it was both isolated and easily within reach of London.

Rex, Hannah and their two sons began to rent Brinkwells probably in the summer of 1905 and a year later paintings of Brinkwells and the surrounding woods began to appear at the Royal Academy. The family's association with the area was made even stronger by the presence of two of Rex's three sisters close by in cottages in the woods (Mrs Louis Paul and Mrs Harry Cargill). For the Cole family, Brinkwells became a home that mirrored their loves and occupations. The landscape became a source of inspiration for Rex and the paintings

---

* The Byam Shaw and Vicat Cole School of Art has continued as a highly successful school of art. In September 2003 it became part of Central St Martin's College of Art and Design within the London Institute. It remains in its present building at 2 Elthorne Road, London N19 4AG, and continues to specialise in the study of Fine Art.

† Cole, *The Artistic Anatomy of Trees*, General Introduction, p. 22.

‡ For a full account of George Vicat Cole's life see Chignell, *The Life and Paintings of Vicat Cole RA* (Cassell 1896).

II Rex Vicat Cole, Under the Lilac Hedge *(1896)*

III Rex Vicat Cole, A Moorland – Bolton Abbey *(1897)*

IV Rex Vicat Cole, The Home Field (1908)

V Rex Vicat Cole, Brinkwells Garden (1916)

VI Rex Vicat Cole, A Young Girl in a Bluebell Wood (1918)

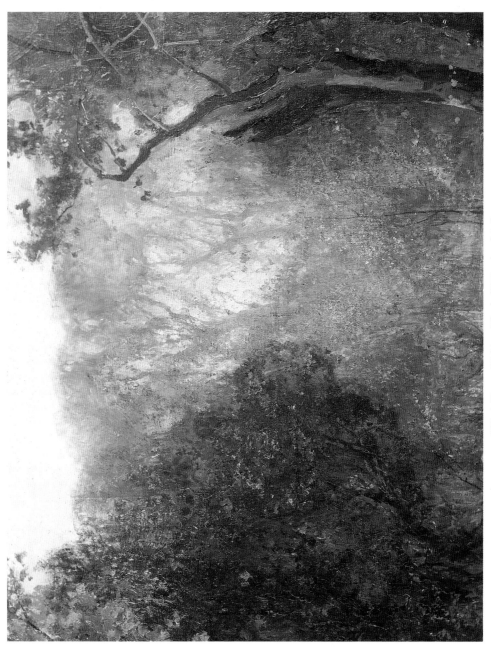

VII A Young Girl in a Bluebell Wood – *detail*

VIII Rex Vicat Cole, A Sussex Granary (1923)

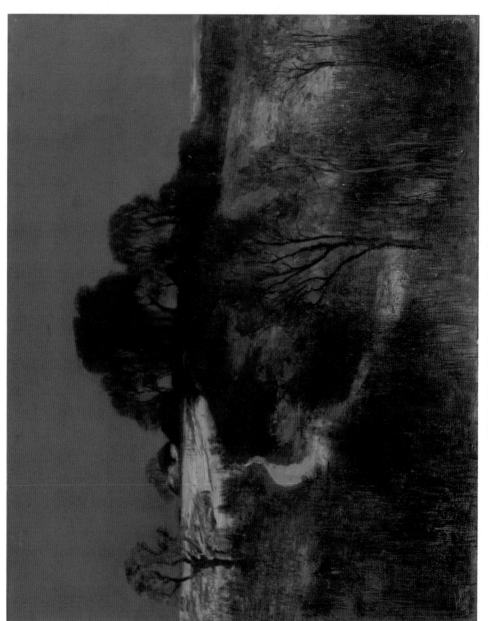

IX *Rex Vicat Cole, Snow on the Copse (undated)*

X *Rex Vicat Cole, Lambeth Palace from Victoria Gardens (undated,* c.1935)

he made there explored his imaginative and subjective response to the truth of nature. He built his own studio, as he had done in Yorkshire, and, as Elgar was to do in his Brinkwells period, he moved between landscape and art, between the woods and their depiction, in one uninterrupted flow of inspiration.

Whilst these years were to see the maturation of Rex Vicat Cole's understanding and interpretation of trees, this preoccupation was already well-established by the time he found the cottage. It was not only his painting that reflected this interest, but the publication of two major pieces of writing on the subject that bore witness to his

34 *Rex and Hannah Vicat Cole with their sons at Brinkwells (c.1910)*

intellectual curiosity and the intensity of his feelings for nature. They showed how his relationship to trees was a curious and potent mix of intellectual curiosity, artistic obsession and love affair.

Clearly there was a sense of spirituality in Cole's passionate attachment to nature and its depiction in art. Whilst his religious views are not really known, from his writings and his paintings it appears that Cole would have felt a considerable affinity with the stories of Blackwood which left no room for a conventional theocentric interpretation of the world around him.

British Trees

The first of his major pieces of writing on trees was *British Trees*. The initial scheme for the project had been drawn up in 1901 when Rex Vicat Cole advertised a publication in monthly parts entitled *British Trees*, illustrated by him. It appeared as a set of 30 monthly monographs published by Hutchinson & Co. and illustrated by drawings made between 1892 and 1906, each month being devoted to one particular tree. The whole series was then bound and produced as a two-volume book in 1907 illustrated with drawings and paintings by the artist.

Rex's intention was to set out the life-history of each forest tree, depicting every facet of its appearance and seasonal cycle. The project was planned as

35 *Rex Vicat Cole,* Bole of an Old Oak, *pencil on paper*

a book of reference for artists and designers which would play the same role as a book on anatomy did for the figure painter. But the resulting study was not merely technical and factual, and the last part of Cole's preface hints at this wider appeal: 'It may also give pleasure to the lover of trees who desires a more accurate knowledge of their growth and character', he wrote. [*]

36 *Rex Vicat Cole, Fallen Chestnut Leaves, pen and ink study*

It is in his publications as well as his paintings that we can see the degree to which trees were central to Rex Vicat Cole's conception of landscape. They appear as characters in their own right, demanding from us the empathy and consideration usually reserved only for our fellow men. In passages of great beauty, Rex Vicat Cole describes the interrelationship between trees and their surroundings, their visual characteristics, their colours, and the legends and beliefs they can engender. It is little wonder that sometimes his name has been coupled with that of Algernon Blackwood, himself a visitor to Elgar at Brinkwells, as a believer in the life force of trees.

The quality of *British Trees* is not only the result of the wonderful illustrations but also of the writing – and in this Cole acknowledged the help of Dorothy Kempe in 're-modelling' his sentences, but the descriptions remained his. Its worth was recognised at the time. 'No amount of instruction could, for instance, have given Mr Rex Vicat Cole that apprehensiveness of the character to be found in trees', was the judgement of Austin Chester in 1910 who went on to praise the richness, vigour and liveliness of Cole's style, finding in the book 'some idea of that worship of the tree which, alive in a more primitive epoch, has since become moribund'. [†]

Each chapter of the 1907 book begins with general remarks about the tree in question, and this is then followed by illustrated sections on the ramification of the branches, the leaf structure, the flower and seed, and the uses of the tree. The drawings include exquisitely fine pencil drawings of details – in particular the tree trunks and bark – more dramatic studies done in pen, gentle gouache sketches on tinted paper of buds and leaves, and simplified diagrammatic drawings in black and white to show different leaf structures. Other drawings concentrate on the complex interweaving of branches and stems. Most of these

---

[*] Cole, *British Trees* (1907), p. 2.
[†] Chester, 'The Art of Mr Rex Vicat Cole', *The Windsor Magazine*, July 1910, p. 376.

studies are clearly drawn from the object they portray and so maintain a sense of life and growth. The paintings also have been chosen to illustrate the particular tree in its natural habitat.

In all these works Vicat Cole's identification with his subject is total. The words he uses also reflect this sympathy in their anthropomorphism; boughs may lose their grace, twigs may be clumsy, the shade cast by a tree can be grateful, the growth of chestnuts impetuous, the strength of the oak stubborn, and the old hollies which crouch above the ground are described as 'magicians all'.

He also manages to convey the pleasure that he felt in being amongst trees. Who can fail vicariously to enjoy his beech wood when he writes:

> To appreciate Beech trees one must be under and among them … In winter the massive grey trunks, lichen-covered and moss-grown, rise in fluted columns from the spreading roots into a network of interlacing boughs and wiry twigs overhead … red-brown leaves underfoot rustle as a rabbit or pheasant runs amongst them. After rain these turn to purple and the pale grey trunks are darkened by the water … while every twig reflects the sky. [*]

Turning from the beech to the willow he describes the haunts of these trees as 'the country of dreams, of peace and quietude: the dreams of the solitary, the peace of lowly places, the quietude that goes with humility. With these, rather than with sad or despairing thoughts, it should be the pleasure of the poet to associate the Willows.' [†] Throughout the book the reader is aware of the painter's eye as Cole describes the 'veil of golden mist' created by larch twigs, or the way that holly leaves 'glitter silver-white in the sunlight', or how the sombre, purplish-grey of the alder bark turns rich red brown where cattle have rubbed against it.

By the time that *British Trees* was published in book form, Rex Vicat Cole had been renting Brinkwells for two years and in Volume 1, in the chapter on the Apple Tree, he included his own drawing of the cottage as well as a wonderful drawing of a Brinkwells apple. He shows Brinkwells from the garden, with someone, probably Hannah, sitting reading in the sun, and in the foreground the twisting branches of an old apple tree. He describes the cottage in these words: 'Close by the orchard stands the labourer's thatched cottage, with its oddly shaped hen coops and well-worn "grin'stone"' (see frontispiece).

Pertinent also to the area around Brinkwells is his description of the chestnut copse throughout the year. His account follows the moods and appearance of the trees as the atmosphere changes from 'the murky airs of a winter's morning' to spring when the open land is swept by March winds and the 'sheltered slope beside the bridlepath in the copse is gilded with daffodils, and the path itself outlined by massed primroses'. He describes scenes which must have been part of the country life around Brinkwells: men and boys cutting the chestnut rods, the bundles of rods glistening white in the sunlight, the fantastic forms of old

---

[*] Cole, *British Trees*, Vol. I, pp. 27-8.
[†] *Ibid.*, Vol II, p. 436.

37 Rex Vicat Cole, Brinkwells Apple, *pencil on paper*

oaks seen against the blue-black sky, and the unseen life of the wood where
'elves hold their revels'.

It is Rex Vicat Cole's fascination with the unseen life of the trees and their
historical and mythical associations which adds a further dimension to the
work – and it is a dimension that would have fascinated Elgar too. In his chapter
on the Mountain Ash, Cole writes of the magic of the woods and the tales of
mystery that developed around trees – sometimes kindly and healing, at other
times darker and less benign. He conjures up a picture of the world-tree of the
Norseman, the sacred trees of the Druids and Celts and the North Country
superstitions surrounding the Rowan. In his eyes trees take on a powerful,

spiritual significance, surrounded by the unseen life of the woods and wrapped in a web of mythical and religious associations.

The Artistic Anatomy of Trees

The second of Rex Vicat Cole's major tree projects was the writing and publication of *The Artistic Anatomy of Trees* in 1915. It was one of a series of books written by eminent practitioners on painting techniques and was designed specifically for the student of landscape painting. Therefore, while Cole used some of the material which had appeared in *British Trees*, everything was recast so that trees were seen relative to their depiction in painting. Once again Cole was in his element and from the very beginning his measure as a teacher and as a man is apparent. His note, which precedes the text, reads as follows:

> It is with considerable diffidence that I undertake the task of attempting a description of Trees from the artist's point of view. A loving acquaintance with them each year brings home to me my shortcomings in rendering them as they should be rendered in the branch of art I follow – painting. To this is added a new terror in having to use words; and the temptation is to relinquish the effort and say instead that only those who can feel the beauty of Trees may attempt to paint them, and that to others their significance must for ever remain a closed door. If my statements appear dogmatic or dictatorial it is not because I think I can draw trees really well; but only because I know that a large number of people draw them worse.

The book was divided into three sections and in these Cole widened the scope of his earlier investigations, particularly in the first section entitled 'Trees considered in relation to Painting'. In this part Rex Vicat Cole surveys the history of tree painting from the 15th to the 20th centuries and analyses the different approaches that had been taken by the artists. By doing so he reveals those aspects of the art with which he was most concerned. He starts the first chapter, for instance, with the name of the Barbizon painter Theodore Rousseau – a surprising choice, perhaps, given the whole range of artists available – but for Rex Vicat Cole he was an artist who could capture the very soul of nature, something that was dear to his heart. When he turned his attention to Dutch 17th- century painters he found Hobbema superior to Ruysdael in his veneration of and fidelity to trees, but in all his named artists, in whatever style or era, what he looked for was the expression of the artist's feeling about the truth of nature allied to an ability to transmute the commonplace into poetry.

Having set out historical and contemporary examples of how trees could be treated in painting, Rex Vicat Cole then discusses what the artist should look for in trees, how they could balance and structure a composition and their visual characteristics. These sections called for a wider range of illustrations than *British Trees* had done, and Cole includes many of his own oils and pencil studies which explore every visual aspect the artist could use: from the patterns

38 *Rex Vicat Cole,* Trees Hanging over a Bank *(1913), pencil on paper*

formed by foliage to how trees were seen against the sky; from the outline pattern of different trees to the variety of curves found in their branches; from how to deal with chiaroscuro effects and distance to the variety of colours and the influence of situation and light. The coverage is extensive and Cole's attention to detail formidable.

Part II of the book examines the anatomy of trees: their outline form, the relationship between twig, shoot and bough, the effects produced by the arrangement of buds and twigs and how the whole tree is constructed. Part III, entitled 'The Details of Trees', contains a comprehensive study of different leaves, flowers, fruits, seedlings etc. No detail appears too small to have escaped Cole's notice and for him to explain how it played its part in the overall effect of the tree to be painted. In order to clarify some of these points and to explain how trees worked he obviously felt it necessary to include many more diagrams than he had in his earlier book. Chapter XIII, for example, goes to great length (16 pages) to clarify the different effects produced on the branch anatomy of a tree by different arrangements of buds – and these 16 pages are packed with diagrams, gouache studies and pencil drawings by the author.

It would be easy to assume, reading this, that Rex Vicat Cole was in danger of losing himself in a welter of details. Yet he does not. We find, in the *Artistic*

Anatomy of Trees, as in *British Trees*, his own pervading sense of delight and respect for his subject which enlivens the whole text. He sets out his own belief that it is both interesting and profitable for an artist to know about what he is painting and for a landscape artist in particular 'to know in what manner one tree differs from another in its growth'. For him, good art could only be achieved by a close, loving, and continuous study, and always he is at pains to explain how nature should be approached by the artist and the balance that should be achieved between knowledge and inspiration. He wrote:

> Care without knowledge of nature may easily be the cause of lifelessness in drawing, so that fact is substituted for the essence of life, movement, sound, and scent … Misdirected energy may give an elaboration of leaves clear and sharp, without the suggestion of movement, and so the flicker and frolic of the pattering Aspen leaves – their chief charm – be lost. [*]

The wealth of knowledge and detail that he includes in his books is tempered by his empathy with his subject and his own overriding need for expression. The reader senses this empathy in a passage towards the beginning of the book. In writing about the naturalism of a painting by the landscape artist Patrick Nasmyth (1787-1831), he describes how the observer can enter into the tree's existence and 'recall its encounters with storms, sympathise with its fresh start in life and marvel at the almost human ingenuity that its parts display while seeking light and air …' [†] Cole writes feelingly of ancient oaks:

> They are just records of time and the stress of life – gaunt fantastic skeletons, survivors of the time past; and they are seen at their best under a thunderstorm such as they have for centuries defied, or in the mystery of nightfall when an owl startles the silence and the nightjar flaps ghostly with a warning cry. [‡]

He acknowledges, too, the almost uncanny analogy between the limbs of a tree and those of the human figure and the 'weird imaginings' suggested by forests. Just such weird imaginings were to possess the Elgars later, particularly in the context of the Piano Quintet. (See ch. 9.)

Above all Rex Vicat Cole exhorts students to make trees their own; to find in them something that the casual observer misses and to remember that painting is an expression of the artist's moods conveyed through the object that he represents – a definition which would have found favour with Elgar.

Rex's teaching, exhibiting and writing carried on through his years at Brinkwells to be interrupted in 1914 by the outbreak of the Great War. Like Elgar, he was keen to do his bit and being a younger man (he was 44 when the war broke out) he volunteered whilst at Brinkwells for the West Sussex Civil Guard and after this was disbanded he joined the United Arts Rifles with Byam Shaw. Ironically, for someone who was never to become an academician, the

---

[*] Cole, *The Artistic Anatomy of Trees*, p. 134.
[†] *Ibid.*, p. 44.
[‡] *Ibid.*, pp. 125-6.

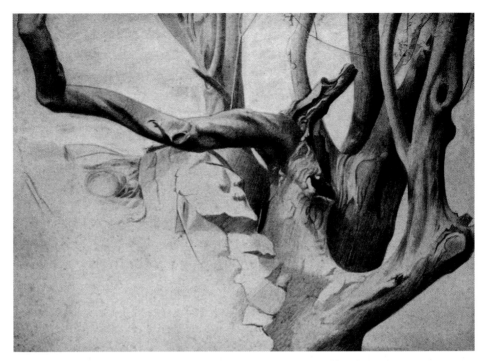

40 *Rex Vicat Cole,* The Twisted Limb of an Old Holly

headquarters of the battalion were at the Royal Academy and its volunteers drilled in the quadrangle in front of Somerset House. In his biography of his friend Cole described how his students were keen to fight, writing that: 'Artists were not behind in joining up … The young men at our art school were soon in Kitchener's army and, presently, most of the girls were on munitions or working on the land. Shaw and I joined the United Arts Rifles (1st Battalion, County of London Volunteer Regiment).'[*]

The war marked a turning point in Rex Vicat Cole's painting and what Elgar must have seen in the studio at Brinkwells were works which represented the development and crystallisation of a style that Cole himself was to abandon in post-war years. So, what were these works like and what do they tell us about Brinkwells and the power of its environment?

The Brinkwells Paintings

Rex Vicat Cole's Brinkwells works included large-scale paintings intended for the Royal Academy, smaller more intimate painted sketches of the surroundings of the cottage, as well as many of the drawings published in *British Trees* and *The Artistic Anatomy of Trees*. These would have been the paintings and sketches described by Elgar. Even before 1905, when he began to rent the cottage, Cole

---

[*] Cole, *The Art and Life of Byam Shaw*, p. 185.

had produced Sussex subjects such as his 1903 canvas *Harvest Time in Sussex* done in collaboration with his friend Byam Shaw, who painted the figures, which was hung at the R.A. that year. In 1905 Cole's Academy painting *The Brimming River: The Arun at Houghton* (R.A. 1905) was the result of working at Amberley and may represent the beginning of his Brinkwells years when the woods and fields around Fittleworth and Bedham provided him with his subject matter. Between 1905 and the outbreak of the war Cole's paintings represent a tribute to that countryside and his commitment to that particular area took on an intense, almost Hardyesque sense of place. From the paintings, from the photographs taken there at the time, as well as from his family's memories, the observer gains a strong sense of his identification with the woodlands. His paintings certainly depict a growing, living countryside and his views are neither exaggerated nor over-composed. Yet, aligned to this naturalism is a deeper emotional attachment. There are elements certainly of Edwardian idyll and pastoral arcadia but Cole escapes from any temptation to drift into over-sentimentality or into an unearthly dream-world. His countryside works as countryside but he also tells you how much it is to be loved and valued.

In his 1908 Royal Academy painting *The Home Field*, Cole depicts one of the fields close to Brinkwells as it is being harvested (see plate IV). It is a balanced, evocative image, full of golden tones and rich late summer air. The landscape rolls away from the foreground into a distant blue haze and everything is caught up and united by this carefully modulated atmospheric space. Here too we can see how Cole could use his knowledge of trees and their appearance under different light conditions, not to add too much detail, but to express their essence and to unify the composition in the most economic manner.

In this canvas, as in his other Brinkwells works, the emotional tone of the paintings has much to do with the way that figures are incorporated into his scenes – they are in fact shown as part of the scene, emerging from the landscape rather than being imposed on it. His intention is not to idealise the country worker nor to see the land as an extension of the inner life of those who occupy it in the way that his friend and fellow artist Edward Stott was to do. There is no way that Cole, like him, could be considered an English Millet.[*] Cole's figures rather share the atmosphere created by their surroundings – they may draw attention to it – but they do not create it and in some instances they almost disappear into it.

Rex Vicat Cole's fine balance between observed nature and personal statement set him apart from some of the contemporary developments in English painting. In 1917, when Elgar saw his work at Brinkwells, Cole could have little in common with those British painters, many of whom had studied in Paris, who were concerned with the development of post-impressionism and who exhibited as English post-impressionists. He had even less in common with the group who gathered around Percy Wyndham Lewis in 1914 as the

---

[*] Jean Francois Millet (1814-75), best known for his paintings of peasants and their labours which he could invest with an almost symbolic intensity.

Vorticists. This is not to say that he was unaware of developments in French and British painting and indeed *The Artistic Anatomy of Trees* commends many contemporary figures for their treatment of landscape, but the 'ideal isolation' of Brinkwells enabled him to pursue a path that was unlike that of his contemporaries. That this direction would not sustain him in the altered post-war world, he was apparently unaware, and therefore what Elgar saw in the studio at Brinkwells was, in some ways, the end of one stylistic era in Rex Vicat Cole's art.

Rex Vicat Cole's dedication to Brinkwells is evident from his 1910 exhibition at the Mendoza Gallery entitled 'English Woodlands'. His paintings included charcoal burners, woodland scenes, views from Bedham and Brinkwells, the hoopmaker's hut and harvest fields at Fittleworth – all scenes that were within easy reach of the cottage and subjects which were to become familiar to the Elgars. In the same year two paintings by him at the Royal Academy demonstrated the blooming of his Sussex woodland style, and a long (14-page) article appeared about him in the *Windsor Magazine*. This article suggests that spring was particularly important for the artist and indeed one of the two R.A. paintings that year, a study of the woods and hills around Brinkwells, was entitled *Awaiting Spring's Return*. The second of the two exhibits, *The Woodman's Home*, was most probably painted to the north of Brinkwells at Bedham and shows the woodman's thatched cottage in the foreground and in the distance a view of the village of Wisborough Green.

In his woodland paintings, Rex Vicat Cole used the contrast of light and shade and the play of light through foliage to order the whole painting. In some canvases this was the main subject. In *Young Girl in a Bluebell Wood* (1918),(see plate VI), the artist's interest is clearly in the atmospheric play of light through the leaves and the sharp tonal contrasts between deep shadow and the occasional sparkling patch of sunlight. Whilst the tree trunks in the foreground support and control the composition, the interior of the canvas is ordered by a tunnel-shaped, womb-like swirl of light which carries the observer's eye into the canvas. It is a compositional device which appears to be organic and to have grown out of the experience of being in the sheltering woods rather than to have been imposed on nature from the realms of other art. Cole has here done what he exhorts his students to do: find something that the casual observer would have missed in the subject itself which is entirely appropriate to the scene.

This picture reveals once again Cole's ability to use his knowledge of nature sensitively. The tops of the far trees, for example, are captured in all their fugitive form and indefinable colour with great brevity (see plate VII). There is no sense of Cole being weighed down by his intimate knowledge and his interest in detail. In fact the canvas, when viewed from close up, is not tightly detailed. Patches of impasto, spots of colour, broken brushstrokes and longer swathes of paint are used to describe the colours, textures and space of the woodland interior and result in a canvas surface that is textured and busy. The colour is sombre and muted except where light catches flowers and bright green blades of grass or leaves, and the blue of the bells themselves is restrained. There is no danger here of Cole falling into the trap of mere 'prettiness' by a subject that traps many artists into that fault. What we see in Cole's work is balance, carefully judged colour, and tonal control that is relative to natural effects. This sensitivity results in a canvas that constantly changes in appearance as light conditions alter. In fact it responds to light just as the woodland itself would respond; sometimes dark and mysterious and at other time alive with colour. The picture also reflects the growing seriousness of his work during the war when the sunnier days of the *Home Farm* painting give way to a more realistic and sometimes sombre vision.

Just how far his landscape had travelled can be seen by comparing this bluebell wood with an earlier one painted in Yorkshire in 1899. The earlier canvas is brightly coloured, higher in tone and obviously attractive in its effects. In the 1918 painting Cole is less concerned to woo his audience and his vision, like Elgar's, has an underlying sense of the sunshine and shade of the world always existing together.

Of course for the Elgar enthusiast Rex Vicat Cole's paintings have an added interest: they tell us what it was like to live at Brinkwells and what the surrounding country looked like. There is the pencil and chalk sketch of Brinkwells itself, made in 1906 and published in *British Trees*; an affectionate portrait of an idiosyncratic cottage (see frontispiece). Then there is his son's photograph of the cottage taken from the same side which gives us the clearest idea of what it must have looked like when Elgar took it over (see illus. 11).

Of great interest also is the 1916 painting of *Brinkwells Garden* (see plate V) which shows the view from Cole's studio across the valley to the Toat Monument on the horizon. This is the view which Elgar 'inherited' and which formed the constant backdrop to his composition. (The end of the studio is just visible on the left of the painting and its large window would have been on the side furthest from the viewer.) Cole's unaffected and direct view of Brinkwells garden under a stormy and brooding sky fully illustrates his powers of selection and observation. The balance between detail and mass, and his mastery of tone, create a powerful, memorable image. The painting carries a strong sense of place and time and we are made aware as viewers that this scene is significant. And yet the means by which this is done are simple and the artist is in full control of his medium and techniques.

The wonderfully strong painting now at Worthing Museum and Art Gallery entitled *A Sussex Granary* (1923) (see plate VIII) has as its subject Springs Farm which belonged to Mr Aylwin, the Elgars' near neighbour and invaluable local carrier. It was a scene that must have been familiar to Alice and Elgar as the walk to Springs Farm was one often taken by them and their guests. The later painting *Snow on the Copse* (exhibited in 1931) (see plate IX) gives another view of the farm, this time in winter, and the path leading up to it. Here Rex Vicat Cole displays a sombre vision, the fluid surface is unrelieved by any prettiness of effect or decorative detail and almost monochrome in colour. These last two works are important also in showing how in the post-war years Cole moved away from the style that had celebrated the sheltering isolation of Brinkwells into another, different vision. (See chapter 11.)

Rex Vicat Cole was not alone in finding a magical landscape in West Sussex. In earlier years the region had been visited by Constable who, at the end of his life in the 1830s, painted near Arundel, whilst Turner had frequented Petworth House where his patron, the 3rd Earl of Egremont, established a studio for him. But near-contemporaries of Cole also worked in the same area. These included Edward Stott (1859-1918) at Amberley and Arthur Rackham (1867-1939) at Houghton. Even nearer were Charles Sims (1877-1928) who worked at Fittleworth before the war, the prolific but sombre Philip Hugh Padwick (1876-1958), another Fittleworth resident who lived at Corner House, and the watercolour painter Berenger Benger (1868-1935), who for a time lived at The Grange, Fittleworth. Lesser figures had also painted the same landscape as the remarkable dining room of the *Swan Inn* in Fittleworth reveals with its 29 panels depicting local scenes completed by artists staying there – sometimes taken in place of payment by the then landlady Miss Hawkins. Rex Vicat Cole had also taken his students to work around Brinkwells, holding sketching classes as he had done in Yorkshire. Yet his work remained distinct from other interpretations of the area.

All the above artists were profoundly inspired by the country around the Arun. For Stott that inspiration was drawn from rural life and labour and his quiet scenes of the countryside honour the lives of those working in it. He had settled at Amberley in 1889 and pursued his vision of the pastoral life and the sentiments of labour portrayed with a stylised quietism in which the landscape becomes an extension of the people in it. Padwick, who was educated at Repton and had studied at the Slade, found in the Sussex countryside a perfect subject for his moody, dark-toned works with their restricted colour and broadly brushed, abbreviated style. In contrast, Cole's works are both closer portraits of the country and more pantheistic in outlook. He eschewed both Stott's visionary element and any trace of Padwickian gloom, to espouse an intimate union with nature in which the artist portrayed the idea suggested both by nature and art. His loving acquaintance with trees, which he expressed in the opening note of *The Artistic Anatomy of Trees*, is clear in his Brinkwells works. Moreover, the ideal seclusion of the cottage and the inspiration of the woods enabled him to build a body of work in which the landscape became a vehicle for the painter's mood and the painter partook of the atmosphere of the landscape without distortion to either. In the next chapters we shall see how Elgar reacted to the 'ideal isolation' of Brinkwells and the surrounding landscape.

CHAPTER SEVEN

The Perfect Guest –
Elgar's Friends at Brinkwells

The Quality of Friendship

Whilst isolation appeared to suit Rex Vicat Cole who needed only nature for his muse, Elgar's requirements were different. Throughout his life, whether composing or not, he needed his friends. Friendship, moreover, was something at which he was gifted, and in her biography Diana MacVeagh makes the point that although Elgar may have been misunderstood by his acquaintances, he was loved by his friends. Difficult as he was at times, at others he could be the most entertaining of companions, and he had the ability to make his friends feel special, something which is clear from his idiosyncratic and lively letters which made the recipient feel that they were in the full beam of Elgar's attention.

He could and did lean on his friends. He could pour out his grievances and worries to them or act impetuously or moodily, but he did not lose their friendship. He engaged their sympathies and there was something too for them in being needed by a creative genius – a need that extended into both his personal and musical life. Many of these friendships were complex in their dynamics, particularly where they involved musical as well as personal issues. But the great key to all of them, as far as Elgar was concerned, was his music – because by the acceptance and championship of his music, his friends were accepting and championing him.

This is apparent from his earliest affections to his last love. In 1890 Ivor Atkins decided, on listening to Froissart, that 'Elgar was the man for me, I knew that I completely understood his music, and that my heart and soul went with it' and Elgar, on seeing this in the young Atkins realised that a 'real friendship' had begun. [*]

Later, it was through his music that Billy Reed became bound to Elgar in friendship and late in life his deep affection for Vera Hockman just before his death was founded on her understanding of him through his music. Elgar's self-identification with his music was total and it is impossible to think of one close friend who was not a wholehearted supporter of his compositions.

This made constructive criticism difficult. Alice could manage it by dropping a hint that things were, well, not quite right, as she did on at least one occasion

---

[*] Atkins, *The Elgar-Atkins Friendship*, p. 26.

by leaving a little note pinned to the manuscript paper for Elgar to find in the morning. But her criticism was so enmeshed in her complete acceptance of Elgar's genius, and so gently done, as to constitute no challenge. The complexity of some of his musical friendships is perhaps best illustrated by his relationship with August Jaeger who did challenge Elgar head on in musical issues and did so by a combination of vigorous encouragement, praise and exhortation to the composer to fulfil the role allotted to him. According to Rosa Burley, Elgar needed constant encouragement not just from Alice but also from his friends and this Jaeger gave, whilst at the same time pushing Elgar to the extremes of his creativity. Of course theirs was a professional, musical relationship as well – but friendship took it over to the point where Jaeger would write in 1907: 'I have worked terribly hard for E.E. and ruined my health over it very likely … I have never loved & admired a man more, made myself a slave for any man out of sheer enthusiasm.' [*]

Friends, therefore, were a necessary ingredient in Elgar's composing life, and however great his love of nature and escaping into the depths of the woods, this escapism was balanced by the need for support and encouragement. There was also the boyish side of Elgar's personality and his need, as expressed by Alice, for someone to play with. The friends who visited Brinkwells answered these different requirements. Alice could not satisfy them herself – of that she had always been aware – and part of the debt owed to her by Elgar was the result of her unselfish generosity in fostering his friendships and standing back from the emotional attachments that he made with other women.

On a more practical level, the Elgars were aware of the benefits of their country retreat when their friends in London were dealing with the privations and dangers of war. 'A. & I have been feeling that it is selfish to have this lovely place all to ourselves & want to be useful in repairing broken nerves', Elgar wrote to the Windflower on 14 July 1918, following this laudable sentiment with a pressing invitation to the Windflower herself. When their friends did arrive they were entertained by long country walks and rural pursuits as well as music. Some guests, amongst them Lalla Vandervelde, did sometimes fall into the 'broken nerves' category and fulfilled the social side of friendship – companions for Elgar's leisure – others acted as muses or performers and audience for his music.

Accommodation

In terms of accommodation, Brinkwells was not ideally suited for entertaining and Elgar was aware that for some of their friends the cottage might have been 'rather too wild'. [†] Brinkwells was far from commodious or even 'convenient'. It is one thing to romanticise about it on a fine summer's day – quite another to have to go down the path for the outside toilet facilities during an October gale.

[*] Powell, *Memories of a Variation*, p. 126.
[†] Letter to Walford Davies quoted in Young, *Letters of Edward Elgar*, p. 259.

There was no electricity, no running hot water nor even a simple bathroom, and it was Alice, now nearly 70, who felt these privations most acutely – they may even have shortened her life. Elgar himself, though blest by then (i.e. without his infected tonsils) with health a good deal more physically robust than he would have readily admitted, was able to escape to his capacious artist's studio in the garden where his muses could be summoned from the air more comfortably.

It has been suggested that their more particular guests may have stayed at the *Swan Inn* in Fittleworth (although there is no mention of their names in the Visitors Book of the period there); others certainly went straight to Brinkwells and stayed the night. (The existence of a *Swan Hotel* at Pulborough confuses the issue. But it would appear possible that certain guests, if they didn't stay in the cottage, may have stayed there rather than at Fittleworth as visitors were more often met by Mr Aylwin at Pulborough Station – the distance being not much greater and another change of trains on to the single line track to Fittleworth and beyond being avoided. Pulborough's original *Swan Hotel*, which had eight bedrooms and had been awarded one star in 1913, was pulled down in 1959.)

In the cottage arrangements were certainly made for visitors. One of Elgar's home-made tables adorned the 'guest room' and Alice's diary contains several references to her rearranging rooms before or after visitors. Elgar also expressed some misgivings about the standard of accommodation they could offer. When the conductor Landon Ronald was about to stay in the summer of 1918, Elgar wrote to the Windflower, 'poor dear, I fear he is very very delicate, he will come here in July but I <u>dread</u> his "delicate" ways & I think our living wd. shock him!' [*] But come he most certainly did in August, and he seemed to survive the experience, turning Alice out of her room in the process: 'A. glad to have her room again', she wrote in her diary the day he left.

Billy Reed was another overnight visitor, recalling how Elgar had appeared in his room at 4.30 in the morning to go and deal with a wasps' nest that they had poisoned the day before. Often there must have been a quick turn-round of guests, with Carice arriving as another visitor left, and on one occasion Elgar made up a bed for her downstairs – 'made drawing – into bedroom for Carice' his diary reads for 21 August 1918. There was also a bed and a couch available in the studio should conditions become too pressing in the cottage.

Most visitors arrived by train and were met by the dependable Mr Aylwin in the pony cart, returning with him to Pulborough railway station. As Elgar began composing in earnest in the early autumn of 1918, these visitors played more of a musical role with Billy Reed making a number of trips in order to help Elgar by playing over new work with him. But, as we have seen, Elgar's musical life rested on a complex nexus of stimulants: environment, mood, mentors, friends, Alice, the female muse, and of course inspiration – that 'fickle Hussey' to use John Clare's words. Three of the visitors to Brinkwells between 1918 and 1919 illustrate aspects of this complex web of interdependence; they are Alice

---

[*] Moore, *The Windflower Letters*, p. 206.

Stuart Wortley, Algernon Blackwood and Billy Reed – or we could characterise them as muse, magician and musician.

The Muse

Alice Stuart Wortley, 'the Windflower', had long been established as Elgar's 'muse' before her visit to Brinkwells in May 1918. She was musically gifted with considerable talent as a pianist and he relied on her musical judgement as well as her understanding. The role of the muse in music has a long pedigree and in this instance it is interesting to consider exactly how the relationship between composer and muse works. The composer Jonathan Harvey in his book *Music and Inspiration* examines this problem and writes: 'The role of the muse, however, is a complex one. She is both the stimulus of the work and the audience at which it is directed. As the stimulus, she is closely aligned with archetypal women: she is seen as something far more wonderful and other-worldly than she really is, with the power to awaken the deepest layers of the unconscious and shake the man with inspiration.'[*]

We find echoes of this in the Windflower/Elgar relationship during the Brinkwells period and, given the Windflower's musical gifts, she was not only the stimulus and audience of his work but also a critic whose judgement was accepted. Elgar relied on his muses to awaken his emotional side. He needed the impetus of a romantic relationship and his feelings for the Windflower kept him within that emotional range – as had the memory of Helen Weaver, his lost love. It seems unnecessary now to try to speculate where the influence of one stopped and the other started as what appears to have been of most importance was the mood and emotion that was generated – for it was this that ultimately fuelled his music. So, as Jonathan Harvey suggests, the muse can be a kind of enabler – a powerful catalyst for the composer's own deepest feelings. In Elgar's case these emotions were often those of loss, regret, and the feeling that the best had somehow passed, and so the unobtainable muse was even more relevant.

And if the Windflower played out this role, what role did Alice play? Not that of muse, certainly, although she had done once at the start of their life together. Rather, what she did at Brinkwells, as she had done for some years before, was to give Elgar the freedom to worship his muse safely. Her accepting presence took on the responsibilty of the relationship for both of them and placed her in a maternal role. It was, however, a position she had gladly accepted before.

Before the Windflower arrived at the cottage for her first stay on 24 May 1918, her visit had been keenly anticipated by Elgar. Letters passed between them making arrangements for her to be met at the station and suggesting any provisions she could bring for the household. 'I am looking forward to your coming with acute joy', Elgar wrote, on 12 May, and later on 17 May, 'the thing is to bring yourself. & rest; there will be a full moon & all lovely & nightingales', as if laying the countryside at her feet. Alice also enjoyed a friendship with the

---

[*] Harvey, *Music and Inspiration*, p. 105.

Windflower, but Elgar's letters often make it quite clear that their relationship is not a threesome. Having described how he had walked to Pulborough with Alice a few days earlier and had a nice lunch at the *Swan Hotel* there, he wrote to the Windflower 'we must do this' – the emphasis placed firmly, and, one feels, exclusively, on the 'we'. [*]

That first visit, which lasted five days from 24 to 28 May, was blessed by good weather and the Elgars took the opportunity to show their guest the sights. Therefore there was a great deal of walking – up to Springs Farm, to Bedham and Bignor Common, and to see the strange group of trees which they had identified on their first stay at the cottage and which Elgar describes in his diary on the occasion of the Windflower's visit as 'eerie' and Alice as 'strange'.

The Windflower was introduced to Lady Maxse, who came to tea. She was there when Elgar nearly swallowed a piece of wire in the gooseberry tart at lunch causing a sore throat for the rest of the day and acute distress to Alice, the accident occurring as it did so quickly after Elgar's throat operation. She was also present to hear the sad news that Charles Mott, the singer, had been killed in France fighting on the Western Front. She helped Elgar in the garden and encouraged him to make changes there which he did after she had left, writing to tell her that he had taken down the wire that she had objected to. Clearly, no sooner had she gone than Elgar wanted another visit and wrote to her three days after her departure: 'All goes on as usual but you are missed … I fear your journey was tiresome but you will make it all again soon.' [†] The Windflower obliged with another visit in August which lasted three days. But on this occasion, wishing to be at her best, she arrived by an earlier train and gave herself time for a rest and for lunch at the *Swan* (probably *The Swan* at Pulborough) before Mr Aylwin arrived to meet her in the afternoon – a ruse that Elgar later described as 'your wonderfully clever journey'. But even without her physical presence, her influence made itself felt at the cottage in many ways – not only through the intangible inspiration that she gave to Elgar but also materially through her gifts, one of which helped to transform the studio into a music room.

Elgar's sudden burst of energy in making this transformation, and his renewed enthusiasm for composition, began only nine days after the Windflower's departure and her presence must have encouraged this turn in his outlook and somehow galvanised him into action. With his enthusiasm for music now returning he arranged for his Steinway upright piano to be brought to Brinkwells. On 15 August with its arrival imminent Elgar turned his attention to the studio floor and, using slabs of pine provided by the resourceful Mark, he laid a covering over what had previously been an earth floor. Of course, he wrote to the Windflower the next day to tell her of his progress and in his letter he makes explicit the association of the studio with her. He writes: 'I have made (sketchily) a floor for the new garden room – your room – but I sadly

---

[*] Moore, *The Windflower Letters*, pp. 202-3.
[†] *Ibid.*, p. 204.

needed help – it was a heavy job and the sun hot.'* This work appears to have
been completed by 17 August, and two days later the piano was duly delivered
and carried into the music room by Mr Aylwin, his son Walter, Mark and three
other men, and placed in a nice position (according to Elgar on the left of the
entrance where the light was good) and Elgar immediately began to play.

Elgar's association of the Windflower with his music and her 'ownership' of
the music room was made more explicit by her gift of a blind for the window
so that Elgar could work there and look at the view without straining his eyes.
This arrived on the same day as the piano and, according to Alice's diary, it was
a 'lovely green shade, & pretty acorns etc' and Elgar busied himself putting it
up. Another letter from Elgar to his muse on the same day once again made
the association between her and his room. He wrote, referring at the same time
to one of her earlier gifts of woodworking tools: 'the blind has arrived & is the
greatest success; you are so clever knowing the exactly right thing in every case
– it is, of course, too good (refined and delicate) like the plane & all of you,
for everyday use, but it makes the garden house yours more than ever.' With
the blind in place Elgar could enjoy the view without worry and in September
Alice noted how much he enjoyed it, finding it like a painting by Turner.

Although the Windflower was not to visit Brinkwells again until August
1919, the music room continued to hold her image for Elgar so that he was
aware of her absence. This longing for her penetrated the cold confines of
Severn House as well, intensified as it was there by Elgar's acute desire to return
to the country. He wrote to her in February 1919 from London: 'It is still all ice
& snow here & very cold … .I long for Brinkwells even in this weather & shall
shut myself up here hermetically I think. London is a desert, alas! And where
are you ….'† This sense of the loss of her presence is felt in the music written
at Brinkwells and it is certainly expressed in the letters that he sent her from
the country. 'I <u>wish</u> you were here', he wrote in November, 'the studio is not
too cold in the early morn. How I remember it all.' And later that same year: 'I
think much of you & it is lovely here but the mornings are cold & dark – and
<u>lonely</u>.' And again, 'There are still sprigs of lavender on the bushes & I think of
you every time I pass them: the blind is taken down & stored away for next year
– we are to be here D. V. & you <u>will come</u> won't you.'‡

By her support, by her presence and, it seems, by her absence the Windflower
kept Elgar's emotions in those areas ideally suited to his musical expression.
There is an eagerness, almost a willingness, in his letters to endure the pain of
loss – both for his absent muse and also perhaps here for his earlier love. Whether
this was conscious or subconscious it is impossible to say – and whether Elgar
himself knew the extent to which his music relied on his willingness to ride
his own emotional rollercoaster is equally impossible to gauge. But although
the exact truth about their relationship can never be known, it is clear that

---

* Moore, *The Windflower Letters*, p. 209.
† *Ibid.*, p. 222.
‡ *Ibid.*, pp. 216, 218-9.

in any assessment of Elgar's creative process at Brinkwells, the Windflower's inspirational part must be acknowledged.

Starlight

With the second of our visitors, Algernon Blackwood, Elgar had an entirely different kind of relationship. Like all Elgar's affections, this was based on his recognition that Blackwood was sympathetic to him and his music. As we have seen in an earlier chapter, they had first met in November 1915 over Elgar's music for Starlight Express, a stage adaptation of Blackwood's story *A Prisoner in Fairyland,* and a firm friendship and mutual sympathy was quickly apparent. Alice also fell under Blackwood's spell for he was an unusual character and a magical storyteller.

41 Algernon Blackwood in 1929

He became a welcome and frequent guest at Severn House. At one stage in March 1916 he stayed two weeks with the Elgars, and introduced them to his brother and sister-in-law. 'Mr Blackwood came to stay', Alice's diary records on 13 March 1916, adding 'Starlight Express records came. Very exciting hearing them, very good …' For a period he became part of their social circle, on one occasion lunching with Elgar and Clara Butt and on another with Alice at her club. Alice's diary gives us glimpses of evenings at Severn House when Elgar and Blackwood – 'Starlight' as they called him – played games at the billiards table far into the night until they were tired. Even at periods when Elgar was unwell Blackwood would come, sometimes for Alice's Sunday tea gathering, and then stay on for dinner; 'E. and he played and played plate pool and he won', Alice wrote approvingly in November 1917 on one of these visits, and on another occasion she noted the 'shouts of delightful laughter' that accompanied their game. On other occasions Elgar would play the piano or they would listen to the gramophone or talk: 'nice evening – just A. Blackwood & our souses', Alice wrote in March 1916.

Elgar was eager for Blackwood to visit him at Brinkwells and tried to 'rig up a picnic party at the Sussex cottage' in August 1917. [*] But the plan came to nothing and Elgar had to wait until the next year before Algernon Blackwood made the journey down to Brinkwells for a night. Even then there were difficulties; initially they were expecting him on 17 July but this had to be cancelled and even when he started out the next morning he was unable to get on the train – presumably due to wartime overcrowding. The day was also very windy with

---

[*] Moore, *The Windflower Letters*, p. 188.

rain storms and Elgar had already walked to the station before hearing that he was delayed. As Mr Aylwin and the pony cart were booked later in the day, Alice and Elgar walked to the station again to meet him at 3.55 pm. 'Much struck with scenery & loved it all. After tea E. and he to sinister trees & octopus & Gog & Magog.' (These were, and are, two old 'eyecatcher' lodges to Petworth House on the edge of woods to the west of Flexham Park that for a period of about one hundred years had been adorned with the sculpted war trophies of Gog and Magog which in the 18th century were returned to the grand entrance to the house in Petworth. The name stuck although the sculpture had long been removed.) Having walked a fair distance before dinner, Elgar and Blackwood were out again in the evening. 'After dinner into woods', Alice reported in her diary for the day.

Blackwood's brief visit remained in their memories and he was quickly designated as 'exactly the Brinkwells guest' by Alice. He dazzled them with a display of pole jumping (a legacy perhaps of his punting skills); 'He jumped wonderfully with a pole' Elgar wrote in his diary at the time, and some time afterwards he 'dreamily' recalled to Wulstan Atkins the excitement of that visit. He described Blackwood as a good walker and talker, a keen athlete and an expert at pole-jumping and told Atkins how he had cut a long pole for him and Blackwood 'had demonstrated his art by leaping on to the top of a tall barred gate, jumping over a hedge, and by long horizontal jumps'.[*] To Elgar, the enthusiastic games player and hobbyist, this must have been irresistible.

That first visit was all too brief. Blackwood returned to London at 9 o'clock the next morning, although even then Alice thought that he looked 'so refreshed' by his stay. It was to be just over a year before Blackwood paid another visit to the cottage – this time with Wilfred Wilson with whom he had enjoyed a canoeing holiday down the Danube in 1900 that was to result in his story *The Willows* (1907). The Wilsons lived in Sussex and Alice's diary reports that they had walked over. 'Did so enjoy seeing him,' she wrote, '& friend quite nice – many a merry laugh.' Elgar and Blackwood took the opportunity to talk over the possibility of reviving Starlight Express which had been particularly dear to them both. 'Do wish something might come of it', Alice wrote, but her hopes were not fulfilled. On this occasion Blackwood, as on his earlier visit, brought a touch of exotic glamour to Fittleworth Wood. 'E. & A. walked thro' the woods with them going back,' Alice reported, 'Starlight's clothes & boots wonderful! But he looked so fine.'

What made Algernon Blackwood such an attractive character to the Elgars? And in the light of the Windflower's contribution to Elgar's Brinkwells experience, what did Blackwood add? To answer those questions it is necessary to look at Blackwood's life, writing and beliefs. But one thing is certain – he was quite unlike anyone that the Elgars had met before.

Hints of his colourful background can be found in his entry in *Who's Who* for 1931. It lists his publications and his club (The Savile) but in the usually

---

[*] Atkins, *The Elgar-Atkins Friendship*, pp. 294-5.

more mundane biographical section where entries summarise the career of the person concerned, his has a certain throw-away, intriguing charm. 'Farmed in Canada; went Rainy River gold fields; ran a hotel etc; joined staff of *New York Sun*; and later *New York Times*; dried milk business; began writing books, 1906; lives abroad.' His appearance too was unusual: over six foot tall, suntanned and, when the Elgars met him, bald; his face was dominated by his lively, intense eyes. His friends likened him to an ancient Egyptian magician [*] and close friends often called him 'Pan', whilst Stella Gibbons remembered his striking personality and penetrating, hypnotic stare.

Blackwood's parents were deeply religious and it was the experience of their religion that set him off on a life-long search for the meaning behind reality. He was a sensitive and imaginative child and found that he could not share his parents' Evangelical Christian beliefs or the mores of their respectable society and instinctively turned for help instead to the power of nature and the mystical side of life. In his autobiography *Episodes Before Thirty*, published in 1923, he described how nature had brought him companionship, inspiration and joy and had remained in his life as a 'truly magical spell'. The discovery of nature's spell had been made early, and, like Elgar, Blackwood would make expeditions out to the countryside where 'night and stars and trees and wind and rain were the things I had to do with and wanted. They were alive and personal ... full of messages and meanings ...'. [†]

His unorthodox outlook was encouraged by his father's taste for ghost stories, by his own discovery of Eastern religions and philosophy and his regard for nature. Unlike Elgar, as a young man he had a deep need to question orthodoxy and this led him into a prolonged engagement with aspects of esoteric beliefs and contact with diverse movements such as the Theosophical Society and the Hermetic Order of the Golden Dawn into which he was initiated by W.B. Yeats in 1900. By the time that he met the Elgars his mystical beliefs had centred around the idea of Earth as a sentient being which was part of a greater collective consciousness, and the possibility of man's spiritual evolution – a possibility only if man was at one with nature.

Blackwood met Elgar at a time when the composer was struggling with his own beliefs and retreating from the orthodox Roman Catholicism he had espoused in his youth – and indeed Blackwood's own reasons for abandoning the 'capricious' and 'despotic' God of Christianity had been expressed in language that Elgar would have understood. Blackwood's pantheistic delight in nature, particularly in the rural isolation of Brinkwells, must also have found some answering chord in Elgar's own reverence for nature as the source of his musical inspiration. But there were other aspects of Blackwood's character too that would have bound him to the composer. Not only was he someone who could entertain Elgar with subjects as diverse as supernatural tales for which they both had a taste (Blackwood had investigated cases of hauntings

---

[*] Ashley, *Starlight Man*, p.1.
[†] *Ibid.*, p. 13.

for the Society for Psychical Research in the 1880s) or details of a new diet for racehorses, but he also was a violinist, who, at one stage, like Elgar, had aspired to be a professional player. He was both in society and at the same time somehow outside it – a position that echoed Elgar's own – and he also had only achieved success relatively late in life after some years of false starts and privations.

Alice's first reaction in her diary to Blackwood was that he was 'interesting' – and this was something of an understatement for he represented a way of life and a wealth of experiences that was unusual in their social circle. He had sat around camp fires in the dark wilderness and told ghost stories in isolated places as far apart as Switzerland and the Great Lakes; he had taken a canoe down the Danube from the Black Forest to Hungary; he had experimented with hypnotism and esoteric beliefs and he was, above all, a free spirit at a time when this may have been looked on with suspicion.

There is little direct evidence that Blackwood influenced Elgar, apart from their collaboration on Starlight Express, but there is enough circumstantial evidence to suggest that he did. This he could have done in two ways. Firstly, through his own attitude to nature – in particular trees – and secondly by his gifts as a storyteller. In the same way that Rex Vicat Cole was to imbue his images of and language about trees with almost human attributes, so Blackwood's writing reveals the extent to which he saw trees exemplifying the magic of nature. This similarity was commented on in 1938 in an article on Rex Vicat Cole in a Sussex newspaper. The reporter emphasised in particular Cole's empathy with trees, writing: 'The artist gets the atmosphere of the country so admirably that in looking at the pictures one can almost hear the wind singing through the trees; he makes one feel that the trees really are living creatures, just as Algernon Blackwood makes one believe it when reading his book *The Education of Uncle Paul.*'[*]

In many of his stories, Blackwood's trees express great natural forces at work and in his writing these forces also become personalised. Sometimes the trees act as messengers from another world. They are often threatening and always powerful.

One of Blackwood's best-known short stories, *The Willows*, illustrates the uncanny powers which he could attribute to trees. Based on his own Danube journey, the story describes how the author and his companion camp for a night on a tiny sandy island surrounded by the foaming streams of the river and constantly being eroded by them. They are surrounded by acres of willow bushes 'pressing upon the river as though to suffocate it' and it is the willows that become the cause of their growing unease. The narrator describes how the serried ranks of willows awake in him a curious and unwelcome suggestion that he and his companion have somehow intruded into a world where they are not welcome. This sense of menace increases as the two men experience and contend with the elemental and primeval forces of the place which animate the

---

[*] *Sussex Daily News*, 'Pictures of Mr Rex Vicat Cole', 10 February 1938 (Cole Papers).

willows. Blackwood's story – based as it was on his own experience – reflects his own awareness of nature and its powers. But it also illustrates the way that his writing transcended the normal 'ghost story' genre in being deeply concerned with aspects of another dimension in life – one that he had tried to reach through study and meditation. Even when he did essay a more traditional story of haunting, as in the early short story *The Empty House* (1906), the authenticity of the story based on his own experiences and his serious approach to the subject makes the tale both chilling and convincing.

Whilst *The Willows* illustrates Blackwood's belief in the spirit of trees, it is another story written a little later that suggests why the woods around Brinkwells may have stimulated his imagination and why they were so immediately attractive to him. In *The Man Whom the Trees Loved*, Blackwood sets a scene which in a curious and uncanny way prefigures the situation at Brinkwells when he visited the Elgars. In his story an elderly couple, David Bittacy and his self-sacrificing wife Sophia, live at the edge of the great old hunting grounds of William the Conqueror. He has a tenacious love of nature, in particular trees which he understands and communes with, which she does not share and of which she is afraid, seeing it as contrary to her own conventional Christianity. David Bittacy forms a friendship with an artist who 'painted trees as by some special divining instinct of their essential qualities'. This artist, Sanderson, stays at the cottage and draws Mr Bittacy out more and more into the woods. Sanderson talks to him of his own beliefs: that there is 'God' in trees and also that which is not God is also, he believes, in trees – something dark and terrible. He suggests that trees show and obtain what they want and have a way of choosing their companions – some of them preferring human companionship to that of the animals and birds. His pantheistic beliefs frighten Sophia who watches as her husband becomes more and more absorbed by the trees. Although she understands that trees made him happy and at peace, she comes to fear the forest and what it will do to her husband. As David Bittacy neglects the rest of his life to wander in the forest, his mind charged with trees, her role turns from wife to mother – seeking only to protect him.

Sophia then enters into a battle with the forest for the soul of her husband and recognises that the trees are jealous of her. On one occasion, having ventured into the woods, she becomes aware of the forest watching her and the trees turning their myriad, vast sight upon the intruder. Gradually, despite her efforts, her husband is lost to her and she acknowledges that the trees were always with him – even in the house – and that they possessed him.

The Man Whom the Trees Loved was published in 1912, some three years before Blackwood and Elgar met in London and six years before he visited the Elgars at Brinkwells. It appeared in a collection of short stories entitled *Pan's Garden* and seems to predict something of the interrelationship between Elgar and the trees of Bedham and Flexham Park. Did Blackwood feel some uncanny sense of recognition when he visited Brinkwells? Did the position of the cottage in old hunting woods, Elgar's deep love of trees, their expedition into the woods at night, Alice's self-sacrificing love and the presence of Vicat Cole's work remind him of his story about the Bittacys, the love of trees and the paintings of the tree artist? Given Blackwood's sensitivity to all psychic phenomena it would be surprising if this were not the case. It would certainly have encouraged him to see human emotions in the trees at Brinkwells, as he had in the trees of his story.

Elgar and Alice had, as we have seen, discovered their group of 'sinister trees' by Bedham in 1917, long before Blackwood visited them the next year. They were the first things that they showed him. Between his visit in July 1918, and the middle of September that year when Elgar was beginning his chamber music, Alice's description of the trees

42 Dead chestnut tree, West Sussex

becomes more fanciful; she writes of the dance of the 'dispossessed trees' and 'a wail for their sins', and by July 1919 she finds the trees 'wicked'. Billy Reed attested to the influence that this group of trees had on Elgar's chamber music and describes their eerie presence. (See ch. 8 and also Appendix 2.)

By the time Basil Maine published his biography in 1933, a legend had become attached to the trees. They were, it suggested, the remains of a group of Spanish monks who had been punished for holding a black mass – this also would account for a 'Spanish' character in parts of the chamber works. There is, however, one flaw in this scenario – no such local legend has ever been found. If there had been one, it would no doubt have figured prominently in Lady Maxse's history of Fittleworth which dealt with local superstitions, but she refers only to the 'witches hill' in that area.

In his Foreword to the Eulenburg Edition of the Piano Quintet, published in 1971, Michael Pope suggests at one point that Vicat Cole might possibly have drawn Elgar's attention to the sinister trees at Bedham, but on the balance of probablility he sees this as unlikely. Certainly there is no record that they ever met at Brinkwells – and only evidence of one brief meeting in London. Neither is there an exact reference to sinister trees in the Bedham area in

Vicat Cole's *British Trees,* a copy of which might well have been at Brinkwells. Contact over the letting of the cottage was, as we have seen, mostly between Hannah Vicat Cole and Alice. Moreover, whilst Rex was clearly absorbed by the mysteries and legends surrounding trees and by their almost human presence, nowhere in his writing does he express the idea that trees could somehow be the metamorphosed forms of humans. This idea finds a more natural home in the writing of Blackwood – a conclusion that Pope also draws. In fact most recent scholars have turned their attention to Blackwood as the source of this story and what evidence there is supports this assumption. In his account of his father's relationship with Elgar, for example, Wulstan Atkins recorded a time in the 1920s when Elgar had talked of the legend to him, said how much the trees had influenced him and had then changed the subject to talk about Blackwood, as if there had been a connection between the two trains of thought. [*]

But as we have seen from his writing, there are further reasons for proposing Blackwood as the source of the legend. Blackwood saw trees as beings with human emotions – that is clear from his stories. It is only after his visit to Brinkwells that Alice's diary takes a moral tone about their 'sins' and eventually designates them as 'wicked'. There is, moreover, an early story by Blackwood about a religious brotherhood in which something similar occurs. In *Secret Worship,* published in 1908, a story about Blackwood's psychic detective character John Silence, the protagonist re-visits the school to which he had been sent to by his father – a deeply religious, German community – to find the school had been burnt down. The Brotherhood who ran the school had turned to devil-worship; as a result their school stood only as a ruin but their evil remained despite the destruction of the buildings. Again, Blackwood's story was based on his life. As a boy he had been sent to study with the Moravian Brotherhood in the Black Forest. [†]

It seems likely that on his visits to Brinkwells Blackwood managed to inject a little magic into the woods there – to stimulate Elgar's creative processes by his vivid imagination and to share his life in the woods. In doing this, he, like the Windflower, made a particular contribution to the Brinkwells experience for Elgar.

The Player – Musician

The final member of the trio of Brinkwells' visitors that we are considering, Billy Reed, illustrates another aspect of friendship – for he was the musical friend and supporter *par excellence*. He first visited Brinkwells on 29 August 1918, only ten days after the piano had been installed in the music room. Alice's diary notes that he 'soon tried the new music & was delighted – very nice evening in the studio – much time over the sonata.' Yet even Reed's presence was not enough to compensate entirely for the Windflower's absence. Elgar

[*] Atkins, *The Elgar-Atkins Friendship*, p. 294.
[†] For a discussion of the influence of the Bulwer Lytton novels on the chamber music see ch. 9.

43 Billy Reed

wrote to her on 11 September that Reed had liked the sonata and that he had copied out a violin part for him and 'we played & thought you ought to be here to help generally: a sad little chair with a pencil is beside the piano now'.[*] Elgar's letter is revealing for the way that it establishes the role of these two friends and also emphasises again how Elgar could bind his friends to him with a sure touch – often by identifying something of his as theirs – as if he were giving something of himself to them. He would do this later with Vera Hockman and the Violin Sonata – 'your sonata' he would write to her, adding on the score that he sent her after his own signature the words 'who only now knows why this was written'.[†] Something of the swiftness of his emotions and impulses is captured by these gestures.

Thereafter Reed made excursions to the cottage to help Elgar with the chamber works. And in this, as in earlier years, his greatest contribution was with the practicalities of composition – with the translation of inspiration into music. He would play passages over and over for Elgar to hear, he would consider the technical aspect of the writing, and he would do all this with absolute conviction in Elgar's greatness. He did not take Elgar on head to head, as Jaeger had done, but supplied him with the unquestioning support and encouragement that was essential for his creative life. And, importantly for Elgar, this was support from someone who knew about music, for although Reed was never in the same league as Elgar, he was a composer.

There was also another facet to their relationship which was no less crucial. When Reed went down to the cottage for the first time, Alice was delighted to see him: 'I am so glad you have come', she said to Reed, 'it is lovely for him to have someone to play with', and she was not only referring to music for Elgar and Billy Reed shared a youthful delight in life and a childlike enjoyment of jokes

---

[*] Moore, *The Windflower Letters*, p. 212.
[†] Allen, *Elgar in Love*, p. 46.

and games. * It is from Reed that we get some of the most informal descriptions of Elgar's life at Brinkwells. Whether it is the sudden relapse into experimental chemistry in order to deal with a plague of wasps, the apparition of 'Sir Edward' appearing beside Reed's bed at half-past four in the morning holding a pair of Wellington boots, or the 'most effective figure' that the composer cut on the river banks when fishing despite catching only 'the smallest and most innocent of fishes', Reed manages to capture something of the pleasure that the two men shared in these ventures. He also shows how the two sides of Elgar's life at Brinkwells were closely intertwined. On his first visit, when he was working through the Violin Sonata with Elgar, he wrote how they used to play up to the blank page and then Elgar would say, 'And then what? – and we would go out to explore the wood or to fish in the River Arun'. †

The presence of Alice and of his friends at Brinkwells was one important facet of Elgar's creative environment and we shall see that, when he returned to Brinkwells after Alice's death, the human spark that would start a fire of inspiration was missing. During the chamber music period, however, all the necessary components were in place. But what was the particular quality that was peculiar to Brinkwells and its surrounding countryside?

---

* Reed, *Elgar as I knew Him*, p. 58.
† *Ibid.*, p. 63.

CHAPTER EIGHT

'The Trees are Singing my Music'

An out-of-doors Spirit

Until Elgar took over Brinkwells in 1917, the area had been known to artists rather than musicians and the profound influence that the countryside around Brinkwells had on the art of Rex Vicat Cole bears witness to its magic. As we have seen, the surroundings of the cottage became a source of inspiration for Cole as he responded to the loving acquaintance he had established with nature. His paintings became ordered and structured by nature in such a way that they appeared to echo the way that nature itself was ordered and the barriers between what was 'artistic' and what was 'natural' became blurred. In this sense, Vicat Cole had only to stroll out of his studio to be presented with scenes that would both inspire him and suggest the way forward in his work. He worked outside drawing and painting directly from life and all the while seeking the kind of truth that would be faithful to nature at its best. It would be fair to say that for him these two activities of observation and artistic expression were inseparable.

But what of musical inspiration? What was there for Elgar at Brinkwells that was relevant both to his way of working and capable of inspiring him to new forms and expressions? For a representational landscape artist, of course, the inspiration of the scene in front of him can influence his work in a very precise way – giving him not only the subject of his work but also ideas about structure, tone and colour. We have seen how this worked for Cole in canvases such as the 1918 Bluebell Wood (see plates VI and VII). For the composer things are a little different. Yet for Elgar landscape also played a significant role in his creative life and often when he talked of his work it would be in conjunction with the natural world. Trees in particular had held him in their spell from his earliest days and were to become for him a source of inspiration. For Elgar trees seemed to share with him in some strange way the music that he plucked from the skies.

His love of being outside was evident from his childhood when his mother had encouraged all her children to respect and enjoy nature. As a schoolboy he had gazed in 'rapt wonder' at the great trees outside his schoolroom at Spetchley Park as they swayed in the wind and increasingly in his own mind he came to identify musical inspiration with being outside. Much later in life he wrote of himself: 'I am still at heart the dreamy child who used to be found in the reeds by Severn side with a sheet of paper trying to fix the sounds & longing

44 *Rex Vicat Cole painting outside in Bedham*

for something very great …'.[*] His identification of music with landscape ran very deep, for it was not merely about being outside but about the nature of inspiration. For Elgar, who believed that there was music in the air all around him and written in the skies for him to note down, it followed naturally that music itself should have above all an 'out-of-doors sort of spirit'. Whilst it is easy to see that he achieved this, it is more difficult to pin down exactly how it is done, for some of his music, and the Brinkwells works in particular, evoke not just a general out-of-doors spirit but specifically English landscape. At times it is clear that that was his intention – his instructions to the orchestra in rehearsal for the First Symphony that they should play a passage 'like something we hear down by the river' leaves us in no doubt that for Elgar the passage evoked a real experience of particular English countryside.

Much of his writing had, of course, been done surrounded by the sights and sounds of the land and throughout his life he maintained this strong attachment. Billy Reed wrote that Elgar 'was in love with the earth' and described how he would delight in revisiting the scenes of his childhood in the country around Worcester. Reed's description helps to explain another aspect of Elgar's out-of-doors spirit, and that is its propensity for nostalgia – the sense of looking back to, or revisiting, a golden childhood spent by the fields and rivers.

---

[*] Letter to Sidney Colvin, December 1921, quoted in Anderson, *Elgar*, p. 151.

Rather like Vicat Cole who would work on even his largest canvases outside as well as in the studio, Elgar used notebooks, or scraps of paper and a pencil, to capture ideas which came to him when he was walking, cycling or working in the woods. From Alice's diary it is clear that he did this at Brinkwells too: 'E. with his music in wood', she wrote in September 1918. But it was not only the first ideas which were prompted by his surroundings. At Birchwood, his cottage near the Malvern Hills, he had, according to Alice, scored Gerontius 'in the deep quiet hearing the sound of summer winds amidst the lofty pines'. The continuing interaction between music and landscape, from first idea to its completion, was to become more marked in that precious period of retreat at Brinkwells.

The Song of the Trees

Whilst landscape delighted Elgar, trees, especially those around the Sussex cottage, were given a special place in his affections. This love had been apparent in his earlier years when the lofty pines around Birchwood, the deep shadows of the woods in moonlight, and the willow-dotted landscape of Longdon Marsh had impressed themselves upon his receptive spirit. In his early homage to the Malvern Hills, Caractacus, he had included a 'Woodland Interval', music that was to have a special place in his heart. There are two instances when he gives us some idea of the meaning that trees had for him. The first is the well known and beautiful passage in a letter to Jaeger where he wrote in July 1900, 'This is what I hear all day – the trees are singing my music – or have I sung theirs? I suppose I have?'[*] – a sentiment which binds together closely the mysteries of nature and artistic inspiration.

The second is as revealing. In 1909 he had received a Christmas present from Edward Speyer and his wife of the scores of Beethoven's String Quartets. In thanking them he tried to describe what it had been like for him when he first discovered such great works as a boy. Not surprisingly the analogy that he uses is one of landscape and he wrote of entering 'shy, but welcomed – into the world of the immortals & wandering in these vast woods – (so it seemed to me) with their clear pasture spaces & sunlight (always there, though sometimes hidden)'.[†] It was, he explained, a holy feeling, and something of this sense of awe was found for him not only in the great works but also in the vast woods which symbolised them. At Brinkwells the woods were always on his doorstep and through Alice's diary we get glimpses of a similar sense of awe as they find long vistas under arched trees and in September 1917 – 'wonderful views thro' firs like a great cathedral'.

From the beginning of the Elgars' stay at the cottage, their delight in the surrounding trees is marked in their diaries. This was to be given an extra boost by the group of 'sinister' trees that they discovered and the strange story that later

[*] Young, Letters of Edward Elgar, p. 87.
[†] Quoted in Moore, A Creative Life, p. 560.

became attached to them. For Elgar, who delighted in ghost stories, the eerie atmosphere cast by these trees was particularly attractive and all their guests would, sooner or later, be taken up the hill to admire them and to experience the strange spell that they cast. Billy Reed gives us a good description:

> A favourite short walk from the house up through the woods brought one clean out of the everyday world to a region prosaically called Flexham Park, which might have been the Wolf's Glen in *Der Freischutz*. The strangeness of the place was created by a group of dead trees which, apparently struck by lightning, had very gnarled and twisted branches stretching out in an eerie manner as if beckoning one to come nearer. To walk up there in the evening when it was just getting dark was to get 'the creeps'.[*] (See Appendix 2.)

Even before such impressions were heightened by the mythical history that the dead trees were really the remains of Spanish monks struck by lightning for performing a black mass, Elgar found the scene stimulated his imagination. Reed was convinced that the spot had a profound influence on the composer in his three chamber works and explained that

> The rather oriental and fatalistic themes in the quintet, and the air of sadness in the quartet, like the wind sighing in those dead trees – I can see it all whenever I play any of these works, or hear them played. Elgar was such a nature lover and had such an impressionable mind that he could not fail to be influenced by such surroundings. There was so powerful a fascination for him there that he was always strolling up to look at the scene again.[†]

This is borne out by Elgar's own inscription at the end of the first movement of the Quintet which is marked 'Bedham'. He had been fascinated by the dead trees long before Algernon Blackwood's visit or the arrival of some novels by Bulwer Lytton at Brinkwells – in particular *A Strange Story*, an eerie and supernatural tale. (The possible significance of this novel is further discussed in chapter 9.)

Inspiration

That Elgar should connect inspiration with trees and landscape, and the world of the great composers with vast woods, speaks not only of his own emotional connection with the land but also about how he perceived inspiration. He was not someone who could naturally be inspired irrespective of his mood; he could not easily go and shut himself up at a certain hour every day and write. Billy Reed attested that he could have written music anywhere, and although once he was sufficiently 'lit up' that was indeed the case, the initial inspiration seemed to demand certain conditions. Reed noted perceptively that Elgar's 'inexhaustible internal fund of music was very susceptible to suggestion from any external

---

[*] Reed, *Elgar as I Knew Him*, p. 63.
[†] *Ibid.*, p. 64.

sound except that of composed music'.[*] And sometimes he would be set off by poetry or by a strange sounding word or phrase, but also natural sounds were a stimulus including the sound of an Aeolian Harp as the wind played its strings. But it is Elgar himself at different times in his life who indicated what he found most stimulating to his creative imagination and suggested from where that 'internal fund of music' might issue.

It is clear that for him inspiration was a mysterious, almost unconscious process. He told the writer Basil Maine that

> I take no credit for the inspiration that people may discover in my music. I cannot tell you how it all comes to me. Of course, I could write out a piece of music here and now as you would write a letter, mechanically, that is to say. But before the real stuff will come, I must be quiet and apart.'[†]

Once inspiration had come Elgar said, 'I am all of a tremble, as if I was in the hands of another person ... .I can only write when the spirit moves me – I cannot write to order.'[‡] When Elgar could be prevailed upon to talk about his music at all, he tended to give the strong impression that he was an impartial observer of what was being written by another person.

This outlook, together with his belief that music was in the air all around him and 'you simply take as much as you require', goes some way to illuminate the process of his inspiration. But it does not go all the way for there were clearly other factors at play. One of these was his own fluctuating mood and restlessness which meant that sometimes he had to wait for the right moment even to think about music. In her account of Elgar, Dora Penny wrote that it often took a long time and a great deal of patience before the mood arrived but that when it did sometimes it was with surprising suddenness. She also gives a convincing picture of the atmosphere at Plas Gwyn when Elgar was struggling with The Kingdom – an uncomfortable time for others in the house – and of his complete absorption in his work when he was in the middle of writing.[§]

On other occasions it was as if Elgar needed physical activity outside in order to liberate his spirits. Walking, cycling, or working in the wood at Brinkwells provided such a space, with his body engaged just enough in doing something to leave the composing side of his mind free. And there is little doubt that the side of his mind that was being left free was not the intellectual but the emotional side. He was always wary of trying to explain his own work and was emphatic that he never 'invented' music but 'felt' it. Faced with a piece of music by Stravinsky that he did not like, he called it 'manufactured' music – music from the head rather than from the heart.

The picture that emerges is of a creative process that is both unconscious, mysterious and at the same time emotionally exhausting. He was not alone

---

[*] Reed, *Elgar as I Knew Him*, p. 148.
[†] Maine, *Life*, p. 76.
[‡] Anderson, *Elgar*, p. 402, quoting a conversation with Fred Gaisberg and Harriet Cohen on 17 August 1933.
[§] Powell, *Memories of a Variation*, pp. 69-73.

45 *Rex Vicat Cole*, Sweet Chestnut Tree

in finding this and it is clear from other composers' experiences that even if, like him, they experienced inspiration as an unconscious, mysterious process it could still take different forms and play different roles in the development of a piece of music. In some instances, the initial inspiration could be a complete phrase or tune, as seems to have been the case with Elgar's Pomp and Circumstance March No I ('Gosh! man I've got a tune in my head', Elgar wrote to Jaeger), in others a 'given' like the song heard at Ynys Lochtyn in Wales in 1901 which later formed part of the Introduction and Allegro, and in other cases an idea came as a result of improvising on the piano as it had for the Enigma Variations.

It could be also that inspiration was not initially musical. Beethoven wrote that his ideas came 'unbidden, spontaneously. I may grasp them with my hands in the open air, while walking in the woods, in the stillness of night, at early morning.'[*] And this seems to have been the case with Elgar as well, so that it was as if by being outside in nature he was putting himself in the way of inspiration. Once that initial spark had been lit the process could develop with extraordinary rapidity – as it did with the chamber works and the Cello Concerto. This was a phenomenon known to other composers many of whom have written on the ecstatic, concentrated, inexorable drive that takes over. Memorably, in his old age, Haydn conveyed something of the obsessive nature of composition when he stated that 'Usually musical ideas are pursuing me, to the point of torture …'.[†]

---

[*] Quoted in Jonathan Harvey, *Music and Inspiration*, p. 29.
[†] *Ibid.*, p. 32.

The language that both Alice and Elgar use to describe Elgar's complete surrender to his work at Brinkwells echoes the same sense of being taken over: 'absorbed', 'possessed', 'deep' in his music, Alice writes, and Elgar describes his concentration on the Violin Sonata as a 'rabid attack of writing music'.

A Divine Madness

The idea that a creative artist might be possessed by his muse is an ancient one. Socrates called this possession a divine madness, which, compared with ordinary sober sense, he believed was a direct gift from God. This possession was held to result in many moods and altered states of consciousness and a little later Aristotle was to make the connection between inspiration and melancholia. [*] In the light of Elgar's own propensity for depression and sadness, it is interesting also to consider contemporary ideas about depression, melancholy and the creative spirit. A degree of melancholia can add positively to artistic expression as it encourages a questioning of life. It directs the gaze inwards, and, as Professor Jamison points out in her book on the relationship between depressive states and the artistic temperament, 'grief and depression often bring with them, for good or ill, the heart of life' – a heightened sense of reality. It has, moreover, the ability to lend a bittersweet quality to the artist's outlook 'adding a tincture of sadness and wistfulness to the creative process'. [†]

The other side of the relationship between melancholia and the creative process is also significant. In his exploration of creativity, Professor Anthony Storr makes the point that creativity itself can be a defence against depression as it bolsters the self-esteem of the artist. For people in the depressive position, he writes, 'rejection and disapproval are a matter of life and death; for unless supplies of approval are forthcoming from outside, they relapse into a state of depression in which self-esteem sinks so low … that suicide becomes a real possibility'. [‡]

The intricate balance and inter-relationship between depression and creativity was something that Elgar had struggled with throughout his life. At one stage he had seemed suicidal – and Alice had taken the threat seriously – whilst at others the delicate relationship between the high of inspiration and his incipient melancholia had been successfully established. At Brinkwells for the brief period that saw the completion of the chamber works and the Cello Concerto, that delicate relationship was sustained. He had the support that he needed in the form of Alice and visits from his friends. He had the isolation that he craved, and he was able once more to express his changing moods without being thrown off balance by them.

It might be that for Elgar the act of composition was a way of structuring his emotions and a way also to know and express his inner self. Yet he saw

---

[*] For a further discussion of these ideas see Jamison, *Touched with Fire*, ch. 3.
[†] *Ibid.*, pp. 118-9.
[‡] See Storr, *The Dynamics of Creation*, chs. 4 and 7.

inspiration as coming from outside. At the back of every discussion of Elgar's inspiration lies his own beliefs that music was somehow part of nature – part of the skies and the trees – and that he had only to take as much as he wanted from the air around him. It was from that base that the drive to compose started. Once the fire had been kindled, Elgar's method of composition relied less on a carefully constructed intellectual plan than on intuition and a process of mental ordering to establish the final form of the work. As with many other artists that ordering process was not necessarily consciously achieved and it is with his life at Brinkwells that we gain some idea of how this worked.

Throughout his diary, and that of Alice, during 1918 and 1919 there is the refrain of 'woods and music' – again and again we are told how Elgar was moving between the two and how his music was bearing him along at a tremendous pace. Four days after the piano had been delivered to the cottage, Alice noted in her diary, 'E. worked out of doors. Music later' and a little later when Elgar had bought the underwood she wrote, 'E. absorbed with his music and delighted with the wood' as if these two things were part of a greater whole. When he was possessed by his music we are told that he varied this by excursions into the wood and Elgar himself joined the two things in his diary when he bracketed together some days in November 1918 and wrote, 'all these days writing music & working a little in the wood'.* With his concentration broken by a trip to London in October 1918 and the worry of Alice's operation for the removal of a wen, Elgar wrote to the Windflower in November that the move had been necessary but had been 'a <u>tragedy</u>' for his music. On his return to Brinkwells he tried to regain his concentration. 'Wrote music and tried to recover the threads broken,' he wrote, 'working in wood'. The same pattern was established in 1919 when Elgar was working on the Cello Concerto: 'E. busy with concerto & working in wood', Alice wrote in June.

Elgar had always found that being outside, moving in landscape, had enabled him to order his own emotions and also to open himself up to inspiration. This, it appears, is just what happened at Brinkwells, where periods spent in the studio were interspersed with work in the woods or walking. Some of this was hard physical activity – chopping down undergrowth and cutting sticks – and its effect seemed wholly to be beneficial, acting as a kind of liberation of the mind and emotions whilst at the same time answering Elgar's restless need to be doing something. His time in the woods therefore answered

46 Elgar selecting sticks at Brinkwells in 1920

* Elgar's diary, 21-23 November 1918.

two needs: it provided inspiration and it enabled him to go through the sub-conscious mental-reordering of that inspiration so that once back at his desk in the studio his ideas could flow without hindrance. This combination of physical exertion and creative liberation was not new in his life, but at Brinkwells it was relatively prolonged, uninterrupted and concentrated.

Convalescence

But there are other factors also which made his time at Brinkwells so special and which are deeply interwoven into the whole experience of the cottage and the woods. One of these was his state of health in the period prior to the start of his chamber music. The short breaks that he had enjoyed at the cottage in 1917 had confirmed his delight in the place but it was his experience in 1918 that was crucial. On 2 May 1918 he arrived there for what was going to be his most prolonged stay, which was to run through the summer until October, and then after a month's break was to continue until Christmas. He arrived, moreover, as a convalescent, having barely recovered from the tonsil operation that had taken place in March. From May until 19 August, when his piano arrived, he did little in the way of composition – the exceptions being the setting of the Rudyard Kipling poem 'Big Steamers' (June 1918) and some orchestration of the 9/8 theme which had come to him in a moment of inspiration after the operation and which was later absorbed into the Cello Concerto. (See chapter 9.) For someone who had been almost insanely busy for many years, this was something unusual.

His illness and operation had cleared the ground for him; there were no pressing commissions, no demands for war music, and no compulsion to write save for its own sake. During the early summer of 1918, his diaries hardly mention music although they do reflect the change in his spirits as he moves to Brinkwells. Compared with Alice's, his diary entries were always terser and less flowery, but, after the almost empty pages of March and April 1918, the entries begin to expand and bloom when he arrives in Sussex. He was, moreover, in a state of convalescence: aware of his own recovering health and receptive to the world of beauty around him. Baudelaire made the point, and it is well made, that the convalescent state is one peculiarly analogous to that of the creative artist and akin to a return to childhood. It is a state, after all, in which a lack of responsibility is united with the ability to see things as if for the first time – 'vividly coloured impressions' is how Baudelaire describes it, a condition in which no edge of life is blunted. *

In this condition Elgar found freedom and an ability to escape into himself and into that region which he had described earlier in his life as his 'insidest inside'. Ernest Newman, who described Elgar in 1900 as an 'exceptionally nervous, self-divided and secretly unhappy man', also made the point that he was afraid of the loss of his spiritual privacy. There can be little doubt that at

---

* See Baudelaire, *The Painter of Modern Life* (1863).

Brinkwells he found that privacy and that whereas Severn House and London had come to symbolise the self-divided Elgar, in Brinkwells he escaped into himself. Nothing else can explain the intimate, self-revelatory intensity of the music written there.

A Changed Voice

Elgar had always been able to open himself up in composing and to present his inner self when he was sufficiently inspired. His 'personal' voice, as opposed to his public voice, was one filled with emotion and self-revelation and this quality had illuminated major works such as Gerontius, the two symphonies and the Violin Concerto. At Brinkwells the personal voice was uppermost, but compared with two major pieces of 'private' work written before the start of the War, the Second Symphony and the Violin Concerto, that voice had changed. It is not only that in three of the four works written at the cottage Elgar is working on a small scale, although this in itself is a significant factor, but that something has changed in the voice that he finds. It would be foolish not to acknowledge that the intimate nature of chamber work itself invites intimacy from the composer but this overlooks the fundamental point that Elgar chose to turn to chamber works and so to deny himself one of the aspects of his work that came to him easily, that is large-scale orchestration.

In turning to chamber music, Elgar made a move akin to that of a visual artist who, having habitually painted in oils, turns to watercolour and in doing so immediately has to question and discard many of the habits and techniques that have become familiar. Elgar's chamber music remains Elgarian, but it is pared down, essential, and courageous in its unabashed revelations about the composer's heart. As well as being less intricate it is also less theatrical – but in a paradoxical way it is still complex in mood. In fact the simplicity of the means reveals and accentuates the complexity of the emotional content. Even when in the Cello Concerto Elgar turns again to the orchestra, the work shows the same pared-down quality and a voice that distils the essence of the composer's feelings.

It may be that the very private world of Brinkwells acted as a spur to private, intimate music, in the same way that Vicat Cole had found the isolation there conducive to the development of a very personal style. There was moreover for Elgar no real pressure to make a public statement, particularly with the ending of the war and the diminution of his desire to do something to help the cause. He had also the opportunity to rest, to gather together his feelings and thoughts whilst walking and working outside, and to listen to the sounds of the countryside safe from the intrusion of the telephone that he so disliked at Severn House. If the privacy of Brinkwells was not the opportunity for music from his 'insidest inside', then what else could be?

We do know that the chamber works and the Cello Concerto were written quickly, within a period of one year, and for that whole period Elgar's ideas seemed to take him over. There were times when he was unwell or moody, but this did not stop his work and there were no episodes of deep depression or sense of personal despair which had frequently surfaced in earlier years. Alice's diary, which usually faithfully recorded the ebb and flow of Elgar's health, gives a picture of someone totally immersed in his work, sometimes too absorbed even to go out or walk. A few days after the arrival of the piano at the cottage, Alice wrote that Elgar was 'busy with his new beloved music' and at the beginning of September 1918 she described how the Violin Sonata was 'vibrating thro' his very being'. Her entries continue to reflect his absorption in the music. Elgar was 'carrying one along at a terrific rate' (of the Quartet), and rising at 5 a.m. in June 1919 to go to the music room and work on his Cello Concerto. A month later, with Elgar 'painting' his Cello Concerto at the cottage, Alice noted that he was loving it so much that he was 'nervously apprehensive that someone might take him away'.[*]

With the return to London in October 1919, their occupancy of Brinkwells as a couple ended. Elgar, with the proofs of his concerto safely posted from Fittleworth post-office, spent some of his last days at the cottage that year clearing the wood and burning the brush with Mark helping. 'Fires of rubbish, great flames shooting up', Alice noted in her diary, a conflagration that was to be her last memory of Brinkwells. Thereafter she was to remain in London until her death only six months later.

The Studio

As we have seen, between Monday 19 August 1918, when the piano arrived at the cottage, and Monday 13 October 1919, Brinkwells acted as the cradle for a group of remarkable compositions. During those months, Elgar's complex needs as a composer were answered in terms of the presence of his wife, the beauty of the surrounding countryside, the insistent demands of inspiration, periods of solitude, time for self-reflection and the right degree of support from friends. There was one further factor, however, in this catalogue of requirements and that was a place to work. The studio at Brinkwells, renamed the Music Room by Alice and Elgar, has hitherto been somewhat overlooked in Elgar literature but it played a significant part in the Brinkwells story.

Even a glance at the ordnance survey map of the period suggests that the studio could not be easily overlooked in terms of scale alone. Alice, on first seeing the cottage, wrote of 'large studio and <u>lovely</u> view' but even this does not fully explain how large the studio was. Its exterior was certainly rustic, but on the 1911 map the ground plan of the studio almost equals that of the cottage and its interior had the dimensions of a small barn. Elgar's music room was totally unlike the kind of summer-house retreat that Bernard Shaw made for himself in the garden of his home; it was not some extended garden shed but a big space perhaps as much as 40 feet in length. The studio had been purpose-

---

[*] See Alice Elgar's diary for 30 July 1919.

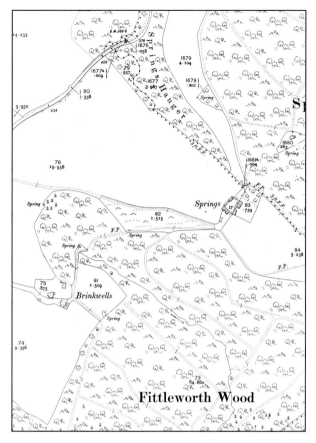

47 Ordnance Survey Map (1911) 25 inches to the mile, Brinkwells, its Studio and Farm Buildings (reduced)

built by Vicat Cole for the production of large Royal Academy canvases as well as smaller sketches. The interior space was carefully lit by a large, multi-paned window that ran almost the entire height of one wall and which overlooked the view across to the Downs and the Toat Monument; hence Elgar's need for a blind to shield his eyes. (As it is now, the studio has four windows let into the roof, one at each corner of the building, but it is not known when they were added. The large window that Billy Reed described, however, is still there.) The beauty of the view from the studio to the distant hills is conveyed in Rex Vicat Cole's painting *From Gardens Gay to Distant View* (exhibited RBA 1907) which also captures the atmosphere of Brinkwells as it was.

But size was not the only significant aspect of the room; its atmosphere was also important. The interior was half-timbered with dark wood and large wooden beams supported the ceiling structure at both ends. Since Elgar's time the interior has been changed slightly with a fireplace added opposite the large window and entrances made to the wings that were added after the studio was

48 *The Studio at Brinkwells (c.1910); photograph by Rex Vicat Cole*

moved, but in essence the space remains how it was, although the interior may have been considerably refurbished. In its original rustic state, with its use of local materials, both its interior and exterior echoed the surrounding woods and countryside. It must have seemed like an extension of the landscape when both Vicat Cole and Elgar moved from the woods to the studio for it shared the light and mood of its surroundings. It was, moreover, totally isolated from the house and at some distance from it – a world of its own and a perfect space in which to write 'wood magic'.

The woods, the views and the magical atmosphere of Brinkwells and the studio inspired both Elgar and Vicat Cole to do something new in their oeuvres. But no-one, probably not even the artists themselves, can say precisely how that worked. There is no spreadsheet or model that can ever explain the workings of a creative mind and how life can interrelate with art, except to acknowledge that it does. For at the centre there will always be a mystery unique to each artist, idiosyncratic, unchartable and magical. The inspiration that came from Brinkwells and its surroundings was in the case of both Elgar and Vicat Cole transformed through their individual experiences and memories. But what we can be certain of is the starting point, the spirit of the woods and hills and their capacity to strike a chord in the hearts of both men.

Influence of English Landscape

There is one more aspect of Elgar's Brinkwells work which cannot be overlooked – its ability to summon up a picture of landscape – and specifically English landscape. This is something which many listeners find in much of his music and the Brinkwells works are no exception. But the question remains as to how this was done. Unlike some of his contemporaries, Elgar did not turn to folk music in order to evoke a feeling of place and nature, and yet a sense of landscape is felt by many in his works. We may label Elgar a 'pastoral' composer, but his music is clearly unlike a piece such as Shepherds of the Delectable Mountains by Vaughan Williams which is deeply and unarguably pastoral in essence. The way in which the two composers approach the depiction of landscape is totally different. Whilst Vaughan Williams is, in this example, descriptive, Elgar is more concerned with how he experienced landscape. When he tells his orchestra to play a passage like something they would hear down by the river, he is not asking for an imitation of the river sound but an evocation of the experience of being there.

Both Jerrold Northrop Moore and Anthony Payne have made the perceptive observation that Elgar's orchestration with its innumerable shifts of colour echoes in some way the ever-changing and elusive play of light in the English countryside. And this point can perhaps be taken further for there also seems to be a significant parallel between the rapid changes of mood in English weather and the rapid succession of mood changes in Elgar's music. He was, as we know, perpetually restless and given to rapid gleams of sunshine or stormy outbursts and this emotional weather runs through his music with its sudden squalls and periods of tranquillity.

Elgar's own love of nature meant that he could identify with its moods because they reflected his own moods. He could also use landscape to modify his own emotions – the relationship was reciprocal. In this context it is interesting to note that Professor Jamison makes a connection in her book between periods of manic or depressive behaviour, creativity, and the natural cycle of seasons, weather and changes in light. She suggests that the varying moods and changes of nature and the shifts of seasonal weather ' may actually be experienced quite differently by those who are artistic and/or cyclothymic by temperament' and that their inner rhythms are 'more similar to those of the natural world'. *

That there are similarities between the inner Elgar and the outside world of nature is something that he manages to capture in his music and it is something

---

* Jamison, *Touched with Fire*, p. 129.

which is transmitted to, and understood, by his audience. (It is interesting that two violinists – widely separated in time – have both found landscape analogies in Elgar's Violin Concerto: Yehudi Menhuin makes this point strongly in his autobiography. More recently the Russian Ilya Gringolts, playing the concerto for the first time at Malvern in 2004, spoke of how being there and seeing the environment helped his interpretation.)

But there are other effects which are more specific and which, amongst other things, appear to have a connection with landscape. One of these is Elgar's use of sequences which have specific compositional roles and a range of emotional connotations. Apart from their structural role they express a range of feelings from nostalgia, longing, loss or change. In some instances they strengthen the feeling of looking back or of some memory receding from the listener while in others they can evoke a sense of space, perspective and recession. In this latter case, they can give the feeling of an expansive landscape that unfolds, hill upon hill, in front of the viewer in diminishing colour and more distant tone. In other instances there are sounds which are 'like' natural ones – in the Piano Quintet, for example, a sound like rain drops falling from branches after a sudden shower or a sudden gust of wind tossing the branches and leaves as it goes past. In September 1918 Alice wrote in her diary that Elgar was writing ' wonderful new music – real wood sounds' and even given Alice's propensity for 'spin', there was obviously something that had struck her as unusual and particular to where they were.

It is apparent, too, from Elgar's letters and diary that he was impressed by the changing effects of light and colour in the Sussex countryside and his response to it does seem to find some musical equivalent in the chamber works. In a letter to Sidney Colvin dated 26 September 1918, the period when he was immersing himself again in music, there is the description of the sun 'climbing over our view in golden mist' – something which made him write, 'I have never seen anything so wonderful … I see now where Turner found such sights as Norham Castle etc.'* It is his sense of wonder at such natural sights which in some passages colours the emotional range of his music, as for example in the slow movement of the Quintet which seems to capture the radiance of the sun emerging and 'climbing over our view' as Elgar had seen it. In finding a musical equivalent to suggest the way that he was moved by nature he could awake a similar response in his listeners.

Elgar had the unerring ability to find something that would speak to other people and in particular the English, the people whom he understood. In part this may be because it takes up the inflections of the English language in its rhythms and cadences, but it also taps into long-standing affections and emotions that are national in character. Elgar reveals the emotional side of the English which they usually keep hidden and unexpressed and he also recalls them to their roots and their love of the countryside. The English have delighted in their landscape for many centuries. This is reflected in a long

---

* Young, *Letters of Edward Elgar*, p. 245.

49 *Rex Vicat Cole*, From Gardens Gay to Distant View, *oil painting*

tradition of landscape painting that is unlike any other European nation and a wide audience for it. They have also a keen sense of history and of the past. In suggesting some of these concerns, by hinting at them through the structure of his music and by using sounds that are analogous to the experience of what you might hear 'down by the river', Elgar engages the imagination of his audience. The strength of his own feeling for nature is reflected as he reveals himself in the accents, colours and structure of his music. That this effect is felt by so wide an audience speaks volumes about his understanding of the human heart. Above and beyond this is, of course, his ability to express unfulfilled yearning – whether romantic or for the past – that is so much part of the human condition, and Elgar's condition in particular.

Elgar was always concerned that his music should be real in terms of its emotions and passions. Having written a piece he would turn to Alice and ask her, 'If you cut that would it bleed?' and he did not spare himself in revealing his own passionate and changeable nature. In doing so, he could connect directly with his audience and suggest by his music a multi-layered world of sunlight and shadow. The sunlight was to him 'always there though sometimes hidden', as he had written in 1909 about the music of the great masters. So in this way he described the complexity of his own music's emotions, always shaded with contrasts.

In his essay on Elgar's use of literature, Brian Trowell wrote that Elgar was aware that 'his power over the listener lay in his ability to conjure forth, by means of musical imagery, emotional responses drawn from the listener's own experience of life that were in some way similar to his own'.[*] Elgar himself, in his analysis of Brahms' Third Symphony given in the course of his Birmingham Lectures, summarised what for him was the goal of great compositions. He wrote: ' It is a piece of music which calls up certain sets of emotions in each individual hearer. That is the height of music', and that is exactly what he also achieved.

---

* Trowell, 'Elgar's Use of Literature', in *Edward Elgar: Music and Literature*, ed. Monk, p. 255.

CHAPTER NINE

The Brinkwells Musical Harvest

Working Assumptions

This particular chapter of our exploration of the effect that Brinkwells Cottage in Fittleworth and its rural and artistic environment had on the complex creative personality of Elgar raises in stark form a perennial problem. How and at what level is an author best advised to write on purely musical matters (assuming a largely non-specialist readership)?

This is a question which would attract a variety of answers. Elgar himself, in this position, tended to favour the broad-brush, no-nonsense, approach to programme notes and get to the essence of the matter with a mere sentence or two. But that would certainly not do here if only because it is part of the thesis of this book that there was a pantheistic 'magic' in the Brinkwells air that helped to explain Elgar's sudden resurgence of creativity, and that this echoes through the chamber works, and needs to be demonstrated. But minute analysis of these works involves the ordinary listener so deeply in the terminological problems inherent in verbal descriptions of music, with all the ripe possibilities of getting lost in a jungle of supertonics and sub-mediants, that we are convinced that any such attempt would be counter-productive. Those readers able and willing to wrestle with Elgar's ingenious key-changing systems and modest but effective variations on classical architectural structures can readily find helpful discussions in existing published work – serious students of Elgar's compositional methods are particularly well catered for.[*] But for the majority of readers who may derive great pleasure from listening to music without necessarily being able to read a score, the author must find a middle way which eschews the 'too technical' while using a small number of musical illustrations to key in the essential points he wishes to make.

And against an over-pessimistic view of the average reader's capabilities is the fact that, over a number of years 'teaching' adults in university extra-mural

---

[*] For example Ivor Keys in 'Ghostly Stuff – The Brinkwells Music' (*Edward Elgar – Music and Literature* (*op. cit.*, p. 112)) makes a technical but fundamental point: 'The gravitation towards plagal cadences in the [Violin] Sonata has already been noticed. The essence of this cadence is that it avoids using the leading note, in E minor the progression D sharp to E ... Elgar would never have been pedantic enough to insist on flattening the leading note in a *cadence,* a tiresome mannerism in some of his feebler 'muscular Christian' contemporaries. There are plenty of D sharps in his E minor.' And see further Trowell, 'The Road to Brinkwells' in *Oh, My Horses!* ed. Foreman, and Brian Newbould's '"Never Done Before"; Elgar's Other Enigma', *Music and Letters*, Vol 77, no 2 (May 1996, pp. 228-41); also *The Cambridge Companion to Elgar*, particularly the contributions by Christopher Kent, Diana McVeagh and Daniel Grimley.

classes, it has always been found beneficial and practical to provide each student with a score of the relevant piece being discussed and played on a recording. If the student thinks that he or she 'cannot read music', almost invariably the art of following the performance is rapidly learned and the piece makes a much greater impression on the mind of the listener with the score than without it.

Accordingly, if readers to whom the above applies buy or borrow the relevant score, together with a good recording, nothing will be lost and there is a good chance of a significant gain. This is simply because each work that is discussed is undoubtedly a masterpiece in its own way and closer acquaintance with a masterpiece, whether of art, music or literature, is always a gain. And in music as with many other spheres of human endeavour, what you get out is related to what you put in. Nevertheless, we realise that following with a score is not going to be practicable for some and have therefore tried to keep technicalities to a minimum.

Elgar's Achievement

By 1918, when work on the chamber music, and what subsequently turned out to be the Cello Concerto, was either well advanced or completed (works which were given the opus numbers of 82-85 on publication) Elgar had proved himself a master of the large-scale forms of oratorio and symphony. As an orchestrator he was unsurpassed and his Violin Concerto had become widely acknowledged as one of the few real masterpieces of this difficult genre. One might have thought that before 1918 Elgar would have published more high quality music for the smaller forces involved in instrumental sonatas or in string or wind chamber music – in other words large-scale compositions but for small forces – but this feature is in fact conspicuously lacking.

He had, it is true, in his earliest years as a composer written a violin sonata in 1887 which was unfortunately destroyed, though some of the material was incorporated into his Sursum corda, op. 11, of 1894. There were also a number of attempts to write string quartets, but these were generally not completed or were destroyed. Nevertheless, Elgar in his smaller scale early 'salon' pieces for violin and piano had shown himself a master of the former instrument (if not convincingly the latter) and all that was lacking was a sustained three or four movement essay in that form.[*] Hitherto, the British public had in any event demanded, particularly, oratorios galore, so chamber music was intrinsically uneconomic for the younger composer. The Brinkwells chamber music harvest was, then, a late flowering one of a new and, for Elgar, hitherto substantially untried crop.

The order in which the pieces were written is complex owing to Elgar's manner of composing which, to the outsider, might seem surprisingly chaotic, and has been remarked on before. So, although the Cello Concerto was the

---

[*] For further details of a number of abandoned and sometimes partially reconstituted pieces, see the comprehensive 'List of Works' in Anderson, *Elgar*, Appendix B.

last of the batch to be completed it is known that the main initial theme of the first movement in 9/8 time (see below) was jotted down long before from his hospital bed when he was recovering from his painful tonsillectomy operation in March 1918, though its precise role in a cello concerto had not then been determined.

Elgar's inspirations tended to come in fits and starts with one being interrupted by another. As with so many creative people the one thing that he despised and resented were interruptions which caused threads to be broken and stemmed the flow. There is always the fear that something vital will have been forgotten, never to be recaptured. But even during this time Elgar periodically had to go up to London or the provinces to conduct, or open up Severn House as a more suitable convalescent home for Alice who had a large 'wen' removed from her forehead in October 1918.

Speed and Order of Composition

For present purposes the chamber works will be discussed in the order in which they were completed and allotted opus numbers, the Violin Sonata (op.82) being followed by the Quartet (op. 83) and the Quintet (op.84).

At the same time it is worth noting that the interval between first starting the Sonata, 20 August 1918, and essentially completing the Quintet on 9 February 1919 (the Quartet, completed on 24 December 1918 and lying in between), was only six months. One can extend the table by the date of completion of the Cello Concerto (8 August 1919) and by any standards one is looking at an exceptionally intense period of creative activity of less than a year.

The Well of Inspiration

Whence did this well of inspiration come? There is no doubt from the diary entries of both Elgar and Alice, and the surviving letters to Elgar's current 'muse-in-chief', the Windflower, that the magic of Brinkwells and its surroundings worked a powerful spell on the composer. Ideas, as we have seen, could come to him even in the now unbenign Severn House in London with its ever-jangling telephone and urban environment. It was there, after all, that he wrote most of Spirit of England, Starlight Express and Falstaff. In fact, Elgar had seemed happy enough in the grandeur of Severn House for quite a few years after buying it in December 1911 and there was no denying the magnificence of its music room and library. But despite this grandeur, he still needed to re-charge his batteries in the country as another more private side of him always missed the vivid inspiration of nature that talked to him so directly.

Style

To the keen-eared Elgarian, well aware of Elgar's major works to date, the style of the Brinkwells pieces will appear to be more conservative, or perhaps, to quote his admirer Richard Strauss, less 'progressivist', than might have been expected. Dr J. Harper-Scott [*] describes this latest stage as being characterised by 'harmonic simplicity and easily understood forms'. He sees three 'phases' in Elgar's development – the first evolves into full-blown post-Wagnerianism, strongly evident in the oratorios with their leitmotifs, and owing much to the harmonic chromaticism of Tristan and Parsifal in particular. This is followed by a second phase of 'early-modernism' when Elgar's style was at its most complex and formally daring (ie to embrace the two symphonies and other work up to about Falstaff, Op.68). Finally, eschewing not only serialism, impressionism, neo-classicism and all the other movements spreading over Europe (and comprehensively dismissed by Elgar as 'cubism') Elgar developed the more Brahmsian, but still highly individual and distinct, style of his last major works. He wrote to the dedicatee of the Violin Sonata, Mrs Marie Joshua on 6 September 1918: 'I fear it does not carry us any further but it is full of golden sounds and I like it: but you must not expect anything violently chromatic or cubist.'

Although the Quartet in particular has a 'pastoral' feeling about it, it should also be noted that Elgar made no bows in the direction of the young, distinctly up-and-coming Ralph Vaughan Williams and his English folk-song movement, either. But, in the first and middle movements of the Quartet, some might feel the influence of RVW's ground-breaking Fantasia on a Theme of Thomas Tallis, – the modal atmosphere, perhaps rather than the actual notes. This was first performed in 1910 at a Gloucester Three Choirs concert at which Elgar was also conducting Gerontius. Elgar's great contemporary, Delius, had by this time also developed a highly distinctive harmonic style grown out of predominantly Wagnerian rootstock which also owed nothing to folksong.

Of Elgar's immediate predecessors, particularly Stanford and Parry, it is perhaps to Sir Hubert Parry that we should look more closely for stylistic, harmonic and structural precedents. Elgar revered Parry but much of Parry's chamber music output, including three violin sonatas, has only recently been published by Musica Britannica (Stainer & Bell) and was hitherto virtually unknown. His settings for chorus and orchestra, often for Three Choirs Festivals,

---

[*] See Elgar Soc. Jo. March 2004, 22.

tend to be uneven in inspiration, with a few exceptions. Both composers venerated Schumann. [*]

Performing the Chamber Music

This is where we should remind ourselves of the warnings given by Sir David Willcocks and mentioned in chapter 2 concerning the need to prepare very carefully for an Elgarian performance of one of the big choral or orchestral pieces. The same applies to these subtly deceptive works.

What do we mean by this? Taking the Violin Sonata, it appears to be technically comparatively straight-forward for either player, and particularly the violinist – certainly when compared with the virtuoso passages in the earlier Violin Concerto or even in some of the 'salon' pieces such as the delightful La Capricieuse, written in 1891 (Op. 17). It compares in its demands more with the three masterly Brahms violin sonatas; but over and above this, there is still an element in it difficult to define, but which if ignored by either player will result in a 'weary, stale, flat and unprofitable' performance. In all three works technical skill has to be taken for granted – that is why performance-wise these pieces are not fodder for amateurs. Concert preparation has to start with complete technical and tonal mastery. One then moves on to questions of tempo, articulation, accentuation and phrasing (always meticulously marked by the composer) and the resultant Elgarian 'discourse', the ebb and flow subtly unconstrained by exact adherence to a particular tempo or even, judiciously, Elgar's own exact markings, since matters proceed instinctively.

Before the first 'official' public performance of the three works on 21 May 1919 at the Wigmore Hall, London, by Albert Sammons, W.H. Reed, Raymond Jeremy, Felix Salmond and William Murdoch, there was a private performance on 7 March at Severn House with a different team and Elgar playing the piano (probably reluctantly since he never considered himself a pianist). The young composer Arthur Bliss turned over for Elgar in the Sonata and was embarrassed at what he should say about it. [†] To him the works seemed to indicate a sad falling off, though he was astute enough to realise that 'the far from brilliant performance' did not help. As explained above, experience strongly suggests that the success of all three works depends on the highest standards of performance – disappointment is inevitable otherwise.

Many aficionados would agree with T.E. Lawrence, speaking to the wife of Bernard Shaw at the end of Elgar's life, and after repeated hearings on records of the Second Symphony, when he remarked that no other composer 'gets inside my defences as he does'. [‡] Similarly the distinguished Dutch conductor Edo de Waart, until recently Director of the Sydney Symphony Orchestra, said about Elgar, a personal discovery of whom he made some 20 years earlier, 'It's

---

[*] See further, *The Strad*, May 2004, p. 519 (Jeremy Dibble).
[†] Bliss, *As I Remember*, p.24.
[‡] Allen, *Elgar in Love*, p. 87.

the sort of music that when I turn on the radio and hear three bars, I know it's Elgar, even if I don't know the piece – he has his own musical language, his own colour, the music has its own feeling, and somehow it speaks to me …' [*]

So in the chamber music too, the essential quality of the Elgarian discourse is critical. There is no richly coloured orchestration to disguise what is going on, nor overt 'programme' as in Falstaff to aid navigation. Leaving aside the pervasive influence on Elgar of the legend of the stricken trees, 'ghostly stuff' according to the composer, this is all 'absolute' music and any 'programmatic' element is emotional.

Elgar's Ghosts

The question now arises – is there a 'quasi-programme' behind these works and if so (a) can it be identified and (b) does it matter in any case? The answers are surprisingly complex.

Ernest Newman blotted his copybook so badly with Elgar by attacking Elgar's proclivity towards oratorios in his earlier life, believing them to represent a compositional cul-de-sac, that Elgar in 1905 tried to prevent Newman returning as critic of the *Birmingham Post*. However their relationship warmed over the years to the extent that by November 1918 Elgar thought it appropriate to offer the dedication of the Quintet to Newman. There was also a long-standing debate between the two men, a debate which may seem largely sterile to sophisticated modern listeners, as to what the real distinction between 'programme' and 'absolute' music was. (The debate arose out of incautious remarks by Elgar in a lecture at Birmingham University in 1905, pertaining to Brahms's Third Symphony.) Newman thought that Elgar was condemning three-quarters of the music of the 19th century by attempting to belittle 'poetic' music as opposed to absolute music. And, Newman rightly asked, on which side of the line, then, did Elgar's own Cockaigne or In the South Overtures fall. Elgar wrote to Newman on 2 January 1919:

> It is true that vital music must be written by a <u>man</u> & must be influenced and tinctured by his life experience, but it need have no literary basis. Beethoven's fifth Sym. is the height. Of course I have written programme music but that does not mean that I think it the highest form of composition – far from it.

So there was probably some irony in the dedication to Newman of a work which, if Alice and other contemporaries such as Billy Reed are to be believed, is shot through with allusions to the legends surrounding the 'sinister trees' that so preoccupied Elgar at Brinkwells (see ch. 8 and Appendix 2). As Reed wrote: 'Elgar was such a nature-lover and had such an impressionable mind that he could not fail to be influenced by such surroundings. There was so powerful a fascination for him there that he was always strolling up to look at the scene again.' [†]

---

[*] See Vol 20, *Elgar Society Newsletter*, July 2003, p.42.
[†] Reed, *Elgar as I Knew Him*, pp. 63-4.

But is this the only, or even the main, source of the 'quasi-programme' which Newman believed underlay the Quintet? Elgar scholars are much in debt to the recently published researches of Michael Allis[*] who makes the case for the primary influence (on the first movement of the Quintet, at least) being the 'occult' novel by the successful Victorian writer Edward Bulwer Lytton – *A Strange Story*. (Lytton (1803-73) was a prolific novelist and poet, as well as a successful politician. Elgar's liking for occult fiction and ghost stories was well known. [†]) The argument is complex and interested readers will find Allis's article a fascinating piece of literary and musical detection – too intricate to be examined here in any detail. Suffice it to say that the argument mainly depends on short notes in the diaries of Alice and Elgar as to the ordering, probably from the London Library, of an unknown number of Lytton novels which Elgar records as arriving at Brinkwells on 3 September 1918. Then on 16 September 1918 Alice records in her diary that 'Lytton's *Strange Story* seemed to sound through it (the Quintet) too' – that is in addition to the weird trees and the possible connection with Elgar's eerie part-song Owls, mentioned in the course of analysing the work later. The author then proceeds with a detailed attempt to match the first movement of the Quintet with the plot of Lytton's convoluted novel.

The plot does not have any obvious connection with the pantheistic influences on Elgar, as noted by Reed (above) in particular, nor is there any other record of the effect of possibly reading this particular novel on Elgar at the time. Furthermore, the theory rather depends on there being sufficient time between the receipt of the novels on 3 September and the earliest relevant sketch of the Quintet – 8 September 1918 – for Elgar to absorb, or possibly reabsorb, a novel of more than 400 pages and translate it into music. In fact, during this short period Elgar was, as far as can be deduced from diaries and dated sketches, busy putting the final touches to the Violin Sonata.

For this and a number of other reasons our conclusion is that whilst this is an interesting theory and there are indeed some striking parallels, there are more convincing alternative explanations. Alice, shrewd though she often was in assessing her husband's work, could also give imaginative constructions that were hers rather than Elgar's – as in her imaginative interpretation of the 1908 First Symphony during the Great War, an 'absolutely triumphant Victory' over the 'Huns'. As Michael Allis himself points out:[‡] 'One could of course argue that Alice was imposing a narrative on the Quintet that represented her own reading of the work, rather than any compositional intent on Elgar's part.' Nor is there any evidence that the theory applies outside the relatively narrow confines of the first movement of the Quintet.

Finally, does it matter, or should we ignore such theories as unnecessary encumbrances to our appreciation of the Brinkwells chamber music? Here we fully agree with Michael Allis as to the importance of the argument, pro

---

[*] See *Music & Letters*, vol. 85, no. 2 (May 2004), p. 198 et seq.
[†] See also Moore, *A Creative Life*, p. 726.
[‡] See Allis in *Music & Letters*, vol. 85, no. 2 (May 2004), p. 201.

and con, rehearsed by Ernest Newman. As Newman pointed out in a review of a professional performance of the Quintet in the *Sunday Times* (11 October 1931):

> The Quintet presents the players with some difficult imaginative problems, rooted in the nature of the quasi-programme that lies at the base of the work. Sometimes one is inclined to think that it would be advisable for the composer to make this public in an authoritative form for the guidance of both players and listeners: then one decides that after all more harm than good might be done by the disclosure, for players of the first class can be trusted to get as near as makes no difference to the meaning of the music without having that meaning put into words for them, while less intelligent performers would be certain to read too much programme into the music and over-dramatise it. On Tuesday evening it was only the swinging tune that first occurs in the opening movement and reappears so mysteriously in the muted violins towards the end of the finale, that I was doubtful whether the players had quite the right intellectual clue.

Is this a slightly tantalising glimpse of another possible enigma – or are the 'ghosts' really the ones which are now familiar to most Elgarians, but not then, in 1931, anything like so well explored? (The first published account of the group of sinister trees and their effect on Elgar is by W.H. Reed in 1929; [*] and see further Appendix 2.) Whichever way one looks at it, there is little doubt that listeners, and probably performers too, are much better off knowing about the trees and the effect that they had on Elgar's imagination as strongly vouched for by Alice, Reed, and Wulstan Atkins [†] as well as other friends, contemporary visitors to Brinkwells and Basil Maine, writing in Elgar's lifetime. That there is an inner meaning, particularly in the first movement of the Quintet, is fairly obvious and what harm can there be in spelling this out?

But there is another sense in which all the Brinkwells works could be called 'programmatic' in that they are *emotionally* programmatic. As Professor Kerry Downes pointed out in a letter to the authors in the context of the Cello Concerto and what it has in common with the chamber music,

> Elgar's piece becomes (emotionally) programmatic though we don't know what the programme is. And then, having dropped his guard and opened a locked casket, private, secret and wordless, he snaps it shut as if we'd never had the glimpse inside it – almost as if he's shown us more than he intended.

Violin Sonata Op. 82

With the arrival of his piano, the 'quite good' one he had used in Hereford (an upright Steinway) in the studio of Brinkwells on 19 August 1918, Elgar started work on this Sonata in earnest. The piano part is somewhat idiosyncratic; but

---

[*] See Cobbett's *Cyclopedic Survey of Chamber Music*, vol 1, pp. 372-3.
[†] Atkins, *The Elgar – Atkins Friendship*, p. 294.

in spite of a certain lack of confidence in his abilities to write effectively for the piano and intermittent requests for help from Ivor Atkins[*] and others, here, in the right hands, it is perfectly well balanced and satisfactory.

The first of the three movements Elgar described at the time to the Windflower as 'bold and vigorous'.[†] The movement is not quite conventional in a number of respects, one being because it starts its journey in the apparent key of A minor rather than in its eventual E minor. Elgar not infrequently used the device of starting in the 'wrong' key, designed, perhaps, to depart consciously from the classical sonata form structure and to better keep the listener's interest – or is this a snide snook cocked at the academics? It will be noted that this ambiguity is deliberately promoted by the composer in not conveniently describing the Sonata as in any particular key, though the music of the first movement has a key signature of E minor with the essential, F#. In fact, the key of E minor, overt or covert, seems to have haunted Elgar in the works of this period. As Ivor Keys has remarked, 'It is not perhaps too fanciful to think of this gigantic ghost [of the rejuvenated composer] coming back to life to write not four works, but one thirteen-movement work in E minor or thereabouts. (The Piano Quintet is the one not 'in' E, but has a big, fairly firm central movement in E major …). All four pieces show a marked unorthodoxy in the use of tonality, whether looked at on the small or large scale.'[‡]

Hardly has the performance started but the violinist almost immediately meets a typically Elgarian challenge in bars 9–12 where the bowing meticulously given by Elgar has the effect of slurring the crochet over the rest to the accentuated quaver *in one bow*, which is not what a violinist faced with that notation would instinctively choose to do. This effect is repeated at the end of the movement (Figure 21) *fortissimo* (fff) and *con fuoco* (with fire).

Apart from a lengthy passage at Figure 5, marked '*tranquillo*' and which requires considerable care by both performers if the movement is not to lose its audience's concentration, the movement well lives up to Elgar's 'bold and vigorous' prescription. The passionate second subject is particularly powerful. When this melody is repeated at Figure 12 high on the G string (unlike Brahms,

---

[*] Letter Elgar to Atkins, 23 September 1918. See *The Elgar-Atkins Friendship*, p. 289.
[†] Letter dated 11 September 1918.
[‡] Ivor Keys, ''Ghostly Stuff': The Brinkwells Music' in *Edward Elgar – Music and Literature*, ed. Monk, p. 109.

no Joachim was needed to instruct Elgar on how to bring out the sonorities of the violin) the movement reaches its climactic moment.

As with the other two chamber works it is in the slow movement, titled 'Romance', that Elgar is at his most affecting and original. Alice wrote in her diary for 24 August 1918: 'Lovely day – sunny & hot. Mr Aylwin's Clover field finished – lovely scent. E. writing wonderful new music different from anything else of his. A. calls it wood magic. So elusive & delicate.'

This movement was clearly also responding to sad external actualities, particularly the news that the Windflower had painfully broken her leg while walking at Tintagel, Cornwall. This apparently accounts for the complete change of character, away from the 'wood magic' via a marvellous transition from a tenuous C# minor to a glorious extended melody in the remote key of Bb major. This, Elgar said in a letter to the Windflower of 11 September, was, according to his friends Billy Reed and Landon Ronald, 'a melody for the violin … as good or better than anything I have ever done in the expressive way'.

As it stands the movement is in a simple ABA form, opening and closing with material which evokes with its guitar-like pizzicato chords and ghostly flourishes the ubiquitous Spanish monks, now metamorphosed into 'sad, dispossessed trees & their dance & unstilled regret'* lodged in the composer's subconscious – a 'fantastic, curious movement' as Elgar himself put it. The fantasy is intensified in the third section which returns (if not quite identically) to the opening themes but has to be played with the violin muted throughout.

Again, this movement poses a considerable challenge to both players. The tone of the violin and touch of the pianist are critical, as is an instinctive elasticity in the tempi. Virtuoso bow control is required for the *fioriture* with which the increasingly wraith-like melody is embellished. [†]

The third movement was described to the Windflower by Elgar as 'very broad and <u>soothing</u> like the last movement of the second symphony'. [‡] It does indeed bring to mind the experience of the flow of the River Severn, or its beautiful tributary and Elgar's favourite, the Teme, as experienced from their banks. Written out this time with a four-sharp signature, a fluid E major, the movement subsequently involves many beautifully gauged modulations in material giving ample opportunity to both players to carry along the audience in the broadly binary form discourse.

However, this particular lotusland was disturbed by news of the unexpected death of the intended dedicatee, and Elgar aficionado, Marie Joshua. As a touching tribute, and when the movement was well advanced, Elgar deftly brings back the expressive 'Windflower' theme from the second movement as a lament for a devoted friend. Elgar employs this retrospectivity in other major works (as did Liszt and Franck, for example) and the device usually gives a

---

* Alice Elgar's diary, 16 September 1918.
† See also Brian W. Harvey, 'The Elgar Sonata on record', *The Strad* (March 1983), p. 792, where a controversy on the bowing of the climax to the movement at Figure 32 is aired.
‡ Letter to the Windflower 11 September 1918.

satisfying cyclic feel. Here the theme is re-introduced at Figure 53 before the music returns (Fig. 55) to a recapitulation of the 'River Severn' themes and ends in a satisfying E major flourish.

The sonata was given its first public performance by Billy Reed and Landon Ronald at the Aeolian Hall on 21 March 1919. After a rehearsal which depressed the composer, who, Alice recorded in her diary, returned 'not liking his own music', the performance itself was, according to Alice, 'beautiful and its reception overwhelming'. But a shrewd critic, having noted that the hall was far from full, went on:

> Like Brahms in the later part of his career, Sir Edward aims at ever-increasing directness, terseness and simplicity of expression. There are in the Sonata no complications of rhythm or harmony, no thematic singularities, it is not exceedingly difficult to play, it seems like a protest against the far-fetched devices of the ultra-moderns – it seems to say: See what can be done with the old forms, the old methods of composing, the old scales … [*]

And H.C. Colles, writing in *The Times* after the first performance of all three works, said:

> An immediate effect of listening to … . Elgar's opp. 82, 83 and 84 in succession is to give one a new sympathy with the modern revolt against beauty of line and colour. A stab of crude ugliness would be a relief from that overwhelming sense of beauty … It is not really ugliness, and still less vulgarity, that one craves as an antidote to the Elgarian type of beauty. It is the contrast of a more virile mind, something less purely visionary and more touched by hardness … [†]

Dare one suggest that this critic was simply waiting for William Walton, the other great 'untutored' English composer, to bring forth (say) Belshazzar's Feast (1931), on an unsuspecting public?

Even shrewder, in retrospect, was the judgement of Ernest Newman, commenting on the Sonata's first Birmingham performance two weeks after its premier:

> Elgar's style has become one of extraordinary slenderness as far as the mere notes are concerned. It may be that he has deliberately rarified the tissue of his music for the occasion; or it may be that his style in general is becoming simpler in maturity, as that of Hugo Wolf did in his last songs. As with Wolf, the simplification is in the texture only; every superfluous line has been eliminated from the design, every superfluous note from the harmony; but the music carries a surprising weight of thought and feeling. It is all calculated, too, with extraordinary certainty for each instrument: many a passage that looks a little unimpressive on paper turns out to be singularly impressive in performance. [‡]

---

[*] Moore, *A Creative Life*, p. 739, quoting L. Dunton Green, *Arts Gazette*, 29 March 1919.
[†] *Ibid.*, 24 May 1919, p. 740.
[‡] Quoted Moore, *ibid.*, p. 739, from *Birmingham Daily Post*, 8 April 1919.

Elgar was clearly touched by this and wrote back to Newman to thank him for his 'beautiful notice' … you are right about the difference of look and sound in the music.'[*] Newman's comments in fact apply neatly to the Quartet and Quintet, too.

Nevertheless, what Colles had pointed out was already beginning to indicate the start of the long process of the decline in popularity of Elgar's music. A feeling developed that it was not keeping up with the post-First World War *zeitgeist* – the same instinct probably drove Rex Vicat Cole to destroy many canvases that had been inspired up to 1918 by Brinkwells. (See ch. 11.) Fortunately, nearly a century after the event the modern listener can take a broader view and appreciate the composer's consummate craftsmanship as well as the 'weight of thought and feeling' so skilfully conveyed.

One of the authors (BWH) must now end this portion on a personal note which really re-emphasises the dependence of the work on a convincing performance and perhaps, thanks to one of the work's great interpreters, adds a tittle to the accumulated knowledge on how to interpret the work which might not otherwise be available.

When I went up to Cambridge in 1954 I secured an admission, *sub rosa*, from one of the college music dons that he liked Elgar, vulgarities and all, but that he had never come across the Sonata and doubted whether it in fact existed. Even in 1983, when I reviewed the available recordings of it for the *Strad* magazine, they were few and far between – whereas the Walton Sonata was copiously recorded. The Elgar was simply not central to anyone's repertoire, if players were conscious of it at all. Happily the scene now is very different.

During the 1980s I was involved in a performance by a small chamber choir as part of the Malvern Festival. Peter Smith, the promoter and keen Elgarian, had managed to hire the young Nigel Kennedy and his talented and much missed piano partner Peter Pettinger to supply the central spot in the programme, the Elgar Violin Sonata. Kennedy was playing a borrowed instrument by J.B. Guadagnini, a maker thought now by many to be quite the equivalent of Stradivari or Guarneri. Additionally everyone had given their consent to the proceedings being recorded by a leading consultant sound engineer, Peter Baxandall, who produced an excellent tape for private study.

Although I already thought that I knew the work fairly well, to say that the performance was a revelation is somewhat to understate the personal quasi-Pauline conversion that ensued. In due course the two artists in question went on to record the work commercially with some of Elgar's shorter violin and piano pieces.[†] Before reviewing this I wrote to Nigel Kennedy asking some detailed questions about tempi etc and he replied on 31 July 1984. Confirming that it was a newly acquired Strad which he was using for the Chandos recording he continued –

_____

[*] 9 April 1919.
[†] Chandos ABRD 1099 (1984).

I think it has a deeper, more suitable sound for the introspective parts of the Sonata and little pieces. I am still using the Guadagnini for concerto work because of its wonderful top register and its power to penetrate through an orchestra … .

I'm sure you're right about the tempo of the last movement. Elgar is such a personal composer that as with all great music, it is impossible to play his music twice exactly the same way. But even if I had been trying to recreate exactly the same effect as in Malvern my reaction to things like the acoustic, change of weather, the football results, might have changed the actual tempo. I've also realised since the Malvern concert that I want the new mood of the third movement to grow from the impression left by the second movement rather than abruptly dispel it …

String Quartet Op. 83

This work, thought by many to be the greatest of the three chamber pieces, was not Elgar's first mature essay in this form, for in 1907 he had planned a quartet for the Brodsky Quartet, of which only fragments, now built into other works, particularly the First Symphony, survive. Adolf Brodsky, the leader, was an accomplished player and a dedicated Elgarian, and the ms. bears a dedication to his Quartet, though this is not carried into the published score. Brodsky led the Halle Orchestra and was Director of the Manchester Conservatoire from 1895. His colleagues were Rawdon Briggs, Simon Speelman, and Carl Fuchs. The ensemble was renowned for its technical accomplishment, artistry and beauty of tone.[*] The composition of the Quartet kept Elgar busy during the period from 9 October to 24 December 1918. For much of this period he was at Brinkwells when it must have been for most people somewhat uncomfortable.

Before looking at it in more detail it is worth remarking that, although many Victorian and Edwardian composers in Britain had tried writing quartets, virtually none of these had secured a place in the repertoire. Sometimes this was because the pieces were overt student exercises and sometimes they were expressly intended for amateur or family use. Even if more ambitious, they often condemned themselves with an irredeemable triviality of utterance. (Occasionally a more commendable effort is disinterred, e.g. a quartet by Charles Wood, an Ulsterman (1866-1926), who succeeded Stanford as Professor at Cambridge, which was played occasionally by a leading British quartet. There may be other undiscovered jewels. Billy Reed is credited with five string quartets!) So Elgar's single essay in this form rose above the existing English rift valley like Mount Kilimanjaro. And some credit for a change in public attitude towards listening to chamber music should be given to Walter Cobbett (1847-1937), an enthusiastic amateur violinist who devoted his life to encouraging chamber music composition and performance.[†] Since Elgar broke the mould

---

[*] There is no genetic connection with the modern eponymous ensemble, one of the best younger British Quartets, who play the Elgar work *con passione* all over the world, but interestingly say that it does not seem to export easily.

[†] See his *Cyclopedic Survey of Chamber Music*, 1929.

there have been a number of successful British quartets which have found a place in the international repertoire. Notably, and arbitrarily taking the 50 years after the death of Elgar, these include a characteristic one by Walton (from 1945-7). This is often coupled in recordings with the Elgar, though Elgar would probably have found it unacceptably astringent, if not actually 'cubist'.

The structure of the Elgar quartet is unusual in that instead of the conventional four movements there are two vigorous outer movements (broadly in sonata form) flanking the central *andante* with its expression mark '*piacevole*' (agreeable, pleasing, not as Percy Scholes in his *Oxford Companion to Music* reminds us 'peacefully, as is sometimes supposed'). This movement particularly commended itself to Alice and was played by four family friends at her funeral in 1920. This was highly appropriate as in his obituary notice in *The Times* for Alice, after careful consultation with Elgar, Fox Strangways recorded: 'She was one of his best critics. He played over the Quartet to her, and she said little; but next morning he found pencilled over the close of the slow movement 'Is this quite? – please!' and so we owe the fine close to her gentle correction'.

Here we start the first movement with a theme in 12/8 time which gives a gently undulating propulsive feel to the music and scope for exploiting the crotchet followed by quaver, swing-along, rhythm – a favourite vehicle of Elgar's. But not all is sweetness and light. Brian Trowell in the course of his perceptive analysis of the work in 'The Road to Brinkwells' (in *Oh, My Horses!* referred to before) hears the 'hoarse whisper of some gaunt visitant in the depressed, modal harmony and strangely spaced homophony of its opening bars'. Elgar advised Harriet Cohen in 1932 not to open a concert with the Quartet because 'it starts in rather a phantom-like way'. In performance these 'phantom-like' features will be destroyed by too brash a tempo or unreflective playing.

In the unusually extended development section he makes much play with the thematic material of the opening bars with their descending fourths, neatly answered by a two-bar ascending phrase.

Another undulating theme is introduced (the second subject, Fig. 4) which a little later manages to stray into the remote key of F major (at Fig. 5) until powerfully restated in its original key (E minor, Fig. 6) and developed. The composer never gives the parts a less than interesting time here and shows a mastery of counterpoint so natural that the listener is effortlessly carried along on the waves of a constantly modulating sea. The players need to judge the tempo carefully so that the detail is not lost but the impetus is maintained. The climax of the movement lies between Figures 9 and 10 where the familiar material is whipped up to storm force before gradually declining to a beautiful '*piu lento*' close. But even here the composer springs a little surprise. We had more than half expected an E minor ending, but after a comma we are treated to a pianissimo chord of E <u>major</u>, which seems particularly sweet.

The middle movement, *piacevole*, has already been briefly remarked on. It starts firmly but gently in C major with 34 bars unusually in three parts, the first violin staying silent or doubling the second violin part an octave higher when it eventually enters. The time signature is a gently ambling 3/8. Alice saw in this 'captured sunshine'. Beautiful though all this is, one feels that there is a danger of nodding off in Elgar's deck chair when the music reaches almost complete stasis (starting five bars before Fig. 25) – another challenge to the tone and concentration of the players. Eventually the opening bars reappear but now in four-part harmony, the first violin in alt., carving out of the air a rich descant and marked *fortissimo*. The central part having run its course, not without passion, the movement ends with some 72 bars marked *piano* or less. The last 32 bars are with muted strings and marked *dolcissimo*, ending in the home key of C major.

In his reminiscences Troyte Griffith, Elgar's old friend and architect, listening with him to a gramophone record of this movement years later, said: 'Surely this is as fine as a movement by Beethoven.' He said quite simply, 'Yes it is, and there is something in it which has never been done before.' I said, 'What is it?' He answered, 'Nothing you would understand. Merely an arrangement of notes.'[*]

This remark has inevitably produced theories as to what Elgar might have meant. Was he referring to the fluidity of his key systems, the Quartet, like the Violin Sonata, being titled without key? Brian Trowell and others have written sophisticated analyses of this aspect of the chamber music for those intrigued by a typical Elgar enigma.[†]

The Finale is marked *Allegro Molto* and the metronome mark of crotchet = 132 indicates an exciting ride. Neither the listener nor the players (facing a severe test of technique) are let down by the composer's seemingly effortless craftsmanship. The jagged, staccato start with its antiphonal semi-quavers leads after five bars into a sweeping, swaggering, Falstaff-like theme, marked *brillante*, and led by the first violin, to be promptly echoed by the viola. There are sufficient permutations of this material, together with a more wistful theme introduced at Figure 43, to justify Alice's diary descriptions of the movement as like 'the galloping of horses' and 'a mighty force'.

There is an odd incident half way through the movement (two bars before Fig.49) where against the first violin's restatement of the jagged opening, the three under parts play an ascending chromatic phrase sul ponticello (or 'on

---

[*] Moore, *A Creative Life*, p. 731.
[†] Trowell, 'The Road to Brinkwells' in *Oh, My Horses!,* ed. Foreman, pp. 373-4.

the bridge'), which produces a weird ghostly effect. Hitherto the Quartet has given little hint of the vision of the 'twisted, sinister trees,'[*] the penumbra of which spreads more overtly over the music of the Sonata and the Quintet. But there is little doubt that this is the composer's bow in that direction. Although the mood is soon enough dissipated, psychologically the legend's influence has probably been more present than might be realised. Basil Maine calls the episode a 'capricious and wilful disturbance of the clear, delightful atmosphere.'[†] However, the mood is quickly restored to the sunny uplands and ends with a virtuoso Coda, the last three bars of which reassert a firm and apparently cloudless E major.

Piano Quintet in A minor, Op. 84

Although the composition of this fascinating piece was intermingled with the String Quartet and Violin Sonata, it is distinct from the others in one or two important respects. Firstly, it is the most Brahmsian of the set and for that reason some continental musicians have dismissed it as simply a tombstone on the grave of the greater master. Yet even to the innocent (if educated) ear, after a few bars of the Elgar it is quite obviously <u>not</u> Brahms. To make a more positive identification it might be helpful to realise that although Elgar did not write particularly idiomatically for the piano, as his friend and often perspicacious critic George Bernard Shaw pointed out:

> There are some piano embroideries on a pedal point that didn't sound like a piano or anything else in the world, but quite beautiful, and I have my doubts whether any regular shop pianist will produce them: they require a touch which is peculiar to yourself, and which struck me the first time that I ever heard you larking about with a piano.[‡]

Elgar's idiosyncratic piano style now presents little difficulty to modern concert pianists who instinctively moderate their tone where, occasionally, there would otherwise be too heavy, or Brahmsian, a texture; thus possible weaknesses are hidden – *ars est celare artem*. (The art is to hide the art.)

Secondly, some find in this work that the inspiration is uneven and that the last movement in particular trespasses even on the verge of 'cheapness',[§] but this subjective reaction is by no means general. One soon realises that despite the bravado (which may indeed exist on the cusp of vulgarity) much of the Quintet is shot through with Elgarian melancholy, an instinctive sympathy with which is one of the factors in the modern listener's appreciation of the composer. So too, in the persistent spectral images of the sinister trees at Bedham, the

---

[*] Elgar wrote to Harriet Cohen that 'the Quartet starts in a rather phantom-like way'. See Anderson, *Elgar*, p. 384.
[†] Maine, *Works*, p. 267.
[‡] Letter dated 8 March 1919, quoted in Moore, *A Creative Life*, p. 737.
[§] See e.g. Anderson, *Elgar*, p. 389, 'a poorish job'.

hamlet near Brinkwells (which Billy Reed says that Elgar often used to visit for inspiration at the time of composition), there is a 'quasi-programme' which makes study and performance of the work all the more rewarding. The nature of this 'quasi-programme' has been discussed in some detail above.

It is also blessed with one of Elgar's most moving and beautiful *adagios* in the middle movement, an early recording of which was often played by the bed-ridden Elgar shortly before he died, reminding him no doubt of the beauties of the lost world of Brinkwells. [*] Bernard Shore, a shrewd writer and eminent orchestral and solo viola player, in his *Sixteen Symphonies* (1949) says: 'I would maintain that the Quintet stands as a peer of the great piano quintets of the 19th century. The slow movement had one of the greatest melodies ever written for the viola.' [†]

The first movement opens with one of the weirdest introductions in roman-tic chamber music. The piano (marked *piano, serioso*) announces the simple AGAD of the commencement of the plainsong chant *Salve Regina*. (Elgar had set this for choir and organ in 1876 when he was organist at the Roman Catholic Church, Worcester.) Meanwhile the strings, *pp* and in unison emit a series of staccato chromatic 'grunts', so that the key is impossible for the listener to determine. Notably also at bar 12 there is an innocent-sounding 'sigh' in the piano part, A-E-D sharp – D natural (descending) which reappears at the end of the first movement and slightly metamorphosed in the other two movements (emphasising the cyclic nature of the work), and finally in the most poignant part (identified later) of the Cello Concerto. 'Ghostly stuff' indeed, as Elgar called it to Ernest Newman to whom he dedicated the piece – but also as Alice pointed out, reminiscent of Elgar's part-song *Owls* (Op. 53, no. 4, published 1908). This is a short, virtually atonal and rarely performed setting of Elgar's own words – 'What is that? Nothing …'

---

* Atkins, *The Elgar-Atkins Friendship*, p. 462.
† *Ibid.*, p. 262.

Some 18 bars from the start (Fig. 1) the upper strings emit another 'plangent wail' (as Ivor Keys has aptly labelled it), with the cello alone in singing an expressive ascending phrase. This turns out to be an important motif in the work's structure. The piano makes its proper entrance a few moments later with a series of arpeggios to establish a clear A major/minor tonality. The mood then completely changes and in roistering 6/8 time we hear music of which Brahms would have been proud. But this lasts for all too short a time before the return of the plangent wail and the cello's acsending phrase (Fig. 4) takes us back into the chilly embrace of the ghosts of Bedham. This time, against an undulating piano part and pizzicato chords from the lower instruments the two violins in thirds play an eerie duet in 2/4 time.

We should not worry too much about whether this in fact is a distorted musical representation of a Spanish dance – perhaps the sub-conscious derivation is more from the gypsy fiddle music with the odd pizzicato of the guitar. Elgar (in common with many other contemporary composers) was well practised in writing Spanish-type music of the traditional rhythmic variety and easily recognised as such by listeners. The superimposed vision of the monks' 'impious rites' comes to mind easily enough. Elgar delightedly develops this material until the *danse macabre* stops with a reinstatement of the sinister opening phrase, but this time in the piano part (Fig. 8). The mood then switches again to a flowing *cantilena* founded on the *Salve Regina* (introductory) theme (Fig. 9). Bernard Shaw, who was present at the first run-through, objected to the *fugato* passage, starting with the cello (at Fig. 10), thinking it too academic and out of place. But a gradual increase in speed in fact makes for exciting listening. Eventually when the 'plangent wail' and 'Spanish gypsy' themes have been developed and recapitulated, what turns out to have been a stirring over-all experience ends with a further pianissimo reminder of the opening 'ghostly stuff'. The movement is significantly inscribed 'Bedham, 1918' – the supposed site of the 'sinister trees' (see Appendix 2).

The middle movement, marked *adagio*, gives the first big six-bar tune to the viola, an instrument whose ingrained melancholy exactly reflects the composer's. It is little wonder that Elgar is reported to have had tears running down his face when he played the 1933 recording of this, with Harriet Cohen[*] and the Stratton Quartet, on his deathbed.

---

[*] She became of friend of Elgar's, although not quite of the 'muse' status, when a young lass.

Later in the movement the cello makes a series of interjections (in the manner but not exact notes of the interjections of the first movement), its tenor register well complementing the viola's tone, and this leads to a second flowing theme. Throughout this movement the piano is used in a very characteristic way with the chords spread.

There is scarcely any musical reference to darker things in this movement which is structurally more complex than might be expected, but its development is so seamless that the listener hardly notices the uncertainty of the underlying tonality. After an unexpected modulation into F major (Fig. 33) which, technically, starts the development section, Elgar brings the music to a rather jarring climax (at Fig, 35) and thus gives the movement a lot more shape than it might have had if it were a mere 'rhapsody'.[*] Moore refers at this climactic point to raising 'the ghost again'.[†] But which ghost is debatable.

Perhaps it was the 'malign influence' which Elgar felt walking through the Second Symphony, when he wrote to the Windflower a propos of a passage in the first movement: 'I have written the most extraordinary passage I have ever heard – a sort of malign influence wandering thro' the summer night in the garden'; and to Ernest Newman, about the same passage, he mentioned 'a love scene in a garden at night when a ghost of some memories comes through it: – it makes me shiver'. (The Rondo movement contains an even more graphic incident, founded on this material, where the tympani threatens to drown out the whole orchestra.)

The movement closes in a warm E major.

The start of the last movement reminds us of what we experienced before the balm of the slow movement – with a restatement of the 'plangent wail' motif. However, this is rapidly dismissed with a rumbustious theme in A major (Fig. 44) with the piano part seeming to rejoice in the arpeggios and spread chords so much liked by Elgar, as we can tell by his recorded piano improvisations and the extant fragments of his Piano Concerto.[‡] Sometimes

---

[*] Elgar avoided 'rhapsodies' popular with other English composers such as Delius and Vaughan Williams.

[†] Moore, *A Creative Life*, p. 736.

[‡] Now recorded by David Owen Norris.

in the Quintet unless the pianist is careful with balance Elgar seems to outdo Brahms at his heaviest, particularly at the climax (at Fig. 53) where there is a *molto crescendo* from *piano* to *fortissimo* with the piano involved in huge off-the-beat unspread chords. Later in the development we have a less equivocal ghostly revisitation (Fig. 55) with first the *Salve Regina* theme followed shortly by the '*danse macabre*' theme, but now in triple time suggesting an eerie waltz. But in animated and brilliant summation the ghosts are despatched once and for all and the movement ends triumphantly in A major. So ends one of Elgar's most popular smaller scale works, one which shows his strengths to great effect if also, occasionally, his weaknesses.

Elgar's Chamber Music and the Great War

The question of how far Elgar was influenced while at Brinkwells by the horrors of the last months of the Great War has not been specifically answered and now is the time to look at the question briefly again.

Fortunately for those interested in the wider question of how far Elgar's output as a whole was influenced by the War, this has been comprehensively dealt with in the collection of essays titled *Oh, My Horses! Elgar and the Great War*,[*] noting especially Andrew Neill, 'Elgar's Creative Challenge'.[†] We also mentioned the problem in Chapter 3 and have compared the response to the War of the artist Rex Vicat Cole in our final chapter. But the Brinkwells chamber music cannot be dismissed on the grounds that only the Violin Sonata was completed by the Armistice on 11 November 1918 and so, in the context of the question, the Quartet and Quintet are not a problem. As we have seen above, the three works were to a large extent conceived quickly together or at least in quick succession, their seeds (and often more than that) lying well within the relevant period. If Elgar was influenced directly by the War in the character of what he wrote we would certainly expect to notice it in all three chamber works. The same applies to the Cello Concerto which had been germinating for some time. The first sketches date from March 1918.

Our conclusion is that any feeling on Elgar's part that he was driven to reflect the horrors of the trenches in his Brinkwells music in the way that the War Poets such as Wilfred Owen and, later, composers such as Bliss and Britten did, was totally absent. Though the Elgars at this period were as susceptible to the bitterness of loss as anyone else, from their diaries it is clear that they also regarded Brinkwells as a magical place from where the War could largely be escaped – despite the occasional audibility of the bombardment in France. In an age where the only available source of what was happening was the newspaper, and that had to be collected from some miles away, escape was superficially not difficult. Accordingly, we have suggested above that a combination of Alice's determination and confidence in her husband's genius,

---

[*] Lewis Foreman, ed., Elgar Editions, 2001.
[†] Foreman, *Oh, My Horses!*, chs 6 and 1.

the Windflower's romantic encouragement and the 'wood magic' of Brinkwells were the subterranean springs which fed Elgar's wells of inspiration here.

None of this is to suggest that the Elgars were unpatriotic or failed to back the war effort in ways that were feasible for people of their age and abilities. Elgar himself had produced earlier on some good, patriotic music, particularly Spirit of England, and, when asked in May 1918 by the Food Ministry to set Kipling's poem 'Big Steamers', Alice noted that in the light of their experience with Kipling before, any such work would be magnanimous indeed. However, Elgar obliged, saying 'Anything for the cause'. But what applied to the War did not also apply to the Peace. So when Laurence Binyon, almost at the end of hostilities, wrote to Elgar to persuade him to set his ode, 'Peace', Elgar replied on 5 November:

> I do not feel drawn to write peace music somehow … The whole atmosphere is too full of complexities for me to feel music to it: not the atmosphere of the poem but of the time, I mean … .I regret (your) appeal to the Heavenly Spirit which is cruelly obtuse to the individual sorrow and sacrifice … a cruelty I resent bitterly & disappointedly. [*]

Although Elgar may have softened his stance somewhat on this later in the month, [†] the outcome remained the same and no 'peace' music was ever written.

Put another way, then, if the Great War had ended in 1917 a year before it did, but the Elgars' circumstances were similar so that the works in question would have been composed in peacetime, would we have noticed any difference? We think not. The real question is whether in any circumstances Elgar would have changed his underlying style of writing, as for example Frank Bridge later did. Whereas Vicat Cole developed a different style after the war to make his painting more relevant to the new zeitgeist, Elgar was aware that he was regarded as old-fashioned and was unrepentant. In writing to Marie Joshua about the Violin Sonata he said: 'I fear that it does not carry us any further but it is full of golden sounds and I like it …'. [‡] This feature of Elgar's character was to lead some of the critics to turn against him, but as is so often the case, time is a great healer and to the modern listener it is immaterial that the late romantic style was giving away to atonality and serialism across the channel. No one now criticises J.S. Bach for writing in what was then considered to be an 'old-fashioned' style, even if this led to such an eclipse of much of his output that he had to be 'rediscovered' in the century following his death by Mendelssohn.

Perhaps the most controversial piece in terms of identifying the inspirations behind it has proved to be the Quintet, particularly the first movement. Of this Michael Kennedy remarks, contrary to the views we express above:

---

[*] Letter 5 November 1918.
[†] See letter quoted in Young, Letters of Edward Elgar, p. 248.
[‡] Letter of 6 September 1918.

There can be little doubt that the agonies of the war are the inspiration behind the first movement. 'The fugato goes wild again – as man does' he told Newman (in answer to Shaw's criticism above). A 'cut-and-thrust dialogue of a ferocity new to Elgar's music' is heard there by Jerrold Northrop Moore. [*]

But Elgar's remark about his 'wild' music could equally apply to earlier works, such as the extraordinary episode in the 3rd movement of the Second Symphony where the work's 'ghosts' are confronted with an aural battering by bass drum and timpani which could certainly be called 'wild'. It has nothing to do with any 'war' in the usual sense.

More ingenious is Brian Trowell's alternative scenario to the Quintet's first movement in which he suggests that the legend of the Spanish monks inspired by the sinister trees is an unnecessary distraction and that Elgar was more likely to be representing the effect of the fighting on the 'bare, ruined choirs' of the smashed churches of Belgium. But this goes against every contemporary witness's account, including those of Alice, Billy Reed, Wulstan Atkins and (subsequently but during Elgar's lifetime) Basil Maine. It is also difficult to tie the theory in with Elgar's remark to Newman that he was then engaged in writing 'ghostly stuff'. [†] And on 16 September 1918 Alice wrote in her diary: 'E. wrote more of the wonderful Quintet – Flexham Park – sad "dispossessed" trees & their dance & unstilled regret for their evil fate – or rather curse – wh. brought it on …'

It seems to us that the solution to this little enigma is neatly pointed out by Dr Moore a propos of the Quintet's last movement:

> It was, Edward wrote to Sidney Colvin, an 'apotheosis'. No such affirmation had closed any work of his since the First Symphony. For then, as now, a war of the spirit had been won. Then the enemy had been the quasi-military ghosts of ambition. Now they were the disintegrating self-doubts which had been faced through the wood magic of countryside peace. Thus the end of the Quintet, though finished at Severn House, was inscribed as the other chamber music with the name of Brinkwells. [‡]

Cello Concerto in E minor Op. 85

This now phenomenally popular concerto was mainly written in May and June and finished by 8 August 1919. It is uncertain how much was conceived in Brinkwells as opposed to Severn House but Elgar felt the connection with Brinkwells to be sufficiently strong to inscribe the score 'Brinkwells, 1919'. Felix Salmond, who had been part of the team involved in performing the chamber music, and was to give the concerto its first performance too, helped the composer with technical questions and joined in run-throughs in both Severn House and Brinkwells.

---

[*] Kennedy, *The Life of Elgar* (2004), p. 155.
[†] Trowell, 'The Road to Brinkwells', in *Oh, My Horses!*, ed. Foreman, pp. 270-1.
[‡] Moore, *A Creative Life*, p. 737.

50 Beatrice Harrison rehearsing the Cello Concerto with Elgar in 1919

It is almost a cliché to say that the concerto has an autumnal or 'valedictory' flavour about it. It has been argued with some conviction that this was Elgar's reaction, not directly to the war itself, but to the changed world he was now finding himself in – and his inner feeling that this might be his farewell statement before lapsing into a rarely broken silence. These remarks have the benefit of hindsight. However, there can be no denying the pervasive sadness running through much of the work. But whether this element is different in kind rather than in degree from what went before is debatable. It is strongly arguable that this melancholic tendency was endogenous rather than reactive, and is to be found as an essential element in all his mature work. Elgar's sadnesses were perhaps more akin to those suggested by Virgil – 'Sunt lacrimae rerum ...' (There are tears in things.)

In late June 1919 Elgar wrote to Sidney Colvin: 'I am frantically busy writing and have nearly completed a Concerto for Violoncello – a real large work & I think <u>good</u> and alive.' Shortly afterwards he offered the Colvins the dedication of the work as we have seen above and in so doing expressed his desire to leave some record of their 'real and precious' friendship.

On 29 June, as the orchestration was being completed, the bell of the local school in Bedham rang out the joyful news that the peace treaty had been signed. Shortly before Elgar was in sufficiently rumbustious form to write for his friend Edward Speyer a notorious 'jape' – his Op. 1,001 Smokers' Cantata, containing a few bars of full scoring (Kindly, kindly, kindly do not SMOKE in the Hall or Staircase!) * – now recorded under the baton of Mark Elder. None of this suggests a composer suffering from Tchaikovsky-like depression! In fact, for most of the months spent at Brinkwells Elgar was cheerful and keyed-

---

* Anderson, *Elgar*, p. 139.

up, the rate of composition being by any standards remarkable (as discussed in more detail above).

Concertos for the cello were not common. Although ancestors can be traced back to Vivaldi, there were only three examples of the genre by romantic composers firmly in the repertoire before Elgar's – those by Schumann (still played less often than it deserves), Saint-Saens (No. 1) and the masterly effort by Dvorak. Tchaikovsky's Variations on a Rococo Theme for cello and orchestra (1876) ought perhaps to be added to the list although not actually a concerto. Part of the difficulty was getting the balance between the soloist and the tutti orchestra correct. As an instrument, beautiful though its voice in all registers is, the cello does not have the extraordinary power to penetrate an orchestra that a well-made violin has. So here, although the orchestra is to all intents and purposes the same as for his Violin Concerto, Elgar took care to see that the solo cello was never swamped by tactless scoring.

Although Elgar's presentation of his orchestral, choral, or other printed scores is by most standards impeccable, showing tempi, expression marks, dynamics, and phrasing meticulously, there is still scope for the minute scholarship involved in compiling an 'urtext'. The Elgar Society Edition covers some 37 volumes towards a complete oeuvre at present, and in the case of the Cello Concerto there is a revised full score (Novello's, Elgar Society Edition Vol. 32, 1988) but the solo cello part remained unrevised in its 1919 version. The unsatisfactory situation arising when the conductor had the revised score and the soloist had learned the 1919 version meant, according to Mats Lidstrom, the distinguished cellist, that most of the rehearsal time was spent reconciling the one with the other so as to accommodate the soloist. The revised solo part appeared in 2004 (Novello's, described in more detail by Lidstrom in *The Strad*, December 2004, 1340).

However, there were still lingering doubts and questions about Elgar's true intentions as to everything from the odd note to phrasing and articulation, and an attempt to produce a definitive edition was made by the editor Jonathan Del Mar derived from all available sources. These were, mainly, the composer's autographs of the score (on permanent loan by Carice Elgar to the Royal College of Music), the cello-piano reduction, surviving earlier drafts, Beatrice Harrison's two recordings with Elgar (particularly the complete 1928 one), and her annotated solo part, and Felix Salmond's solo part as bowed and fingered by him for the 1919 first (and disappointing) performance (Barenreiter Urtext, 2006).

Not unnaturally Elgar's view of the work tended to be swayed by the person with whom he was playing it, regardless of incidental anomalies between the notes played and printed. The reviewer of this edition in *The Strad* (April 2006, 95, Jeffrey Solow), quotes Breatrice Harrison's autobiography (*The Cello and the Nightingales*) as recalling Elgar's advice to her before going on stage, c.1922, in Manchester, in which the words ring very true: 'Give it 'em Beatrice, give it 'em. Don't mind about the notes or anything. Give 'em the spirit'.

The concerto is unusual in being in four, rather than the usual three, movements. Here we have a 'will-o-the-wisp' Scherzo and a fine Adagio flanked by the bulwarks of two outer movements. The work opens with an introductory E minor flourish of great determination (marked *ff* and *nobilmente*) which has the effect of focusing the listener's ear on the voice of the solo cello from the start (though it is in fact discreetly accompanied by lower strings).

Soft woodwind then tentatively echoes the first two bars, leading in turn to a further recitative by the solo cello of an ascending nature over another two bars. Those who know the work well (most readers we suspect) might try to put themselves into the position of someone hearing this for the first time. Is the note on which the cello ends the note we were anticipating? Most of us would probably say that we would have expected the soliloquy to go on one more note up the minor scale to the G, which would keep the key in a firm E minor. But in fact it stops on the F# (Fig. 1) and leads into the gently ambling theme on violas, then cellos, starting on the F# and reproduced above on page 138.

This theme was first introduced so far back in the text to remind us of two things. Firstly, that, given the necessary energy, Elgar composed by taking inspiration from the air anywhere, preferably with notebook at the ready. This tune derives from the unlikely environment of his sickbed at Dorset Square Nursing Home when Elgar was recovering from the painful tonsil removal operation in March 1918. Carice reminisced that despite the absence of modern painkillers and sedatives 'nevertheless he woke up one morning and asked for pencil and paper and wrote down the opening theme of the Cello Concerto'.[*] For good measure he copied it out and sent it to the Windflower 'as a thank-offering'. At that stage, though, it had not been allocated to any particular work. Secondly, the theme's apparent 'wrong note' start reminds us of Elgar's capacity to keep listeners on their toes by 'twists' such as this, though here it takes but little time to re-establish the key of E minor.

A little later a memorable moment occurs where the soloist takes the cello in a scale almost to the top of its register, showing what a huge range the instrument has, the listener hoping that the player proves up to it – since the challenge recurs (see Fig. 16) and this is a notorious trouble-spot! Another prominent theme emerges in 12/8 (four, instead of the preceding three, groups of three beats per bar) (Fig. 7) as the movement develops before leading to a repetition by the cello of the opening chords *pizzicato* (Fig. 18) – which links in turn with the second movement.

---

[*] Anderson, *Elgar*, p. 133.

This is marked *allegro molto* and in classical terms is a scherzo (though not here so called). The cello is immediately involved in a nervous, scurrying figure in semiquavers:

This tune makes a coruscating subject for Elgar to construct a quick-witted dialogue between soloist and orchestra. Notice that in the chase the orchestra seems to be very unsympathetic to the soloist's pleas to take a breath here and there (Fig. 22)! In contrast a short but typically Elgarian theme (with its initial dropping 7th familiar from e.g. the Nimrod *Enigma* variation) emerges –

though this is not allowed to impede the soloist's semi-quaver momentum for long. The movement takes on the character of a *perpetuum mobile* requiring considerable agility to keep together to the good-humoured close.

The elegiac slow movement, marked *Adagio*, is a heartfelt utterance which can easily be spoilt by over-indulgence – the composer being Elgar not Mahler. Its speed is clearly marked and to help resolve any doubts a recording conducted by the composer is readily available. A firm Bb tonality is established from the start and after a preliminary eight-bar paragraph we are taken into a true lotusland with a seamless webb of melody in 3/8 time (metronome marked quaver = 50) during which the cello plays almost continuously. This heartfelt outpouring eventually comes to a half-close on the dominant as if the composer could not face ending it unequivocally in the tonic. This upset Novello's who thought that the movement might be published separately and needed a full close. Elgar did try, but found it quite impractical. He replied: 'I fear I cannot think of anr. ending for the slow movement – it will do as it is if played separately.' *

The final movement contrives to be exciting and poignant in turn, and rests as a skilful summation of what has gone before. The preliminary statement (Fig. 42) announces a swaggering theme in B flat minor.

---

* Quoted Anderson, *Elgar*, p. 358.

This is tried out *legato* (*quasi recit*) by the cello and this dialogue prompts a brief and spectacular cadenza before the movement properly starts (Fig. 44). There are echoes of Falstaff here in the cheerful orchestration; the use of woodwind in the bucolic proceedings may also suggest gathering in the harvest from Farmer Aylwin's fields on a hot summer's day. But there are also echoes from the earlier movements. As the movement develops a new and wistful 'sighing' theme emerges (Fig. 66). This is interesting because it represents about the only direct thematic link with the immediately preceding chamber music. It is the same 'sighing' theme as the piano first announces at almost the beginning of the first movement of the Quintet and noted above (see page 152). As Brian Trowell remarks (in 'The Road to Brinkwells' above) – 'This extraordinary but tightly-organised lament [is] the most dense and chromatic music that Elgar ever wrote.'

The mood then alters (Fig. 67) with a change to triple time and the emergence of a passionately beautiful sequence (Fig, 69):

This in turn gives way to a restatement of the main theme of the slow movement, The nostalgia is palpable. But almost before we can dry our eyes the solo cello restates the opening chords of the first movement (Fig. 73). Having firmly re-established the key of E minor, the orchestra, with a final glance at the main finale theme and with the soloist in tow, scampers home.

The Harvest's Gleanings

So far as the Brinkwells harvest was concerned the making of the Cello Concerto was the final creative act. Alice's death on 7 April 1920 a few months after its first disastrous performance (due to inadequate rehearsal time), understandably fed Elgar's depressive tendencies. The long-promised Piano Concerto, to a large extent inspired by the keyboard capabilities of the Windflower, remained fragmentary. * Elgar separately identified the main slow movement theme in 'your Piano Concerto' to the Windflower in a letter to her early in 1917. On 3 August 1919 he wrote to her: 'I want to finish or rather commence the Piano Concerto which must be Windflowerish so I hope you will come but I know you will not.' (This recalls the Third Symphony's evolution some 14 years later when Elgar referred to the work as being 'practically complete' when on paper at least it was very far from it.) It is significant that Elgar wrote 'Finis. R.I.P.' after the Cello Concerto entry in his personal catalogue of works.

---

* Percy Young produced a performing version of the slow movement from these bits and pieces and Robert Walker has produced a full realisation of the work which was recorded in 2005 by David Owen Norris.

But there was other evidence that the magic of Brinkwells was beginning to lose its potency. On 22 September 1919 Elgar wrote to the Windflower: 'Here we are, very cold and I want to get away – strange: but the Studio is sad sad and I feel I have destroyed the best thing I ever wrote and it had to be so … the world is a changed place & I am awfully tired of it.' Quite what Elgar meant by this remark has been the subject of much speculation. [*]

Before leaving Brinkwells finally on 21 August 1921, with Carice loyally stepping into her deceased mother's shoes, Elgar had roused himself sufficiently to complete his arrangement, with what would now be considered the acme of political incorrectness, of J. S. Bach's Organ Fugue in C minor BWV 537 (followed later with the preceding Fantasia.) In May 1921 he copied out the score for publication by Novello's at Brinkwells and received a fee of 100 guineas for the copyright. [†] 'I wanted', he wrote to Atkins, 'to shew how gorgeous & great & brilliant he would have made himself sound had he had our means.' As one would expect it is a virtuoso display and, like Rachmaninov's piano transcriptions of Bach, reveals the composer's personality at every turn. The piece was performed to great acclaim under Eugene Goossens in October that year and from time to time, for those brave enough, since. Although something of a step-child, it was in its own way a fitting farewell for the happiness and inspiration that he had taken from Brinkwells.

---

[*] Trowell, *op. cit.*, p. 363.
[†] Moore, *A Creative Life*, p. 759.

CHAPTER TEN

Aftermath – 'No Human Spark'

The Decline of Alice

With Alice's death in April 1920 Elgar was cast adrift into the uncertain post-war world without the anchor which she had always provided for his quixotic spirit. Although intimations of her illness had been apparent for many months, her condition deteriorated so as to cause real worry in the autumn of 1919.

Alice had always been extraordinarily responsive to any change in Elgar's health and her worries about him may well have eclipsed those she had about herself. However, even her diary begins to record some concern in 1918. Soon after the operation that she had to remove a wen from her forehead on 29 September 1918 – an operation which Elgar informed the Windflower had been 'much more of an event than we anticipated & than she knows even now'[*] – she fell ill at Brinkwells and had to keep to her room. Immediately on their return to London at the beginning of December she consulted Sir Maurice Abbot Anderson again about a persistent cough but was reassured by him that there was nothing wrong with her lungs. Even so she did not seem to improve for some time.

Her health again caused some concern in the autumn of 1919 and her diary begins to contain increasing reference to her own health. A 'wretched cold' in November kept her in bed and required the attentions of Sir Maurice who found her 'rather badly'. The diary entries then become shorter and some days there are only a few words pencilled in instead of the more usual full page of writing. By the middle of November she was clearly very unwell. Sir Maurice called and ordered her to bed and when she did try to get up nine days later she was 'rather too shivered to enjoy it'. She still saw some visitors and on Wednesday 10 December invited Rex Vicat Cole to tea to talk about the future of Brinkwells. 'Serious conversation re Brinkwells', she wrote, 'Whether they wd. give it up etc – Do hope so.' The fact that she intended to negotiate with Rex rather than Hannah suggests that what she was intending was the purchase of their remaining lease.

Alice had always planned ahead for Elgar's comfort and aware of the financial impossibility of keeping Severn House she sought to find an answer that would please him by obtaining Brinkwells for their use. Was she also anxious to plan for him in case she was no longer with him? It would have been in her character

---

[*] Moore, *The Windflower Letters*, p. 215.

to do so and she knew that he loved their Sussex cottage. The outcome of the meeting with Rex, however, was not clear and no long-term arrangement was agreed. Indeed the only consideration that might have persuaded the Vicat Coles to give up the lease was the financial one as their attachment to the cottage ran very deep. In the end they must have decided that their last few leasehold years were beyond price.

By the beginning of 1920 Alice was still less than well although her diary reveals that she continued with her Sunday tea parties and visitors at Severn House. But her old energy seems to have gone. Elgar wrote to the Windflower on 6 January that Alice 'does not get on much but comes down to breakfast'. [*] Alice's diary entries also start the year in an air of foreboding: 'The year opens with many heavy clouds – continued financial anxiety for E. & A.' she wrote. Then a little later on 16 January – 'A. out for short walk' as if this were an unusual occurrence whereas in previous years this would have passed without comment. The entries themselves are often very short as if the effort of keeping her diary was almost too much for her. By the end of the month Sir Maurice was again needed to advise about her cough. He came on 30 January but her cough persisted and five days later she went on the bus to see him – 'tired of cough' she wrote in her diary, while Elgar noted in his diary that there was 'much coughing in night'. Even by late February she had not regained her former health: 'Poor dear Alice does not really improve in strength', Elgar wrote to the Windflower, 'So after all I did not go away to Stoke; it seemed too lonely for her.' [†]

Then once again she tried to take up the threads of her life with visits to her club, lunching out and shopping. She went to the cinema with Elgar on 10 March and shopped at Maples and Heals the next day, but by Saturday 13 March she was once again clearly ill. 'A. feeling very badly', she confessed in her diary for 14 March, 'returned to bed till dinner time.' She went to a concert at Queen's Hall on 16 March and then, with Elgar away at Ridgehurst, she went to see Sir Maurice again who gave her some new medicine and sent her back in his car. He had, she wrote, 'relieved her mind of some anxiety'.

A few days later she made a trip to Woking with Elgar who worried that the car was too shaky for her and although she was clearly not well enough to go to Leeds with him on 22 March she did make one last effort to get to the concert of his chamber music on 23 March. She then seemed to go downhill very rapidly. Elgar wrote to the Windflower on 26 March: 'Carice & I are in much trouble of mind about poor dear Alice who seems really very ill & weak and does not improve', a letter which reflects Elgar's alarm at the seriousness of the situation. [‡] Three days later the same tone permeates a short note to Ivor Atkins: 'This is a sad little note to tell you that my poor dear Alice is really ill, very ill, I fear.' [§] Billy Reed summed up the insidious downward path which had led Alice to this point. He wrote: 'In the beginning of the New Year, 1920,

---

[*] Moore, *The Windflower Letters*, p. 233.
[†] *Ibid.*, p. 236.
[‡] *Ibid.*, p. 238.
[§] Atkins, *The Elgar-Atkins Friendship*, p. 306.

Lady Elgar seemed to be ailing. She who had always been so full of vitality and energy was now often listless. She would creep up close to the fire and look so fragile that I began to feel anxious about her. She would brighten up for a little while; but every time I saw her she seemed to be getting smaller – she was never of any great stature – and I am sure she must have been losing weight.'[*] His judgement was also shared by Rosa Burley who remembered finding Alice 'shrunken and terribly depressed' early in 1920. [†]

Alice's Last Illness and Death

Alice was attended in her last illness by Sir Maurice's deputy, Dr Rose, but in reality he could do nothing and Elgar's diary simply shows a steady decline. 'A. awake during most of the night – alas!' (28 March), 'A. no better' (31 March) – a refrain that was repeated in his diary for the next few days – then he wrote 'A. bad night & C. slept in her room' … A. took 2 sleeping draughts but ineffectual' (5 April). By the next day she was clearly at the end of her life and in great pain. 'My darling in great distress cd. not understand her now – very very painful', Elgar wrote. A specialist (presumably for cancer) was called but gave a bad report and Elgar described a 'long dreary restless night' that followed. The next day she was given Extreme Unction and eventually died in the early evening of 7 April 1920. Elgar then wrote the closing entry for Alice's diary that day: 'Died in my arms at 6.10 pm … .'

Her death certificate, signed by the Registrar on 9 April, gave as the cause of death Chronic Interstitial Nephritis and Anaemia Coma, causes certified by T. Rose MRCS. The widely held belief now, however, is that the cause of death was most probably undiagnosed lung cancer.

The shock for him was terrible. She had always been there as a fixed point in the maelstrom of his emotional world. She had enabled him to work; she had given him the freedom that he wanted – but it was a freedom made possible by her protecting love, and whilst he sometimes placed her in the background, she had always had him in her thoughts. One instance in 1917 illustrates this. Elgar was in Manchester and Alice also away in Hereford and Gloucester where she visited her old family home, Hazeldine, at Redmarley. On 16 August Elgar wrote to the Windflower who had visited his sister's house at Stoke Prior: 'I am glad you "feel" Stoke – that is a place where I see & hear (yes!) you. A. has not been there since 1888 & does not care to go …' Whilst Elgar's feelings were with the Windflower, Alice's were with Elgar. On the same day she wrote to the Windflower but her theme was how much she missed Elgar: 'I have been longing for him to be here' and again the next day her diary reads 'Thought so much of E. & when he was at Hazeldine & our walks there …'.

However, Alice as much as Elgar believed in the overriding importance of the creative artist, and must have known the sacrifices that she would be called

---

[*] Reed, *Elgar as I Knew Him*, pp. 66-7.
[†] Burley, *The Record of a Friendship*, p. 201.

upon to make in the name of music. She knew that genius was uncomfortable to live with, and that it could also be selfish. Even if she did resent his behaviour, she certainly never showed it, and her diary gives no hint of censure. Rosa Burley, in summing up their relationship, wrote that Alice 'really did worship him with a blindness to his faults, and indeed to his occasional cruelty to her that seemed almost incredible.' *

It would be easy to portray Alice in the guise of a martyr – but that would not be the whole story for she willingly accepted and believed in the importance of her role – a point clearly made by Carice when she wrote that Alice 'gave up her lifelong ambition to be a writer of note because she was so sure that a genius had been given into her charge.' † She loved Elgar in a way that was almost maternal, worrying about him compulsively when he was not with her. Separated from him one day in 1917 in London during rehearsals for the Fringes of the Fleet, Alice had been enjoying a quiet half hour at the National Gallery when an air raid was suddenly suspected. She wrote in her diary, 'All were herded into basement, raid said to be on way. A. cd. not bear not being with E. if raid came so an official let her out at some back door & she 'sprinted' up to the Coliseum.' ‡

But there was more to her commitment than just worrying and wanting to be with Elgar, for she made him work when he had to and recognised his need for entertaining diversions as well. Even if she did not fully understand all the intricacies and depths of his music, she could sometimes tell Elgar when something he wrote was not 'right'. Moreover, when she died he stopped writing and completed little of any great weight in the long winter of his life – and this in spite of the continuing presence of the Windflower who was more musically gifted than Alice and who had previously inspired him . His love affair with Vera Hockman in 1931 brought him to the brink of creativity again only to be thwarted by his declining health and waning musical energy. Clearly Alice was an enormously powerful presence in his life, one all the more unexpected because of her small stature, her ultra-conventional conduct and uncritical acceptance of him.

Some contemporaries did realise the extent of her role in his career. In 1933 when Elgar's commitment to finishing the Third Symphony was obviously diminishing, Frederick Gaisberg spent the weekend with him and observed – 'I think he misses the inspiration and driving force of Lady Elgar. Some sympathetic person, lady or man, of strong character should take him in hand and drive him on.' § Others had been aware of the other, strong side of Alice's character during her life – 'ruthless' was the word used by Carice about her mother whilst one of Carice's friends called her 'an excessively difficult character'.

---

* Burley, *The Record of a Friendship*, p. 202.
† Carice Elgar Blake, 'A Family Retrospective', in *Edward Elgar: Centenary Sketches*, p. 6.
‡ Alice Elgar's diary, 14 June 1917.
§ Anderson, *Elgar*, p. 174.

Rosa Burley suggested that in many ways the marriage had been irksome to Elgar. But even if that had been so, his initial reaction at her death was to realise what he had owed her. It is clear also that in some respects he was constantly aware of aspects of this debt throughout their marriage. When he had received his knighthood in 1904, Carice had made a telling point about her mother: 'I am so glad for Mother's sake that Father has been knighted. You see – it puts her back where she was.'* If Carice at the age of 14 was aware of the social obligation that Alice had imposed on Elgar, then how much more must Elgar have been aware of his debt. But this quotation also highlights the point that Elgar too gave something to Alice in this marriage and that by marrying him Alice gained the kind of life that she would never have been able to attain on her own. In devising words for the tombstone that Troyte Griffith was to design for her, Elgar sought for the appropriate phrase that would summarise her life with him; what he suggested in the end was her own family motto 'Fortiter et fide' – strong and faithful – because it 'suited dear A. so well.'†

Desolation

In a letter to Walford Davies written a month after Alice's death, Elgar's words reveal a man overwhelmed by loss: 'I am just back to a cold & empty house – alas! – & find your sympathetic note – I can only say thank you for it. All I have done was owing to her and I am at present a sad & broken man – just stunned.'‡ His diary entries become short and factual – one simply reading 'the empty house' when he returns to London from being away – and the thought of new music was out of the question to him. He described himself as 'a weary & a much broken man' to Ivor Atkins in May 1920, making it quite clear that 'It will not be possible for me to write anything new – you cannot fathom the loneliness & desolation of my life I fear'.§

In the empty, cold space of Severn House during the weeks after Alice's death, Elgar attempted to deal with her affairs – a process that he found unearthed much of the past and the hostility that her family had originally felt about the union. With the imperative urgency of bereavement he was also concerned to do everything that Alice would have wanted to do in the way that she would have wished. In a letter to his old friend Sidney Colvin in April he wrote: 'It is all too sad & too lonely to bear thinking of. I try to busy myself by 'setting to rights' in such manner as she would like ….'¶ His friends rallied round, he went to the cinema with Carice --nearly every evening at the beginning of May – and eventually he wrote to the Windflower. His first letter to her after Alice's death, written on mourning stationery on 16 June 1920, paints a picture of a man who felt himself to be at the mercy of life. 'I cannot tell anything of the

---

* Burley, *The Record of a Friendship*, p. 174.
† Kennedy, *Portrait of Elgar* (1987), pp. 290-1.
‡ Moore, *A Creative Life*, p. 755.
§ Atkins, *The Elgar-Atkins Friendship*, p. 307.
¶ EBM, letter no. 3509.

future: I do not like the outlook & cannot control events any longer … I only mean that we are drifting & at the mercy of the waves – and human beings.'[*]

The shock of bereavement and loneliness brought on physical symptoms – he was troubled by dizziness which kept him in bed. He was, according to Carice, limp, tired and depressed, and in need of medical attention. By June, wishing for some retreat from London, his attention had turned to Brinkwells and another short lease was negotiated with Hannah Vicat Cole. Carice in particular had been apprehensive as to whether a return to the cottage would be the best for Elgar but her fears were initially groundless as the environment there proved to be helpful, full as it was with happy and peaceful memories. From that first visit in June 1920 both Carice and Elgar were eager to obtain the long-term lease from the Vicat Coles. 'In fact we do nothing but long for it to be our own', Carice wrote to the Windflower shortly after their arrival, and this desire must have been intensified by the knowledge that Alice had also wished it and had begun the process of negotiation before her death.

Setting to Rights

There was no doubt in either Carice's or Elgar's mind about the sympathy of their friends in the country and the reception they would receive. When the news reached Fittleworth of Alice's death, many of their friends and acquaintances had sent letters, and in Elgar's 'setting to rights' on her behalf he arranged for small gifts to be sent to Fittleworth. The care with which this was done speaks volumes about the affection in which both she and Elgar held their dear villagers. Elgar carefully drafted a letter on black-edged mourning stationery to go with the small sums of money: 'All the dear 'wood folk' at Brinkwells

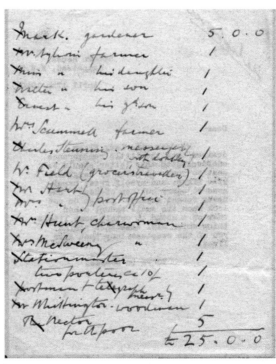

51 Elgar's list of gifts to the 'wood folk' after Alice's death

have received some remembrance – even to her hedgecutter', he wrote to Sidney Colvin with a mixture of sadness and pride, adding, 'I hear that Mark – our gardener is overwrought with grief'.[†]

---

[*] Moore, *The Windflower Letters*, p. 242.
[†] EBM letter no. 3509.

Elgar's list of recipients ran to 15 names all of whom were to be given one pound, apart from Mark Holden who was left five pounds, and the list included four members of the Aylwin family. He also remembered 'two porters' at the railway station who were to receive 10 shillings each. Another five pounds was designated to go to the Rector for the poor. Elgar in his graceful letter made his intentions clear – he wrote, 'Please do not look upon the small amount other than as a means to obtain some little thing which will sometimes remind you of the sweetest lady that ever lived. Yours in sorrow …'. [*]

Brinkwells Revisited

Although sure that they would be welcomed at the cottage, Elgar had to face up to the many memories that Brinkwells held – all of them reflecting his life with Alice. He had never stayed one night there without her and her hand had been behind many of the improvements they had made. Algernon Blackwood realised the way that her presence had permeated Elgar's life at the cottage and in a letter sent to Elgar soon after Alice's death he wrote:

> Your life companion and comrade, and oh how dear and sweet she was to me always. My dear friend, I do feel and pray for you and Carice, and Severn House without her is unthinkable, and little Brinkwells … It all makes me ache so for you – and the impossibility of helping or comforting is terrible. [†]

Elgar and Carice eventually left London by car on the morning of 22 June and were driven to Brinkwells. They were met by Mark and another domestic help, Mrs Hurst, – 'very, very tenderly sad, alas!', Elgar wrote in his diary. There were domestic arrangements to make and repairs to supervise: the pump for the well water was not working and it took two days to get it repaired. Carice, taking over Alice's responsibilities, fetched the letters from the Fittleworth post office and used her bicycle to go over to Pulborough. Although there were some difficulties in getting staff, and Carice had to organise breakfast herself, she did find some help and wrote to the Windflower three days after their arrival that the house was settled and should work quite easily. She explained that she had her bicycle and so could go out and collect things but that she had found an 'overwhelming' abundance of fruit which needed preserving and a garden which needed weeding – 'I want to weed & do everything at once', she wrote. [‡]

Elgar spent the first few days settling in. He rested, busied himself with the wood, cleared out the workshop and did some woodwork. One of the first letters he wrote from the cottage was to Ivor Atkins and it showed the depth of his sadness. 'We are down at the cottage', he wrote,

---

[*] EBM, letter no. 510.
[†] Simmons, 'Elgar and the Wonderful Stranger: Music for Starlight Express', in *Elgar Studies*, ed. Monk, p. 184.
[‡] Moore, *The Windflower Letters*, p. 243.

& it is quiet and restful but very, very, very sad. I do not get on in health as we could wish but the shock has been too great ... I wish you could see this place, but it is uncertain how long we remain; it is difficult to get service – servants out of the question. [*]

As Carice had suspected the first day, so filled by memories as it was bound to be, had been 'dreadful', but then the air and the abundance of milk, butter and eggs appeared to do Elgar good and she thought that he was physically a little better.

They had one friend to stay, Lalla Vandervelde, but Elgar declared that they could not really cope with visitors and apart from this interlude their time was spent quietly walking in the woods or to the river and working in the garden. In a long letter to the Windflower a month after their arrival, Elgar gave an extended account of his health and state of mind since Alice's death. The shock had brought on an attack of his ear problem and he was having to lie down for a day or two at the time, but, as he explained: 'I, to all intents and purposes, am an invalid – you see the stronger I get (& I am fairly well) the worse my ear is – if I am low in health & unable to get about, my ear is less troublesome: so there it is – in a vicious circle.' His physical problems were matched by a sense of unwelcome and inevitable change in all aspects of his life. He wrote that he loathed music, adding that, 'I did get out some paper – but its all dead'. Severn House was to be sold, and to add to his acute sense of loss three places which he had always regarded as 'havens' in his life were put on the market in the same week: Birchwood, his sister's house at Stoke Prior, and all the Wye fishing where he used to 'lie & fish & write & dream'. Neither had Brinkwells escaped unscathed: 'They have cut down the woods so much & made a road etc which alters the look of the place but of course dear A. made it & it is full of remembrances – too sad for words.' [†]

The next two weeks were spent away from the cottage – Carice wanted a change although Elgar said that he did not – and they returned to Brinkwells again at the beginning of August. All Elgar's letters from Brinkwells at this period show him in the depths of early bereavement – the sense that the world was going on as usual and that the beauty of the landscape was untouched by Alice's death moved him to despair. In a letter to Sidney Covin he wrote, 'I find everything as usual but sad, sad & sad beyond words; inscrutable nature goes relentlessly on, birds, flowers, everything as of old. But I could not see the beauty in it –.' [‡] The woods were still beautiful but the absence of Alice had taken something from him. Again to Colvin he was to write: ' I feel these woods all aglow – a spark wd. start a flame – but no human spark comes.' [§] He lost any interest in his diary, leaving the pages almost blank, and his letters to the Windflower reveal that he is both anxious to ask her to come to see him at

[*] Atkins, *The Elgar-Atkins Friendship*, pp. 308 and 311.
[†] Moore, *The Windflower Letters*, p. 244.
[‡] EBM, letter no. 3511.
[§] McVeagh, *Edward Elgar*, p. 70.

Brinkwells, as of old, but resigned to the fact that this could not happen. 'I wish we cd. ask you – but it is too primitive … I wish you cd. come!', he wrote to her, 'there is no train service allowing for a day visit I fear & it is really too far for such a journey alas!' [*]

He did however ask Billy Reed and his letter dated 15 August 1920 is less conditional in its invitation: 'If you could bring yourself to consider a few days here we shall be delighted …', he wrote with no mention of the inherent domestic difficulties. With memories of past times when Reed had visited the cottage he adds rather touchingly, 'we might fish again' but then waves this optimism away by continuing, 'I am not very well & have lost all interest in life & I fear nothing will ever revive it –'. [†]

Elgar and Carice returned from Brinkwells at the end of August and his ill-health continued to be a worry through the summer. Writing to Ivor Atkins near the end of their summer stay at the cottage, he described himself as 'very shaky' and their final visit to Brinkwells that year lasted only three days in November, probably to take some of their things back to Severn House and close up the cottage before the winter.

Nevertheless, both Carice and Elgar were still eager to obtain the long lease of the cottage and in April 1921 Carice visited Hannah Vicat Cole for tea to sound her out on the possibility. But she was unsuccessful and her diary entry for 5 April expresses the disappointment that both she and Elgar felt when they realised that the Vicat Coles wanted it themselves at the end of the year and that there was no prospect of its being sold. [‡] That Elgar's own hopes had been high that they might be able to retain the cottage is reflected in the letter that he wrote to the Windflower nine days after Carice had visited Hannah. He wrote, 'Brinkwells alas! is not to be ours – the Coles intend to keep it after all; naturally we cannot blame them only it seems rather hard after we were led to believe we could have it.' [§] Whilst the last few words imply some kind of unwritten understanding, it is impossible now to say whether this was based on fact, although a letter written by Elgar to Frank Schuster in July 1920 suggests that something had been said. He wrote: 'It is devastating that our landlord here has changed his mind & will not give the place up to us as he suggested nine months ago – which is piggish for us. It wd. have been a shelter anyhow ….' [¶] It is likely here that Elgar is thinking back to Alice's unresolved meeting with Rex Vicat Cole in December 1919 when she discussed the possibility of having the cottage.

Although the long-term ownership of the lease had been denied to them, Elgar and Carice still had the use of the cottage for short periods for one more year and during 1921 they visited Brinkwells twice. Carice, having taken on Alice's mantle, was busy arranging the move after her meeting with Hannah in

---

[*] Moore, *The Windflower Letters*, p. 246.
[†] Young, *Letters of Edward Elgar*, p. 265.
[‡] See Carice Elgar Blake's diary 1921.
[§] Moore, *op. cit.*, p. 255.
[¶] Young, *Elgar O. M.*, pp.203-4.

April. There were still difficulties with staff and their first attempt to get down to West Sussex was foiled by a possible rail strike. They eventually set out for Brinkwells at the end of May and drove down, stopping for a picnic lunch en route. On arrival Elgar was again struck by the sadness of the place without Alice. 'It is divine but sad beyond words & empty', he wrote to the Windflower, adding, 'I do not know how long we shall, or can rather, stay …'. *

Although their visits in 1921 were still marked by the profound sadness of Alice's death, Elgar did spend some time at music, copying the orchestration that he had made of Bach's organ Fugue in C minor. The presence of Carice's dog, Meg, also served as a distraction and perceptibly lightened the mood. Meg, it appeared, was, to use Elgar's words, 'very naughty but a dear', and her various escapades and moods kept him well entertained. Carice had taken her camera down to the cottage, as she had also in 1920, and it is to her that we probably owe the few images of Elgar in the woods selecting sticks for his wood work. They also had some visitors – at the end of May Billy Reed and Percy Hull arrived in order to talk about the details of the forthcoming Three Choirs Festival and Elgar drew Reed a map so that he could walk from Pulborough station to the cottage.

However, in spite of the beauty of the surroundings and these mild distractions Elgar could not find himself or consider the future direction his life might take. Carice's forthcoming marriage to Samuel Blake and move to Chilworth and the necessity of selling Severn House meant that the future was by no means certain for him. In July during what was to be his last stay at Brinkwells he wrote to the Windflower:

> I have let the days go by to see if it is possible to say anything not melancholy about this dear place – but it is too sad. I do not sleep & can do nothing all day but wonder what it is all for, what it means & what the end will be … Living here is difficult, – worse than in wartime – milk & eggs very scarce so we can ask no one here. †

Inevitably the place turned Elgar's mind to past happiness: 'I think of nothing but the dear, hard-to-remember days when you were in Lucas's house at Tillington – my dear ones', he wrote to the Colvins in July ‡ and not even Meg's adventures with snakes, wasps and the muddy horse pond could in the end divert his mind from the memories which flooded back. He did not put up the blind in the now unused studio and told the Windflower how the ferns they had planted were all withered and dry. Although the nightjars were still heard and all the wild things still lived in the woods, he told her that he found everything altered – as indeed it was for him.

He and Carice spent their last few weeks at the cottage quietly. Carice wrote that Elgar was tired and very sleepy and the weather was dry and hot. The ever

---

* Moore, *The Windflower Letters*, p. 257.
† *Ibid.*, pp. 258-9.
‡ EBM, letter no. 3523.

52 Elgar with Meg in Brinkwells Garden in 1921

faithful Mark still tended the garden and brought his six-month-old sheepdog puppy with him to play with Meg. At the beginning of August Elgar spent a few days at Crowborough with Landon Ronald and then returned to Brinkwells for the last time. He wrote to the Windflower: 'I have really nothing to say – we are sorrowfully putting things on one side here for the final departure & marking things to be given to the villagers … it is all very depressing but necessary & must be faced & is being faced.'*

Carice's diary records that Elgar was unwell and very depressed as the time for leaving the cottage grew nearer. Just before he left, Sir Julian Corbett from Stopham called for tea and Elgar walked some of the way back with him, just as he used to with Alice and their visitors. As they walked through the woods, Carice noted that Mr Aylwin's son, Walter, had made fires of rubbish in the cornfield and what a wonderful sight this made under the moon. So just as Alice's last memories of the cottage were of fires in the woods, so too Elgar's – a final, almost Wagnerian conflagration to mark the end of the Brinkwells era.

On 17 August Elgar wrote to the Windflower for the last time from 'this dearest little place' and then on Sunday 21 August he left the cottage and walked to Pulborough station to catch the train to London. Carice remained a few more days to pack up. It was, for Elgar, one more loss in a series of losses which he believed had punctuated his life. 'What a blight has come over my life in the last eighteen months,' he wrote to the Windflower in August, 'Stoke, Worcester, Birchwood, Brinkwells – all gone.'

On Friday 23 September at Severn House Carice unpacked the trunks that had arrived from Brinkwells, so ending an episode that had witnessed some of the happiest and most fruitful times in her father's life. By the next month Elgar had moved into a service flat that she had found for him at St James's Place, SW1, and Severn House was eventually auctioned.

But the links that bound Elgar to that 'divine' place were not totally broken. In November Mark Holden wrote to let Elgar know that he had left a new scythe blade at Brinkwells and to ask what he should do with it and to ask for 8s. to cover the expense of sending various shrubs and plants to Carice at

---

* Moore, *The Windflower Letters*, p. 260.

Chilworth. * Elgar too kept in touch by sending Mark gifts of tobacco. In reply to one of these, Mark wrote again in February 1922 and told Elgar how Brinkwells was getting on. 'No one living there all winter', he wrote, and added that the removal of an elm tree in the lane had 'given a great light into that end of the garden'. Mark added local news and what the weather had been like before ending, 'Dear Sir I trust you are keeping in the best of health – I am well myself.' †
A further gift of tobacco (the

53 *Carice with Meg at Brinkwells in 1921*

'best sort of tip' according to Mark) – probably for Christmas 1922 – brought about another reply, but this time with bad news. 'You will be sorry to hear that Mr Aylwin is dead. It happened yesterday after he had been in bed eight days. We shall miss him very much.' ‡ Elgar was also touched by the news and wrote almost immediately to the Windflower about it: 'Our dear old farmer [Aylwin] at Brinkwells – he drove you in the old ponycart – is dead; so another link with all that was sweet, peaceful & lovely is gone.' §

Carice also found it hard to let go. A year after they had left Brinkwells she visited the cottage with her husband and then told Elgar. The news upset him greatly and he wrote to the Windflower: 'They motored over to Brinkwells on Sunday – (shut up) but she saw all the sweet old villagers & said it was lovely, peaceful & sad. The thought of it has made me ill – so I have to lie down.' ¶

It is hard to say definitely whether after Alice's death Brinkwells would ever have been a satisfactory home for Elgar but many factors suggest that it would not. It was isolated, living conditions were basic, and it was full of memories which might have prevented Elgar from ever moving on. It was not until November 1921, after his connections with the cottage had been finally broken, that Elgar could really accept that Alice had gone. He wrote to Troyte Griffith from London: 'I have at last realised that my dear wife and beloved companion has left me: until two months ago I always felt – subconscious that she <u>must</u> return as of old – now I know & submit.' **

---

* EBM, letter no. 6245.
† EBM, letter no. 6248.
‡ EBM, letter no. 6137.
§ Moore, *The Windflower Letters*, p.276.
¶ *Ibid.*, p. 275.
** Young. *Letters of Edward Elgar*, p. 275.

54 Carice at Brinkwells in 1935

But it is clear that Elgar did not wish to leave Brinkwells and all the memories that it contained for him and was profoundly sad to say good-bye to the cottage. In selling Severn House and leaving Brinkwells he stepped out of the protective aura with which Alice had surrounded him, for these were the homes that she had found for him and Brinkwells was the place in which she had at one point envisaged their future. Thereafter Elgar's association with Brinkwells was broken for the rest of his life – although he continued to be remembered by his neighbours in Bedham and Fittleworth. (One postcard from Rex Palmer of Bedham congratulating Elgar on a performance of the Second Symphony and dated 1933 exists in the EBM.)

But one poignant episode still remained to be played out. In May 1936, a little over two years after Elgar's death, Carice took Vera Hockman to see Brinkwells. It seems entirely fitting that the final link between Elgar and the cottage he loved so much should have been made in this way. It was Vera who, at the end of his life, turned his enthusiasm once again to music and it was to her that he 'gave' his Violin Sonata by calling it 'my Sonata – our sonata'.* The fact that Vera wished to see where the Sonata had been written and Carice wanted to take her speaks also of the powerful magnetism of the place in which Elgar's chamber music had been born.

---

* Allen, *Elgar in Love*, p. 46.

CHAPTER ELEVEN

Epilogue – The Lost World of Brinkwells

Not of This World

Writing to the Windflower on 4 July 1927 from his home at Napleton Grange, Kempsey, Elgar described the recital of his chamber music that Frank Schuster had arranged at The Hut to celebrate Elgar's 70th birthday. (The Windflower had been unwell and was unable to attend.) 'I need not say that you were sadly missed last Sunday at the Hut …', he wrote. 'The music was well played – the Quintet <u>quite</u> satisfactorily … I <u>wish</u> you could have heard the things which seem to me to be of my best & the Quintet is not of this world; but you know more of this than I do.' [*]

There are many ways in which this last sentence could be interpreted – one of them being the ghostly quasi-programme of the Quintet. And yet the phrase 'not of this world' with all its overtones appears to suggest more.

55 *Elgar in 1922*

There is in Elgar's letter the implicit recognition of the Windflower's role as muse and her understanding of the nature of inspiration, a recognition that is the same kind of 'giving' that we have seen before between Elgar and his friends – an expression of his quick affection and warmth. But is there something else as well? For the phrase seems to echo through with memories of the past. Billy Reed also stresses the way that the music talked of something other than reality when he described it as 'a message from another world'. [†]

By 1927 Elgar had truly moved into a new world and it was a world with which he was less emotionally in tune. (His judgement on post-war life made to the Windflower was, 'I am dreadfully unhappy at everything'.) The world of Brinkwells, which saw the final, vigorous burst of his creative energy and in which he was securely held in the web of affections and associations necessary for his inspiration to flourish, belonged to the past. It had become a distant

---

[*] Quoted in Moore, *The Windflower Letters*, p. 313.
[†] Reed, *Elgar as I Knew Him*, p. 65.

56 Brinkwells in 1999

world relegated to memory alone. The Windflower would have known this. He had written to her in 1919 of the 'holy peace of Brinkwells in the early morn' but even by his last visit with Carice that taste of arcadian isolation was already receding into the distance. 'The place is not the same as it was in the lonely war years', he wrote to the Windflower in 1921, 'there are so many men at work in the woods now & in the quarries – quite a dozen men in one – & the vast loneliness of it, which was its charm, is (<u>in a measure</u> only) gone.'*

Elgar's Brinkwells was changed even further when the studio which had seen the creation of his chamber works and the Cello Concerto was physically moved away from the cottage and taken to Bedham. This radical removal marked the end, too, of Rex Vicat Cole's association with Brinkwells. Thereafter the exact conditions which had inspired both men to create individualistic and self-generated works could no longer be experienced.

The Great War marked most of those who lived through it in some indelible way. But for Elgar, already in his early 60s when the war ended, its effects were overlaid, even eclipsed, by the death of his wife. The accumulated effect of these experiences was to be a diminution of the extraordinary vigour and creative energy which had been so clearly evident in the Brinkwells era. He maintained his friendships with those who had visited the cottage but it was as if his musical inspiration was somehow on a lower plane and hard to sustain.

So what of the three Brinkwells guests that we looked at earlier? How did their friendships fare with Elgar in this new world? He continued to write to

---

* Moore, *The Windflower Letters*, p. 260.

and meet the Windflower but, with his move away from London in the late 1920s, they met less and the intensity of their earlier relationship diminished although their deep affection continued to Elgar's death. Elgar's Windflower survived him by only two years, dying in 1936.

Similarly his friendship with Algernon Blackwood survived the war years. Carice's 1921 diary notes Blackwood's presence at Severn House for dinner and plate pool – as in old times – and she and Elgar went to a performance of his new play 'Through the Crack' which elicited only reserved praise from Elgar who thought it 'might have been improved'. But the war had also changed Blackwood – and drained his energy through his work in Intelligence and with the Red Cross. His biographer, Mike Ashley, makes the point that the war stripped him of some of his optimism: 'The old Blackwood, the Starlight Man, the man who hoped to make the world aware of beauty, had his vision despoiled. It was an older, wiser, more mature, and, alas, less visionary Blackwood who rose from the ashes.'* Blackwood lived on until 1951 having spent much of his time abroad but towards the end of his life he established a considerable following through his BBC broadcasts. However, with Elgar's move out of London this too was another friendship that suffered and became a memory. Elgar's circle was further diminished in the 1920s by the deaths of both Frances (1924) and Sidney Colvin (1927) – 'my dear ones' as he had called them.

Elgar's closeness to Billy Reed, however, survived both the war and innumerable changes of house. Reed, it appears, could always bring out the youthful, playful side of Elgar's personality. In their delight in japes and games they were alike – something that Reed recognised when he wrote about Elgar: 'He was like a child in many respects; and although when I suggested any frivolous amusement or did anything boyish he would rebuke me with 'Oh, Billy, when, if ever, will you grow up?' he was much the

57 Elgar and Billy Reed in 1922

* Ashley, *Starlight Man*, p. 232.

same himself.' * As Elgar's confidant and compassionate friend to the end of the composer's life, it was to Billy Reed that the dying Elgar entrusted his wishes about the unfinished Third Symphony – not to let anyone 'tinker' with it. The selfless Reed died in 1942, eight years after Elgar.

Elgar reacted to the new world by withdrawing from it – by retreating behind the persona of an English country gentleman much concerned with dogs and horses. For many of his outlook and background the effects of the upheaval on their way of life and social assumptions were hard to take. Edward Heron-Allen, like Elgar, was shocked at the end of the war by the disappearance of the old values and could only face the future in a spirit of pessimism, holding that 'we are on the verge of – if not the throes of – a revolution of all our preconceived ideas and habits of life … The world is mad.' †

Rex Vicat Cole

For others of a younger generation, coming to terms with the aftermath of the war had to be achieved actively. For Rex Vicat Cole, the architect of the Brinkwells studio and the first to translate the magic of the place into works of art, the post-war years posed particular problems. With the premature death of Byam Shaw in 1919 Cole lost a close friend and was left to re-establish the reputation of the art school that they had co-founded after its closure during the war years – something that he did with great success until his retirement as Principal in 1926. But he too had been marked by the changes brought about during the war and his response to these was every bit as profound as Elgar's. At some stage during or shortly after the war he destroyed many of his earlier canvases – including some of those works painted at Brinkwells and half of all the works that he had exhibited at the Royal Academy between 1900 and 1919. Some canvases from those years were sold or given away but in all 20 major works were cut into pieces. No facts are known that might explain this episode in a life that was, apart from this singular act of savagery, one of great balance and achievement.

Soon after the war Rex Vicat Cole turned again to writing, publishing another successful book for art students – this time on perspective. *Perspective; The Practice and Theory of Perspective as Applied to Pictures, with a Section dealing with its Application to Architecture* was published in 1921. Again Cole dealt with a complex subject with thoroughness and clarity using 436 of his own drawings and diagrams as well as 36 paintings by old masters to illustrate the book. He himself well knew the difficulties inherent in the subject and in his Preface acknowledges, 'I have known students to attend a course of well-delivered lectures on Perspective and yet say they did not understand a single word of what the lecturer was talking about'. His book sets out to remedy this

---

* Reed, *Elgar as I Knew Him*, p. 96.
† Harvey and Fitzgerald, *Reflections on Heron-Allen's War Journal* (Opusculum V, Heron-Allen Society, Chichester 2002) pp. 24-5.

by suggesting that students sketched the object to be drawn first before putting it into correct perspective. That he succeeded in his aim to make perspective understandable was recognised by the anonymous reviewer of the book for *The Studio* in 1921. He suggested that Cole had saved young artists from the fate suffered by Paolo Uccelli who, according to Vasari, suffered poverty and depression to the day of his death as a result of his devotion to perspective. 'The modern student is more fortunate', the reviewer wrote, 'in having the difficulties of the subject smoothed away for him.' *

In his post-war paintings, including those canvases painted during his last years as tenant at Brinkwells during the 1920s, Cole consciously moved away from the atmospheric, arcadian image of his pre-war paintings and developed a broader, simpler and more selective style. His work had always demonstrated a toughness of vision that was unlike the refined and elegant images of his father's paintings. As his work had developed, moreover, his ability to observe, select from, and simplify the wealth of information presented to him by nature had become more and more apparent. Alongside this ability was an openness to change and the courage to take on new challenges. All these qualities came to the fore in his later work.

After the end of the war, his interest in perspective prepared the way for paintings in which forms were more solidly and more simply shown, as in the 1923 painting of Mr Aylwin's barns (see plate VIII). His emotional range also widened to include a stronger and sometimes sombre vision. This was apparent as early as 1916 in the picture of Brinkwells Garden with its stormy and brooding sky (see plate V) and in the dark, snow-filled emptiness of *Snow on the Copse* (see plate IX) which again depicts Mr Aylwin's 'Springs Farm' near Brinkwells. In later paintings of the 1930s, when his attention had turned to depicting the streets of London, he was to bring the same attention to detail and commitment to understanding this subject that he had demonstrated in his publications on trees. He planned another publication, *The Streets of London*, which was to be illustrated by his paintings and in manuscript ran to 700 pages. But the finished book never saw the light of day as at the time of its completion war-time conditions made publication impossible. The manuscript was subsequently lost. However, in his many London paintings he left not only an artistic legacy but also an historical one.

In approaching this huge task, Rex Vicat Cole had immersed himself in the history and appearance of London streets. The many resulting paintings present the viewer with a comprehensive portrait of the city at one period in its development. His views ranged from the beautifully balanced and tonally controlled views of London churches, streets and arcades to atmospheric nocturnes which capture the smokey night skies and the dim street lighting of London before the Second World War. His interest in and mastery of perspective enabled him to capture the idiosyncrasies of buildings with the same brevity of style that he had evolved in landscape. Vicat Cole's late paintings have a weight

---

* See *The Studio*, Vol 81, 1921, p. 168.

of experience behind them which in part explains how much they manage to convey through a simple painterly language. A fine example of this late style is his canvas *Lambeth Palace from Victoria Gardens* (see plate X) painted in the 1930s. What stands out in such works is a sense of balance in tone, composition, colour and emotion, a visual honesty that matches the language of the artist with the reality of his subject.

Rex Vicat Cole died in West Sussex in 1940 carrying out an act which seems wholly in keeping with what is known of his character. He collapsed and died whilst helping to rescue a family whose car had become stranded in flood water. He was 70 years old. His wife, Hannah, died just one year later aged 61 and they were both buried in Fittleworth churchyard, as was their artist son John who died in 1975. A stone commemorating all three has recently been erected.

Elgar's 'Divine Place'

The countryside around Brinkwells today is not so different from the descriptions left to us by Rex Vicat Cole and the Elgars – a sense of isolation and remoteness still remains in spite of the intrusions of modern life. The woods are still thick, flowers carpet the ground in spring and nightingales still sing in the dark of summer evenings. It would be a tragedy if this were ever lost. We have as evidence of its beauty the surviving paintings by Rex Vicat Cole which document both the idyllic life of the country and the changes brought about in his vision by the experience of the Great War. These works are a permanent record of the inter-relationship between the artist and that small, distinct area of West Sussex around Fittleworth and Bedham. And we have too Elgar's response to his 'divine place'. The legacy of the music he wrote there will always speak clearly about the magic of Brinkwells and gives us an extraordinary glimpse into the composer's complex and intuitive heart.

APPENDIX ONE

The Elgars at Brinkwells – Calendar

1917

2 May   Alice and Carice saw Brinkwells for the first time on a day visit from London.

24 May–4 June   Elgar and Alice's first stay at Brinkwells. Carice joined them from 26 May and stayed on after their departure until 18 June. (At some period during her sole stay she may have been joined by Rosa Burley.)

26 July   Alice and Carice made a day trip from Severn House to Brinkwells.

29 August–8 September   Alice and Elgar at Brinkwells.

1918

This year saw the Elgars' most prolonged stay at the cottage.

2 May–11 October   Alice and Elgar at Brinkwells. Elgar left for Ridgehurst to stay with the Speyers on 31 August and returned to Brinkwells on 3 September. Carice travelled down with them on 2 May and returned to London the next day. Thereafter she joined them in West Sussex between 7 June and 10 June, then between 24–26 June, 26–28 July, 22–31 August, and from 3–6 September (a planned visit later in the month had to be abandoned because of the railway strike.)

11 November–27 December   Alice and Elgar at Brinkwells. This stay was broken by a short trip to London between 4 December and 6 December. They were joined by Carice on Christmas Day. She then returned to London with Elgar on 27 December whilst Alice remained until at least 31 December to close up the cottage for the winter.

The two short periods in 1918 when Alice was alone at the cottage were the only two instances in which either Elgar or Alice was there without the other. Although Alice left Elgar at Brinkwells to go to Severn House to organise things after the burglary there on Tuesday 17 December, she returned the same day.

1919

Again the Elgars spent a considerable time at the cottage during this year, making five visits in all.

16 May–20 May   A short stay at Brinkwells for Elgar and Alice where they were joined by Carice 17–19 May.

13 June–2 July   A stay for Alice and Elgar without Carice.

16 July–27 July   Elgar and Alice were joined by Carice between 18 and 21 July.

30 July–29 August   A longer summer stay when they were joined again by Carice 2–5 August.

16 September–13 October   Another longer stay. Carice arrived before Alice and Elgar and stayed with them until 6 October. This was to be Alice's last visit to Brinkwells before her death in April 1920.

In 1920 and 1921 Elgar made a number of visits to Brinkwells always in the company of Carice.

1920

22 June–19 July   Elgar and Carice at the cottage.
3 August–30 August   Their second stay.
5 November–7 November   The last stay in 1920 made to close the cottage for the winter.

1921

23 May–8 June   Elgar and Carice again at cottage.
21 July–21 August   Elgar left for a short stay at Crowborough with Landon Ronald on 3 August and returned on 6 August. They then both stayed until the 21 August when Elgar left Brinkwells for the last time. Carice stayed on, packing up and sorting things out in the cottage. She eventually left on 24 August.

Thereafter Elgar was only to hear about the cottage through letters sent by Mark Holden (the gardener) and through Carice. She visited Brinkwells on several subsequent occasions including a visit with her husband in October 1922 and then, 14 years later in May 1936, she took Vera Hockman to see the place in which the Violin Sonata had been written.

In Search of those 'Sinister Trees'

The text contains detailed discussion of the undoubted effect on Elgar of his arboreal surroundings at Brinkwells and on the music he wrote there. In particular there is the problem of the nature of the hidden 'programme' behind the first movement of the Piano Quintet. Whatever the detailed position might be on that issue, there is absolutely no doubt that, as Billy Reed points out in *Elgar as I knew him* (1936), Elgar was obsessed with the view of a group of dead trees on a plateau nearby. Their dead branches seemed to be gaunt arms held up in derision, beckoning one to come closer – 'a ghastly sight in the evening'. Reed goes on to point out that Elgar was such a nature lover and had such an impressionable mind that he could not fail to be influenced by such surroundings. 'There was so powerful a fascination for him there that he was always strolling up to look at the scene again.'

The Legend of the Dispossessed Trees

The legend in question is founded on this group of dead trees in or near Flexham Park, the trees being transmogrified Spanish monks involved in impious celebrations before being struck dead by lightning. Because of its attraction as a mild horror story the legend appeals to the listener to the Piano Quintet (in particular) as a way of entering into the composer's mind. Its provenance is therefore of some interest.

The first reference in print to this legend and its link to Elgar was by W.H. Reed, writing in Cobbett's *Cyclopedic Survey of Chamber Music,* published in 1929. There he talks about Brinkwells and Elgar's studio, with its wonderful views across the old-world cottage garden and adds that nearby on a strange plateau were a number of trees with gnarled and twisted branches, bare of bark or leaves, 'a ghastly sight in the evening, when the branches seemed to be beckoning and holding up gaunt arms in derision' (p. 372). Reed then goes on to analyse all three chamber music works in some detail and points out the places in each work where the 'ghastly sight' inspires an episode in the relevant movement. Reed does not mention the impious Spanish monks and their fate, nor does he in a similar passage in his later biography, *Elgar as I knew him* (1936). Perhaps the nearest Reed gets is to pick out the passage with a distinctive dance-measure in the Quintet (five bars after Figure 4) and describe it as being 'Spanish, Moorish, or possibly oriental in character'. Reed refers in the later work to the trees having been struck by lightning and as being in Flexham Park. As to the monkish flavour of the Quintet generally, the perspicacious H.C. Colles, writing in the *Musical Times* as early as November 1919, alluded to the 'cold plain-song melody' at the opening piano octaves, this being the Solemn Tone of the Antiphon Salve Regina, as mentioned in the text.

It seems to have been left to Basil Maine, writing in Elgar's lifetime, (see 'Works' *op. cit.* p.268, 1933) to be the first in print to explain, in a footnote to his analysis of the Quintet and the 'Spanish' theme, the full story. He wrote, 'Possibly this theme is a clue to the underlying programme. The withered trees near Elgar's cottage in Sussex have inspired a legend in those parts. Upon the plateau, it is said, was once a settlement of Spanish monks, who, while carrying out some impious rites, were struck dead; and the trees are their dead forms. The Spanish character of this theme suggests that the composer had this legend in mind.'

After the publication of Percy Young's *Elgar O.M.* in 1955 it was realised that Alice's diary, mostly unpublished and in her manuscript, was a valuable additional source and often illuminated what before was obscure. Her diary for 15 September 1918 notes with considerable acuity the resemblance of the spirit of the music, then in the course of being written, to Elgar's part-song *Owls* 'reminiscent of sinister trees & impression of Flexham Park'. On 16 September she refers more explicitly to the 'sad' and 'dispossessed' trees, referring to their dance and their unstilled regret for their evil fate and the curse which brought it on. She also refers a week or so later to a possible link with Bulwer Lytton's *A Strange Story*, which in our view appears to be unfounded as regards any programmatic, as opposed to atmospheric, influence and this is discussed elsewhere in our text. [*]

By the time that Michael Pope published his invaluable Introduction to the Eulenburg miniature score of the Quintet in 1971 he could find no trace of this legend, though Alice seems to speak of it as an existing one that required no elaboration from her in 1918. The authors' impression is similar to Michael Pope's, but we suspect that many legends of the area have evaporated unless they happen to be recorded in one of the few 'memoirs' which have some credibility. So the alternative explanation, namely that the impious monks were a product of the remarkable Algernon Blackwood's imagination, probably passed on to the Elgars during his visit to them in July 1918 (indeed a seminal time), still seems to be the best available.

Wulstan Atkins, writing in 1982, described his clear memories of Elgar's remarks about the writing of the Quintet in Brinkwells, and of his description of the 'haunted trees, and the legend about them …'. Elgar implied that these trees and their ghostly appearance had been much in his mind at the relevant time. Atkins also makes the link, apparently spontaneously, with Algernon Blackwood who, he suggests, 'wove the legend' on their walks together through the woods. [†]

Pope also raises the possibility that Elgar's artistic sub-landlord may have given Elgar the idea, but concludes that the balance of probabilities makes this unlikely. Rex Vicat Cole, as we have seen, was a true 'man of the trees' – to him they lived in a pantheistic way and must be thoroughly understood before the artist portrays them. But we agree that to suppose that he introduced the like-minded Elgar to the scene is not a viable theory either, since so far as is known the men only met once, briefly, at Severn House in London. Even if a copy of Vicat Cole's *British Trees* was available at Brinkwells, Elgar would have found no suggestion of a similar legend being attached to dead trees. Although the text is imaginative and is concerned with myths and the 'weird imaginings' that can be occasioned by the almost human forms of some branches, Vicat Cole makes no mention of monks being transformed into dead trees.

Of course, taking the larger view, it hardly matters whether the legend exists or not. The trees were certainly there. Similar dead Chestnuts can be seen in the area to this day conforming to the descriptions given by witnesses. If the composer was gripped by the story at the time, this provided the necessary ignition to creative achievement.

A Perambulation in West Sussex

Aficionados may wish to obtain a large-scale Ordnance Survey map of this intensely wooded area, put on their green wellies and try at least to find the site of these trees – for

---

[*] See p. 142 and the recent publication of a contrary view by Michael Allis there discussed.
[†] Atkins, *Elgar-Atkins Friendship*, pp.294-5.

it has to be accepted that disappointingly the trees themselves have long gone. This leaves a nice Elgarian enigma as to what type of tree they really were, why they seemed to be associated with music written in the Spanish style, and their precise former whereabouts.

As pointed out in the text, such explorers will to a large extent be treading in the footsteps of Michael Pope who describes in considerable detail the results of his own researches in 1969-70 when preparing his illuminating notes on the Quintet for the Eulenburg miniature score published in 1971. His conclusion is that the trees were not actually in the ancient hunting ground of Flexham Park as Reed seems to suggest. If we look at Alice's diary entry written on 7 September 1917, soon after they had identified the group of trees for the first time, it reads 'walked to Bognor Common then by the pine walk & around by Bedham & the sinister trees'. In the 3rd edition of the OS map of the area published in 1914, Alice's itinerary would seem to suggest that the pine walk was situated on the eastern edge of Flexham Park and so the sinister trees are likely to have been somewhere in the area where Bedham Copse merges into Flexham Park. One must also bear in mind that the existing road was cut through the woods at this point after the First World War probably following the route of an earlier footpath.

Pope plumps for Bedham Copse as the likely site of the trees, a plateau lying adjacent to Flexham Park and clearly marked on the large-scale maps of this area, (map ref. 015221, Explorer 134). There is a short account in the Elgar Society's Newsletter of January 1974 of an expedition led by Michael Pope to Brinkwells and Bedham Copse in the preceding September, taking the existing minor road. There is now no trace there of the remains of any group of dead trees, nor had the West Sussex Wildlife Trust that manages land in that area ever heard of them. On the other hand, on the authors' interviewing the only identifiable person who had known that area intimately for fifty years or so, it was apparent that as a child she and other children had been told about these trees, though her strong impression was that they were much nearer Brinkwells in the Warren Barn Copse area.

So what did Elgar signify by subscribing the end of the first movement of the Quintet '(Bedham 1919)', while the whole work is subscribed at the end '(Brinkwells 1919)'? It could strengthen Pope's theory as to Bedham Copse being the scene of the sinister trees. But Bedham is a scattered hamlet of several houses, some of considerable age (Bedham Farmhouse is early 17th-century), and Brinkwells is in fact much nearer Bedham's epicentre than to the village of Fittleworth. If Elgar had wished to put the matter beyond doubt he could have added the word 'Copse' – or indeed 'Flexham Park' – to the subscription, but he chose to leave the topography more general, perhaps as a slightly enigmatic tribute to the *atmosphere* of the whole surrounding area including Flexham Park.

Although it seems intrinsically unlikely that lightning should have struck so as to produce not one but a group of dead trees, there is a very heavy plantation of Sweet Chestnut trees (*Castanea sativa*) throughout this area. The popular name for these trees used to be 'Spanish' Chestnut. In Cole's magnificent treatise on *British Trees*, Vol. I, readers will find a fine drawing and description of just such a tree, about which he says, 'the boughs are stiff and contorted, and assume many grotesque forms' (p. 582), and can come to their own conclusion.

Ultimately the Quintet is atmospheric music, with its plainsong melody and weird, stuttering passages right at its commencement, 'ghostly stuff' according to Elgar writing to its dedicatee Ernest Newman. It must be allowed to speak for itself in the 'absolute' terms favoured by the composer. As in Elgar's setting of his own words in the part-song *Owls*, atmosphere, not detailed narrative, is all.

The Legal Status of Brinkwells and its Tenant

Elgar's tenancies of Brinkwells pinpoint to some interesting legal problems which may have led some commentators to misunderstand the position. Brinkwells is a cottage of great antiquity going back in parts at least to the 16th century. It has belonged to the Stopham Estate for many years – at least 150 – and is surrounded by woodland – mainly chestnuts used traditionally for the hoops of beer barrels etc (until replaced by iron ones), for fencing or for charcoal burning.

Unfortunately, the records for the relevant period are largely missing and the agents then dealing with it have long since gone out of business. However, it is clear that in about 1905/6 Brinkwells was let to Rex Vicat Cole, probably on a lease for 21 years. (The fact that he appears finally to have left the cottage in 1926 supports this assumption.) The lease would have made it clear what the repairing obligations were (the general principle being that the longer the lease the more onerous on the tenant are the repairing and other obligations). This would be classified as a lease of intermediate length and probably at a rent which represented the full unfurnished annual value of the cottage and the grounds. It would almost certainly have obliged the tenant to insure, obtain the landlord's permission to any assignment or sub-letting or to any alterations, and pay any rates and taxes and to return it at the end of the lease in good order. It is probable that the landlord retained responsibility for external repairs, as is the present position.

By the time the Elgars came on the scene in 1917 for two short lets, the Coles had erected the artist's studio and workshop in the garden, presumably with the landlord's consent. Elgar, by virtue of a sub-lease, would have been responsible only to Cole for the rent and any other imposed obligations. It would quite likely have been an oral lease only since the common law allowed valid informal leases provided that the term did not exceed three years and was at the best rent reasonably obtainable without taking a fine (or premium). Otherwise a deed was, and still is, always required. Again, the landlord's consent would probably first have been needed by the terms of the head lease.

It is interesting to note that Brinkwells is thought to have been decorated with wooden panels painted with sketches of flowers and leaves by Rex Vicat Cole * which would have been put up by the time the Elgars were involved. The legal implications of any decorations in the cottage are mentioned below.

So the Elgars obtained a decorated and furnished cottage and grounds in return for a rent which would normally be significantly more than Cole as head tenant was paying. The increment would have represented the additional annual value to Elgar of the furniture, workshop and studio paid for by Cole.

In 1920 Elgar attempted to 'buy' Brinkwells from Rex Vicat Cole but, because Cole decided that he wanted the cottage back, Elgar was disappointed. This is somewhat

---

* See T. Barringer, *The Cole Family*, p. 127.

enigmatic. Cole could only have had the fag-end of his lease left, and whilst this was perfectly saleable and would have involved an assignment of what was left of the term for a modest capital sum, it was hardly an attractive investment, being a wasting asset. The Stopham Estate, if asked, would have made it quite clear that the freehold of Brinkwells was not for sale. *

Another matter in need of clarification arises from Elgar's love of cutting and working wood. Such rights as went with the cottage were clearly inadequate for Elgar's needs and on 8 September 1918 he makes a diary entry that he 'wrote proposing to buy underwood'. On 12 September he writes that he has heard from the Stopham Agent that the wood reeve would call regarding the underwood. On the 16th Elgar notes: 'The Reeve came. I bought the near underwood for £3 and proceeded to cut a boundary.' But what was encompassed in the expression 'underwood'? As Billy Reed, on his first visit to Brinkwells, rapidly discovered, the meaning is not quite straightforward. Reed charmingly relates apropos his first visit:

> Then, as we walked up to the house, he told me which part of the wood went with it, and how he had the right to cut any wood there except forest-trees, which I gathered from him, included oaks, beeches, and elms …. He set me at once to cut down some chestnut poles. Happily, before I had time to cut myself down, Lady Elgar wanted a tub for some domestic purpose or other; and as there was a big barrel at the house doing nothing, he produced a long-handled saw with which he sawed the barrel in half quite successfully and presented Lady Elgar with two tubs. †

It follows from this that the right to cut wood in this way exists as a right separate from ownership of the land and is open to the estate owner to trade in it without selling the land to which it is attached. This is still the practice there today.

More complicated is the question of entitlement to the studio building so important to Elgar (subsequently removed from Brinkwells and re-erected at Bedham) and any painted panelling that there might have been in the cottage. These points involve the law of fixtures and fittings which still arises today in a number of different situations – but particularly when someone sells a house or other building or when a tenancy ends. Taking the latter situation, here the question arises as to whether the landlord is entitled to retain items put in by the tenant as 'landlord's fixtures'. In principle any building tranfers itself on the ending of a lease or on sale to the purchaser or landlord as 'land', a widely defined word which includes without specific mention all buildings, trees, growing vegetation etc annexed to the land. Similarly, within a house, if the tenant puts in a new sink (for example), being firmly plumbed in and affixed to the building, the sink is also 'land'. Common sense suggests that this must be right since purchasers and re-possessing landlords do not inherit a hole where the original sink was.

However there are inevitably marginal situations where matters are not straightforward. Here it has long been established that the court in adjudicating has to look at two tests: 1) the degree of annexation and 2) the purpose of annexation. So, in the case of buildings, it has long been accepted that if a building rests on its own weight like a Dutch barn and can be removed without damage the tenant may remove it on his vacating the premises. This rule applies only to buildings – dry stone walls are normally irremovable landlord's fixtures as are statues on plinths forming part of the architectural design. This probably

---

* Information by courtesy of Col. Sir Brian Barttelot Bart.
† Reed, pp.57-8.

explains why in the Brinkwells case it was possible to move the garden studio building out of its original habitat and re-erect it elsewhere. It assumes that there were no substantial foundations and that it primarily rested on its own weight. (It is of course open to parties to renegotiate their strict positions if they wish, but the starting point will depend on the underlying law.)

In the case of any painted wooden panels which might have adorned the walls of the cottage, although they might be securely affixed to the wall, because the purpose of so exhibiting them is to enjoy them as chattels and there is no other way of doing so, it is likely that they would have been regarded as chattels rather then fixtures to the land, and consequently could be removed at any time by the tenant. In modern times, though, the court has tended to take a stricter view if the panelling pictures are of historic interest and form part of the décor of a listed building when removal may even constitute a criminal offence.

APPENDIX FOUR

Elgar's Doctors

After his move to London and the acquisition of Severn House in December 1911, Elgar began to seek medical advice from distinguished practitioners in the face of his increasingly worrying symptoms. His doctors were eminent figures in the medical profession and their biographies reveal that these were men of great experience with wide interests.

Sir Maurice Abbot-Anderson (1861-1938), physician and botanist

Abbot-Anderson became the Elgar family's chief physician whilst they were at Severn House. He regularly answered Alice's calls for help as Elgar's health declined in 1916 and 1917 and obviously enjoyed the confidence of both Elgar and Alice whose worries would often be alleviated after consulting him. On some occasions he put his car at their disposal and during periods when both Elgar and Alice were unwell – as in January 1920 – he visited Severn House to treat them both. Abbot-Anderson was educated at University College, London, and at Durham. He had a distinguished medical career and became Honorary Physician to the Princess Royal and Household, and a Fellow of both the Medical Society of London and the Royal Society of Medicine. He was created Knight in 1912, CVO in 1925, and in 1922 was created Knight of the Order of the Hospital of St John of Jerusalem in England. His great interest outside medicine was botany and he was the Founder of Flora's League. He also supplied an 'afterword' to the book by Henry Salt, *Our Vanishing Wildflowers and Other Essays*, in 1928 – a publication that reflected the author's love of wild nature and his essentially Thoreauvian approach to the subject. It was Abbot-Anderson's deputy, Dr Rose, who attended Alice in her last illness with the help of a specialist, Dr Larkin.

Sir Victor Alexander Haden Horsley (1857-1916), physiologist and neurosurgeon

Sir Victor Horsley examined Elgar in 1912 when the composer was afflicted with bouts of giddiness. Horsley, who had studied medicine at University College Hospital Medical School in London, was known for his work on the thyroid gland, on the treatment for rabies and his interest in the functions of the brain. He played a leading role in the development of cerebral surgery, particularly after 1886 with his appointment as surgeon to the National Hospital for the Paralysed and Epileptic in London. In 1887 he carried out the first surgical operation to remove a spinal tumour. Horsley was knighted for his medical work in 1902. A believer in reform both politically and in the medical profession, he also played a prominent role in the British Medical Association. He was politically committed to temperance, to National Sick Insurance and to the support of women's suffrage – so much so that he often offended people by his persistent and committed attitude. [*]

---

[*] See *DNB* entry by Stephen Paget, *rev.* Caroline Overy.

With the outbreak of the First World War, Horsley, then 57 years old, first served at the British Hospital in Wimereux but less than a year later was appointed consultant to the Mediterranean expeditionary force. He then went to India and to Mesopotamia where he died from heatstroke in July 1916. An insight into his last months is given by Edward Heron-Allen in his War Journal.[*] His diary entry for 29 June 1917 reads:

> My old friend, Sir Victor Horsley, the greatest English surgeon of his time, volunteered for service in Mesopotamia and died there of sheer overwork and lack of proper medical appliances ... his letters home to his wife were frightful. There were not even splints or beds for the wounded, and wounded and dysentery patients were all huddled together in the same straw in tents under the burning sun – there were no hospital ships in which to remove them. He wrote too that the only food for soldiers, officers, and wounded was often only a little porridge.

Heron-Allen then added this account in a postscript dated 26 December 1919:

> I have recently read Stephen Paget's 'Life of Sir Victor Horsley' who was killed in Mesopotamia in 1916 ... by heatstroke. He was a fanatic about total abstinence ... Poor Victor who was a great friend of mine in the early 'eighties' really died by his fanaticism for he argued that a total abstainer was immune from the effects of heat and used to go about his work quite unprotected from the sun.

Horsley died at the British General Hospital in Amara, near Baghdad, where he was buried.

Dr Stanley Melville (1867-1934), radiologist

Elgar visited Dr Stanley Melville on 11 January 1918 at the suggestion of Sir Maurice Abbot-Anderson for an x-ray examination which would most probably have involved a barium meal. As a result of this appointment the diagnosis of a dropped stomach was made and, according to Carice's diary, Elgar was given 'electric treatment and a special belt'. At this period in the development of radiology, when doctors could for the first time study anatomy in a living and standing patient, there was considerable interest in the subject of visceroptosis (dropped stomach) and the usual treatment for this condition could have involved the use of belts, laxatives, a tonic diet and electrotherapy (high-frequency current). Although the diagnosis of a dropped stomach was well-recognised at the time of Elgar's illness, the diagnosis became less fashionable in the 1930s. In seeing Dr Melville, Elgar was going to one of the leaders in that new field of study. After initially training in law, Melville turned to medicine and the discovery of x-rays in 1895 influenced his future which was devoted to radiology. He had a distinguished career in that field, becoming President of the Electro-Therapeutical Section of the Royal Society of Medicine and in 1934 the President of the British Institute of Radiology where a Memorial Award is still given in his name.[†]

Sir Arthur Peregrine Thomson (1890-1977), physician

Sir Arthur Thomson treated Elgar later in his life and obviously knew the composer well. He movingly describes Elgar's death and the courage with which the dying man faced

---

[*] *Edward Heron-Allen's Journal of the Great War*, ed. Harvey and Fitzgerald (Phillimore, 2002).
[†] The authors are greatly indebted to Dr Adrian Thomas, Honorary Secretary, The British Institute of Radiology for information about Dr Stanley Melville.

his crisis. Thomson was also connected with another artistic near-contemporary of Elgar, Dr Francis Brett Young. Thomson graduated from the Medical School of Birmingham University with many prizes in 1909 and during the Great War was awarded the MC and the Croix de Guerre, retiring with the rank of Major in 1919. He became President of the British Medical Association in 1958-59 and was knighted in the latter year.

Thomson was a member of the elite 'Octette' Society of medical graduates of Birmingham along with, amongst others, Francis Brett Young (1894-1954) who by 1925 or so had become a hugely successful author and poet. Since much of Brett Young's best work concerns the 'sweet borderland' of Worcestershire and westward, often contrasted with the Black Country and Birmingham to the north, it would be surprising if Elgar was not well acquainted with his work. Brett Young married a professional singer, Jessica, with whom he attended a moving performance of *Gerontius* in Worcester Cathedral, conducted by Elgar, in 1905. The score they used is in the University of Birmingham Main Library Collection of Brett Young papers. In his *This Little World* the experience is recalled through the character 'Dr Selby' (p.592). In his earlier days Brett Young had some well-written songs published in Germany and these were apparently well thought of by both Elgar and Granville Bantock. Francis Brett Young's ashes are interred in Worcester Cathedral where he is memorialised by a plaque. *

Mr Herbert Tilley (b. 1866), ear, nose and throat surgeon

Elgar's diary entry for Wednesday 6 March 1918 reads: 'E. to Mr Tilley with Sir Maurice. Tonsils condemned.' Nine days later Herbert Tilley operated on the composer at a private nursing home in Dorset Square, London, and removed his tonsils which were badly infected. By the time of the operation Tilley was well known for his work on diseases of the nose and throat and the fourth edition of his book on that subject appeared a year later in 1919. Tilley trained at University College Hospital, London. He worked as surgeon at the Golden Square Throat Hospital and became Laryngologist to the Radium Institute, President of the Laryngological and Otological Sections, Royal Society of Medicine, Vice-President of the Medical Society of London, and in 1910 President of the Laryngology Section of the British Medical Association. He published widely on diseases of the ear, nose and throat. In going to him Elgar was putting himself into the hands of a leading specialist and once his tonsils were removed and he had recovered from the painful operation, his health improved greatly.

Sir William Hale-White (1857-1949), physician

Sir William Hale-White was called in by Sir Maurice Abbot-Anderson to examine Elgar in December 1917 when the composer's health was fragile and he was exhibiting a variety of symptoms. Elgar's health had caused considerable concern throughout the month and Sir Maurice had called on Christmas Eve to prescribe new medicines which Alice then fetched on Christmas Day. But Elgar did not respond and Sir Maurice decided to get another opinion. Alice's diary for 27 December reads:

> Sir Maurice came & decided to bring a tummy specialist Dr Hale White evidently very disappointed & puzzled over E. Hale-White attended at Severn House two days later

---

* See, on Thomson, Moore pp. 818-9 and *Journal of the Francis Brett Young Society* No. 50, 2003, p. 25 (Dr R.D. Bridgewater). Alan Rankin, Editor of the above Journal, kindly supplied invaluable detail about FBY.

and Alice again recorded the outcome: Sir Maurice brought Dr Hale White to see E
… They decided … that there was no organic trouble. Urged smoking, golf, change
etc etc.

Hale-White had trained at Guy's Hospital, London, and worked as demonstrator of
anatomy there between 1881 and 1885. By the time he saw Elgar he had established a
reputation as a physician with wide interests, publishing on many branches of medicine,
and his textbook, *Materia medica, Pharmacology and Therapeutics* (1892) had reached its
28th edition by his death in 1949. During the Great War he served with the rank of Colonel
as consulting physician and in 1919 he was knighted for his services to medicine. He was
an approachable figure, esteemed as a teacher by his peers and his students, and with a
wide range of interests outside medicine which included golf (hence perhaps his advice to
Elgar), travelling and photography.

Catalogue of Colour Plates

Rex Vicat Cole Paintings and Drawings

(Ledger numbers refer to the artist's own painting ledger)

Under the Lilac Hedge (1896)
Signed and dated: *R VICAT COLE 1896.*
Oil on canvas, 30.5 x 46.1 cm.
Painted at Headcorn, Kent.
Private Collection.

A Moorland – Bolton Abbey (1897)
Inscribed on verso: *A Moorland Bolton Abbey R. Vicat Cole 1897.*
Oil on wooden board, 13 x 23 cm.
Private Collection.

The Labourer's Home (1906)
Signed: *R.V.C.*
Pencil and Chalk on Paper.
Reproduced: Rex Vicat Cole, *British Trees*, p.218.
Private Collection.

The Home Field (1908)
Signed and dated.
Oil on canvas, approx. 127 x 152.5 cm.
Ledger no. 234. Exhibited at RA in 1908.
Private Collection.

Brinkwells Garden (1916)
Signed and dated: *REX VICAT COLE 1916.*
Oil on canvas, 35.5 x 46.0 cm.
Private Collection.

A Young Girl in a Bluebell Wood (1918)
Signed and dated: *REX VICAT COLE 1918.*
Oil on canvas, 70 x 94 cm.
Private Collection.

A Young Girl in a Bluebell Wood – detail

A Sussex Granary (1923)
Signed: *REX VICAT COLE.*
Oil on canvas, 50.8 x 61.0 cm.
Ledger no. 356 described as *Aylwyn's granary & trees & straw yard.*
Worthing Museum and Art Gallery.

Snow on the Copse
Signed: *REX VICAT COLE* (undated).
Oil on canvas, 40.8 x 50.8 cm.
Ledger no. 406 described as *Aylwyn's farm on hill, copse with road of snow. Given to George for New Hall.* Exhibited at the ROI in 1931.
Private Collection.

Lambeth Palace from Victoria Gardens
Signed *REX VICAT COLE* (undated).
Oil on wooden board, 30.7 x 41 cm.
Ledger no. 510. Exhibited at Colnaghi's June 1935.
Private Collection.

Select Bibliography

Manuscript Sources

Diaries and letters of the Elgar family and their friends at the Elgar Birthplace Museum (EBM) and at Birmingham University Library Special Collections. Records of Rex Vicat Cole and his work in the Cole Papers Private Archives.

Published Books and Essays

Allen, Kevin, *Elgar in Love – Vera Hockman and the Third Symphony* (published by the author, 2000)

Allis, Michael, 'Elgar, Lytton, and the Piano Quintet, op. 84', *Music & Letters*, vol. 85, no. 2 (May 2004)

Anderson, Robert, *Elgar* (Dent Master Musicians. J.M. Dent, 1993)

—, *Elgar and Chivalry* (Elgar Editions, 2002)

Ashley, M., *Starlight Man: the extraordinary life of Algernon Blackwood* (Constable, 2001)

Atkins, E. Wulstan, *The Elgar-Atkins Friendship* (David & Charles, 1984)

Barringer, T.J., *The Cole Family: Painters of the English Landscape 1838-1975* (Portsmouth City Museums, 1988)

—, 'Rex Vicat Cole' in *Oxford Dictionary of National Biography*, Oxford University Press, 2004)

Bax, Arnold, *Farewell my Youth* (Longman, 1943)

Blackwood, Algernon, *A Prisoner in Fairyland* (Macmillan & Co., 1913)

Blake, Carice Elgar, 'A Family Retrospective', in *Edward Elgar: Centenary Sketches* (Novello and Co. Ltd., 1957)

Bliss, Arthur, *As I Remember* (Faber and Faber, 1970)

Buckley, R.J., *Sir Edward Elgar* (John Lane: The Bodley Head, 1905)

Burley, Rosa and Carruthers, Frank, *Edward Elgar, the Record of a Friendship* (Barrie & Jenkins, 1972)

Catt, Phyllis, *A Miller's Daughter* (Midhurst and Petworth Printers, n.d.)

Chambers, H.A. (ed.), *Edward Elgar – Centenary Sketches* (Novello and Co. Ltd, 1957)

Chester, Austin, 'The Art of Mr Rex Vicat Cole', *Windsor Magazine* (July 1910)

Chignall, Robert, *Life and Paintings of Vicat Cole R.A.* (Cassell and Co., 1896)

Cobbett, W.W., *Cyclopedic Survey of Chamber Music* (London, 1929)

Cole, Rex Vicat, *The Art and Life of Byam Shaw* (Seeley Service and Co., 1932)

—, *The Artistic Anatomy of Trees* (Seeley Service and Co., 1915)

—, *British Trees, Drawn and illustrated by Rex Vicat Cole* (Hutchinson and Co., 1907)

—, *Catalogue of an Exhibition of Pictures in Oils Painted in the Neighbour of Bolton Abbey, Yorkshire* (Dowdeswell Gallery, 1901)

—, *English Woodlands*, Exhibition Catalogue of Paintings by Rex Vicat Cole (Mendoza Galleries, *c.*1910)

—, *Perspective; The Practice and Theory of Perspective as applied to Pictures* (Dover Publications, Inc., 1976 republication of the 1921 original)

—, Review of Vicat Cole's *Perspective, The Studio*, vol. 81 (1921)

Collett, Pauline, *Elgar Lived Here* (Thames, 1981)

De-la-Noy, Michael, *Elgar the Man* (Allen Lane, 1983)

Dunhill, Thomas F., *Sir Edward Elgar* (Blackie and Son Ltd, 1938)

Fitzgerald, Carol, 'Edward Heron-Allen, the War Journal and Women' in *Reflections on Heron-Allen's War Journal* (Heron-Allen Society, 2002)

Foreman, Lewis (ed), *Oh, My Horses! Elgar and the Great War* (Elgar Editions, 2001)

Grimley, Daniel and Rushton, Julian (eds), *The Cambridge Companion to Elgar* (Cambridge University Press, 2004)

Gundry, Doris, *Petworth Today and Yesterday* (published by the author, 1981)

Harrison, Beatrice, *The Cello and the Nightingales* (John Murray, 1985)

Harvey, Brian W., 'The Elgar Sonata on Record', *The Strad* (March, 1983, p.792)

—, *The Violin Family and its Makers in the British Isles* (Oxford University Press, 1995)

Harvey, Brian W. and Fitzgerald, Carol (eds), *Edward Heron-Allen's Journal of the Great War* (Phillimore & Co. Ltd, 2002)

Harvey, Jonathan, *Music and Inspiration* (Faber and Faber Ltd, 1999)

Hodgkins, Geoffrey, *Providence and Art – A Study in Elgar's Religious Beliefs* (Elgar Editions, 2002 revised edition)

Hudson, Derek, *Arthur Rackham* (Heinemann, 1960)

Hunt, Donald, Programme Notes for the Medici String Quartet, Worcester Cathedral (October 1985)

Hurd, Michael, *Elgar* (Faber and Faber, 1969)

Jamison, Kay Redfield, *Touched with Fire* (Free Press Paperbacks, Simon & Schuster Inc., 1994)

Jerome, Peter, *Tread Lightly Here* (The Window Press, 1990)

Jose, Everard, *The Significance of Elgar* (Heath Cranton Ltd, 1934)

Judd, Alan, *Ford Madox Ford* (Harper Collins, 1991 revised edition)

Kennedy, Michael, *Portrait of Elgar* (Oxford University Press, 1987, revised edition)

—, *The Life of Elgar* (Cambridge University Press, 2004)

Leigh, Rhoda, *Past and Passing – Tales from Remote Sussex* (Heath Cranton Ltd, 1932)

Lucas, E.V., *The Colvins and their Friends* (Methuen & Co. Ltd, 1928)

—, *Highways and Byways of Sussex* (Macmillan and Co. Ltd, 1921)

McVeagh, Diana, *Edward Elgar – His Life and Music* (J.M. Dent, 1955)

—, 'Elgar', *New Grove Dictionary of Music and Musicians* (Macmillan and Co. Ltd., 2001)

Maine, Basil, *Elgar – His Life and Works* (G. Bell & Sons Ltd, 1933)

Masefield, Joan, *Stopham Remembered* (Mrs F. Knight, 1991)

Maxse, The Hon. Lady, *The Story of Fittleworth* (The National Review, n.d. [1935])

Monk, Raymond (ed.), *Elgar Studies* (Scolar Press, 1990)

—, *Edward Elgar Music and Literature* (Scolar Press, 1993)

Moore, Jerrold Northrop, *Elgar: Child of Dreams* (Faber and Faber, 2004)

—, *Edward Elgar: A Creative Life* (Oxford University Press, 1984)

—, *Elgar: A Life in Photographs* (Oxford University Press, 1972)

—, *Edward Elgar: The Windflower Letters* (Clarendon Press, 1989)

—, *Spirit of England* (Heinemann, 1984)

Mundy, Simon, *Elgar* (The Illustrated Lives of Great Composers, Omnibus Press, 2001, revised edition)

Neill, Andrew, 'Elgar's War: from the Diaries of Lady Elgar, 1914–1918' and 'Elgar's Creative Challenge 1914–1918' from Foreman (ed.), *Oh, My Horses!* (Elgar Editions, 2001)

Parrott, Ian, *Elgar* (The Master Musicians Series, J.M. Dent and Sons Ltd, 1971)

Pentecost, Evelyn, *A Shepherd's Daughter* (The Window Press, n.d. [1987])

Pope, Michael, *Foreword* to Piano Quintet (Ernst Eulenburg Ltd, 1971)

Porte, J.F., *Sir Edward Elgar* (Kegan Paul, Trench, Trubner & Co., 1921)

Powell, Mrs Richard, *Edward Elgar – Memories of a Variation* (Methuen, 1949, 3rd Edition)

Price, Bernard, *Sussex – People. Places. Things.* (Phillimore and Co. Ltd, 1975)

Reed, William H., *Elgar as I knew him* (Victor Gollancz, 1936)

—, 'Elgar' in Cobbett's *Cyclopedic Survey of Chamber Music* (London, 1929)

Saunders, Gil, *Fittleworth, Village of the Artists* (www.sussexlife.com/gils_guide)

Shore, Bernard, *Sixteen Symphonies* (Longmans, Green and Co. Ltd, 1949)

Storr, Anthony, *The Dynamics of Creation* (Penguin Books, 1991)

Strudwick, Ivy Linda, *Pulborough: A Pictorial History* (Phillimore & Co. Ltd, 1983)

Tolanski, J., 'Elgar and the LSO', LSO programme note, 1998

Trowell, Brian, 'The Road to Brinkwells: the Late Chamber Music' in Foreman (ed.), *Oh, My Horses!* (Elgar Editions, 2001)

Vine, P.A.L., *Images of England. Around Pulborough* (Tempus, 2002)

Ward, Yvonne M., 'Edward Elgar, A.C. Benson etc', *Elgar Society Journal*, vol. 13, no. 5, pp. 13-37 (2004)

Willcocks, David, in *Edward Elgar – Centenary Sketches* (Novello & Co. Ltd, 1957)

Young, Percy M., *Alice Elgar – Enigma of a Victorian Lady* (Dobson, 1978)

—, *Elgar O.M.* (Collins, 1955)

—, *Letters of Edward Elgar and Other Writings* (Geoffrey Bles, 1956)

Index